Archibald Hamilton

Report of the Trial of Archibald Hamilton Rowan, ESQ

An Information General, for the Distribution of a Libel

Archibald Hamilton

Report of the Trial of Archibald Hamilton Rowan, ESQ
An Information General, for the Distribution of a Libel

ISBN/EAN: 9783744745925

Printed in Europe, USA, Canada, Australia, Japan

Cover: Foto ©Suzi / pixelio.de

More available books at **www.hansebooks.com**

REPORT

OF THE

TRIAL

OF

ARCHIBALD HAMILTON ROWAN, ESQ.

ON

AN INFORMATION,

FILED, *EX OFFICIO*, BY

THE ATTORNEY GENERAL,

FOR THE

DISTRIBUTION OF A LIBEL;

WITH THE

SUBSEQUENT PROCEEDINGS THEREON.

CONTAINING

THE ARGUMENTS OF COUNSEL,

THE OPINION OF THE COURT,

AND

MR. ROWAN'S ADDRESS TO THE COURT,

AT FULL.

DUBLIN:

PRINTED FOR

ARCHIBALD HAMILTON ROWAN, ESQUIRE,

AND SOLD BY

P. BYRNE, GRAFTON-STREET.

1794.

THE FOLLOWING

INFORMATION

WAS FILED BY

HIS MAJESTY'S ATTORNEY GENERAL,

EX OFFICIO,

AGAINST

ARCHIBALD HAMILTON ROWAN, ESQ.

OF TRINITY TERM *in the thirty third year of the Reign of our Sovereign* LORD GEORGE THE THIRD, *now King of Great Britain, and soforth, and in the year of our Lord one thousand seven hundred and ninety-three.*

County of the City of Dublin, to wit. } *B*E *it remembered that the Right Honourable Arthur Wolfe, Attorney General of our present Sovereign Lord the King, who for our said Lord the King prosecutes in this behalf, in his proper person comes into the Court of our said Lord the King, before the King himself, at the city of Dublin, in the county of the said city, on the eighth day of June in this same term, and for our said Lord the King gives the court here to understand and be informed, that Archibald Hamilton Rowan, of the city of Dublin, Esquire, being a person of a wicked and turbulent disposition, and maliciously designing and intending to excite and diffuse amongst the subjects of this realm of Ireland, discontents, jealousies, and suspicions of our said Lord the King and his government, and disaffection and disloyalty to the person and government of our said Lord the King, and to raise very dangerous seditions and tumults within this kingdom of Ireland; and to draw the government of this kingdom into great scandal, infamy, and disgrace,*

B   *and*

*and to incite the subjects of our said Lord the King to attempt, by
force and violence, and with arms, to make alterations in the government, state, and constitution of this kingdom, and to incite his
Majesty's said subjects to tumult and anarchy, and to overturn
the established constitution of this kingdom, and to overawe and
intimidate the legislature of this kingdom, by an armed force, on
the sixteenth day of December, in the thirty third year of the
reign of our said present Sovereign Lord George the Third, by
the grace of God of Great Britain, France, and Ireland, King,
defender of the faith, and so forth, with force and arms, at
Dublin aforesaid, to wit, in the parish and ward of Saint Michael
the archangel, and in the county of the said city, wickedly, maliciously, and seditiously, did publish, and cause and procure to be published, a certain false, wicked, malicious, scandalous, and seditious libel, of and concerning the government, state, and constitution of this kingdom, according to the tenor and effect following,
that is to say,——" The Society of United Irishmen at Dublin, to
the volunteers of Ireland. William Drennan, chairman, Archibald Hamilton Rowan, secretary.—Citizen soldiers, you first took
up arms to protect your country from foreign enemies and from
domestic disturbance; for the same purposes it now becomes necessary that you should resume them; a proclamation has been issued
in England for embodying the Militia, and a proclamation has been
issued by the Lord Lieutenant and Council in Ireland, [meaning a
proclamation which issued under the great seal of the kingdom
of Ireland, the eighth day of December, one thousand seven hundred and ninety-two,] for repressing all seditious associations; in
consequence of both these proclamations it is reasonable to apprehend danger from abroad and danger at home, for whence but
from apprehended danger are these menacing preparations for
war drawn through the streets of this capital [meaning the city of Dublin] or whence if not to create that internal commotion
which was not found, to shake that credit which was not affected,
to blast that volunteer honour which was hitherto inviolate, are
those terrible suggestions and rumours and whispers that meet us
at every corner, and agitate at least our old men, our women, and
children; whatever be the motive, or from whatever quarter it
arises, alarm has arisen; and you volunteers of Ireland are therefore summoned to arms at the instance of government as well as
by the responsibility attached to your character, and the permanent
obligations of your institution. We will not at this day condescend
to quote authorities for the right of having and of using arms,
but we will cry aloud, even amidst the storm raised by the witch-
craft of a proclamation, that to your formation was owing the
peace and protection of this island, to your relaxation has been
owing its relapse into impotence and insignificance, to your renovation must be owing its future freedom and its present tranquility; you are therefore summoned to arms, in order to preserve
your country in that guarded quiet which may secure it from
external*

*external hostility, and to maintain that internal regimen through-
out the land, which, superseding a notorious police or a suspected
militia, may preserve the blessings of peace by a vigilant preparation for war.—Citizen soldiers, to arms, take up the shield of
freedom and the pledges of peace—peace, the motive and end of
your virtuous institution—war, an occasional duty, ought never to
be made an occupation; every man should become a soldier in the
defence of his rights; no man ought to continue a soldier for offending the rights of others; the sacrifice of life in the ser-
vice of our country is a duty much too honourable to be intrusted
to mercenaries, and at this time, when your country has, by public authority, been declared in danger, we conjure you by your
interest, your duty, and your glory, to stand to your arms, and
in spite of a police, in spite of a fencible militia, in virtue of two proclamations, to maintain good order in your vicinage, and tranquility
in Ireland; it is only by the military array of men in whom they confide, whom they have been accustomed to revere as the guardians of
domestic peace, the protectors of their liberties and lives, that the present agitation of the people can be stilled, that tumult and licen-
tiousness can be repressed, obedience secured to existing law, and
a calm confidence diffused through the public mind in the speedy
resurrection of a free constitution, [meaning that the people of
Ireland had not at the time of the publishing aforesaid a free
constitution] of liberty and of equality, words which we use for
an opportunity of repelling calumny, and of saying, that by liberty
we never understood unlimited freedom, nor by equality the levelling of property or the destruction of subordination; this is a calumny invented by that faction, or that gang, which misrepre-
sents the King to the people, and the people to the King, traduces one half of the nation to cajole the other, and by keeping up
distrust and division wishes to continue the proud arbitrators of
the fortune and fate of Ireland; liberty is the exercise of all our
rights, natural and political, secured to us and our posterity by
a real representation of the people; and equality is the extension of
the constituent to the fullest dimensions of the constitution, of the
elective franchise to the whole body of the people, to the end that
government, which is collective power, may be guided by collective will, and that legislation may originate from public reason,
keep pace with public improvement, and terminate in public
happiness. If our constitution be imperfect, nothing but a reform
in representation will rectify its abuses; if it be perfect, nothing
but the same reform will perpetuate its blessings. We now address you as citizens, for to be citizens you became soldiers, nor
can we help wishing that all soldiers partaking the passions and
interest of the people would remember, that they were once citizens, that seduction made them soldiers, but nature made them
men. We address you without any authority save that of reason,
and if we obtain the coincidence of public opinion, it is neither by*

force nor stratagem, for we have no power to terrify, no artifice to cajole, no fund to seduce; here we sit without mace or beadle, neither a mystery nor a craft, nor a corporation; in four words lies all our power—universal emancipation and representative legislature—yet we are confident that on the pivot of this principle, a convention, still less a society, still less a single man, will be able first to move and then to raise the world: we therefore wish for Catholic emancipation without any modification, but still we consider this necessary enfranchisement as merely the portal to the temple of national freedom; wide as this entrance is, wide enough to admit three millions, it is narrow when compared to the capacity and comprehension of our beloved principle, which takes in every individual of the Irish nation, casts an equal eye over the whole island, embraces all that think, and feels for all that suffer; the Catholic cause is subordinate to our cause, and included in it; for, as United Irishmen, we adhere to no sect, but to society—to no cause, but Christianity—to no party, but the whole people. In the sincerity of our souls do we desire Catholic emancipation: but were it obtained to-morrow, to-morrow would we go on as we do to-day, in the pursuit of that reform, which would still be wanting to ratify their liberties as well as our own. For both these purposes it appears necessary that provincial conventions should assemble preparatory to the convention of the Protestant people; the delegates of the Catholic body are not justified in communicating with individuals or even bodies of inferior authority, and therefore an assembly of a similar nature and organisation is necessary to establish an intercourse of sentiments, an uniformity of conduct, an united cause and an united nation; if a convention on the one part does not soon follow, and is not soon connected with that on the other, the common cause will split into the partial interest, the people will relapse into inattention and inertness, the union of affection and exertion will dissolve, and too probably some local insurrections, instigated by the malignity of our common enemy, may commit the character and risque the tranquility of the island, which can be obviated only by the influence of an assembly arising from, assimilated with the people, and whose spirit may be, as it were, knit with the soul of the nation, unless the sense of the Protestant people be on their part as fairly collected and as judiciously directed, unless individual exertion consolidates into collective strength, unless the particles unite into one mass; we may perhaps serve some person or some party for a little, but the public not at all; the nation is neither insolent, nor rebellious, nor seditious; while it knows its rights, it is unwilling to manifest its powers; it would rather supplicate administration to anticipate revolution by well-timed reform, and to save their country in mercy to themselves. The fifteenth of February approaches, a day ever memorable in the annals of this country as the birth-day of new Ireland; let parochial meetings be held as soon as possible, let each parish return delegates, let the sense of Ulster be again

declared

declared from Dungannon on a day auspicious to union, peace and freedom, and the spirit of the North will again become the spirit of the nation. The civil assembly ought to claim the attendance of the military associations, and we have addressed you, citizen soldiers, on this subject from the belief, that your body uniting conviction with zeal, and zeal with activity, may have much influence over your countrymen, your relations and friends. We offer only a general outline to the public, and meaning to address Ireland, presume not at present to fill up the plan or pre-occupy the mode of its execution, we have thought it our duty to speak.—Answer us by actions; you have taken time for consideration; fourteen long years are elapsed since the rise of your associations; and in 1782 did you imagine that in 1792 this nation would still remain unrepresented? How many nations, in this interval, have gotten the start of Ireland? How many of your countrymen have sunk into the grave?"——In contempt of our said Lord the King, in open violation of the laws of this kingdom, to the evil and pernicious example of all others in the like case offending, and against the peace of our said Lord the King, his crown and dignity.—WHEREUPON the said Attorney General of our said Lord the King, who for our said Lord the King in this behalf prosecutes, prays the consideration of the court here in the premisses, and due process of law may be awarded against him the said Archibald Hamilton Rowan in this behalf, to make him answer to our said Lord the King touching and concerning the premisses aforesaid.

ARTHUR WOLFE.

THOMAS KEMMIS, *Attorney.*

Received the 8th of June 1793.

(Copy.)

To this information Mr. ROWAN appeared by *Matthew Dowling*, gent. his attorney, and pleaded the general issue—Not Guilty—and the Court having appointed Wednesday the 29th day of January, 1794, for the trial of the said issue, the undernamed persons were sworn upon the jury:

Sir F. HUTCHINSON, Bart.	JOHN READ,
FREDERICK TRENCH, Esq.	ROBERT LEA,
WILLIAM DUKE MOORE,	RICHARD FOX,
HUMPHRY MINCHIN,	CHRISTOPHER HARRISON,
RICHARD MANDERS,	GEORGE PERRIN,
GEORGE PALMER,	THOMAS SHERRARD.

Upon calling over the jury, *John Read* was objected to, as holding a place under the crown, but the Attorney General insisting upon the illegality of the objection, and observing that it went against all that was honourable and respectable in the land, it was

over-

over-ruled by the court. *Richard Fox,* when called to the book, was interrogated whether he had ever given an opinion upon the fubject then to be tried, to which he anfwered, that he did not know what the fubject of the trial was. The fame queftion was put to *Thomas Sherrard,* who returned a fimilar anfwer.

Joſhua Dixon, who had been fworn upon the jury, with-out any objection, here ftated, that he had given an opinion upon the fubject, upon which Mr. Attorney General confented that he fhould be withdrawn, but protefted againft the right of the defendant's counfel to examine the jurors as they had done. If they had any objection, they ought to make their challenge, and fupport it by evidence.

The counfel for the defendant anfwered, that they would not acquiefce in the confent of the Attorney General to with-draw the juror, if their examination was to be objected to, and intimated that the juror ought to be withdrawn upon the *defire* of the Attorney General, without any confent whatever being entered into.

Hereupon the Attorney General defired that the juror might be withdrawn.

Counſel for the Proſecution.	*Counſel for the Defendant.*
Mr. ATTORNEY GENERAL,	Mr. CURRAN,
PRIME SERJEANT,	Mr. RECORDER,
SOLICITOR GENERAL,	Mr. FLETCHER.
Mr. FRANKLAND,	*
Mr. RUXTON,	
Agent, Mr. KEMMIS.	*Agent,* Mr. DOWLING.

Mr. *Ruxton* opened the pleadings.

Mr. ATTORNEY GENERAL—*My Lord and Gentlemen of the Jury,* In this cafe, between the KING and ARCHIBALD HAMIL-TON ROWAN, Efq. it is my duty to profecute on behalf of the crown. The traverfer in this cafe, gentlemen, ftands accufed upon an information filed *ex officio,* by the King's Attorney General, for publifhing a feditious libel. It is my duty to lay the facts of this cafe before you—it will be the duty of another of his majefty's fervants to obferve upon the evidence. I fhall ftate the nature of the charge and the queftions you are to try : I will then ftate fuch circumftances as are neceffary to be taken into your confideration, for the purpofe of underftanding and expounding that paper which the information charges to be a malicious and feditious libel. The information charges, that

* *Mr. Emmet,* and fome other gentlemen, who had been originally con-cerned in this caufe, as counfel for the defendant, feeling a perfonal inte-reft, declined any longer acting in that capacity.

ARCHIBALD

ARCHIBALD HAMILTON ROWAN, malicioufly defigning and intending to excite and diffufe amongft the fubjects of this realm difcontents, difaffection and difloyalty to the king and government, and to raife very dangerous feditions and tumults, and to draw the government into fcandal, infamy and difgrace, and to incite the fubjects to attempt, by force and with arms, to make alterations in the government, and to excite the fubjects to anarchy, to overturn the conftitution and overawe the legiflature of the kingdom, did publifh the libel fet forth in the information. In this cafe, therefore, it will be for you, gentlemen, upon the evidence which fhall be laid before you, to determine, whether the traverfer has been the publifher of that paper or not. I fhall, in the courfe of what I am to offer to the court and to you, read the very libel itfelf, and make fuch obfervations as occur to me to be proper in the prefent ftate of the bufinefs. Previous, however, to my doing fo, I will take the liberty, gentlemen, of ftating to you fome facts and circumftances that appear to me deferving of attention in the inveftigation of the matter before you ; and in doing fo, I fhall carefully avoid mentioning many facts and circumftances which thofe difgraceful times have furnifhed, that might lead your verdict one way or the other. I fhall not attempt to excite your paffions.. I am happy at length that this cafe has come before an impartial jury. It has long been the defire of every good man that this matter fhould come to trial before that conftitutional tribunal who ftand arbiters in this cafe, to protect the accufed againft the power of the crown; not refembling any of thofe profecutions which the turbulence of former times have excited, you are affembled with that coolnefs which the folemnity of the occafion requires, to determine whether Mr. ROWAN be guilty, criminally, of the offence charged againft him. Take the libel into your confideration, and determine, as the law now allows you to do, whether it be a libellous publication, tending to excite fedition, to overawe the government ; or tending to produce any of the effects imputed to it. I fhall now proceed to ftate a few facts which I faid it was my duty to do. I fhall call your attention to the hiftory of the times about which this libel was publifhed :—No man, let his fituation be what it may, can be too cautious in uttering what ought not to be faid, which might influence your judgment upon your oaths ; and in that office which I hold, which is the office of the people, as well as of the crown, it is more than a common duty to take care not to ftep beyond that 'line which leads to common juftice. I am warranted by the authority of a court 'of juftice, by the proceedings of the King's Bench in England ; by the opinion of a Judge of as much fpirit and independence as any man, I allude to the cafe of the printer of the Morning Chronicle, in which Lord KENYON informs the jury, That it is neceffary, in cafes of this kind, to

attend

attend to the circumſtances and hiſtory of the times in which the
libel was publiſhed. They tend to explain the motives which induced the publication, and the meaning of the libel itſelf. He
ſays it is impoſſible for the court or a jury to ſhut their ears
againſt the hiſtory of the times. Beſides that common principle, I am the more juſtifiable in what I ſhall ſtate, becauſe
the libel charged comes from that body of men who have
conſtituted themſelves by the name of " *The Society of* UNITED
IRISHMEN *in Dublin.*" From the time of the reſtoration of
our conſtitution—from the year 1784 to the year 1792—this
country advanced in proſperity with a regular progreſs and grada-
tion. The agriculture, commerce and police improved ;—the ci-
vilization of the country proceeded uniformly from year to year ;—
the commonalty began to enjoy bleſſings they had been ſtrangers
to—ſhips crouded in our harbours—commerce occupied our ports
—culture in our fields, and peace and happineſs every where prevailed. The French revolution took place, when there were found
many men, who from ſituation, from circumſtances, from ambi-
tion, were deſirous of commotion. Clubs were formed in the
metropolis with the avowed intention of improving the conſtitution, for they muſt aſſume ſome pretext, but with a view, I fear,
under colour of that, to overturn it. They ſubſiſted here in
this town under different names, till at length in 1791, they
formed themſelves into a club, called the Society of *United
Iriſhmen*, conſiſting at firſt of a ſmall number, compoſed of various claſſes of men, certainly ſome of them of the learned profeſ-
ſions, ſome of the loweſt members in the community. In 1791
they continued to pour upon the public daily publications, ſetting forth the diſtreſſes of the people, teaching them to be diſ-
contented with their ſituation and the government of the country. Things thus proceeded down to the latter end of the year
1792. In the latter end of autumn, 1792, the allied armies
retired from the kingdom of France : the convention of that
kingdom began to hold a high language, and to talk of overſet-
ting the government of kings. An attack was made upon re-
gal authority, a ſpirit was ſtirred among thoſe deſirous of ſuch
ſchemes—it ſeemed to inſpire them. There was a talk of over-
turning the government of king, lords, and commons—ſucceſs at
the ſame time ſeemed to crown the arms of the French ; they
advanced beyond their own territory, and menaced an attack upon
the United States of *Holland*. In this ſituation of things, there
did pervade a gloomy apprehenſion for the ſafety of the country.
Emiſſaries from France were ſpread throughout Europe ; a new
array of a new corps was made in Dublin in the noon day, de-
corated with emblems of ſedition ; they were to parade in your
ſtreets, and to be marſhalled in your ſquares. The Volunteers of
Ireland, a name revered by this country and by every good man
loving the conſtitution, that ſacred name was made a cloak for
arming

arming a banditti, that arraigned the conſtitution and degraded the name of Volunteer; a National Guard was formed upon the plan of thoſe in Paris. It is notorious to every man in Ireland, to every man in the Britiſh dominions, that ſuch men aſſembled with clothing of a particular uniform, with emblems of harps diveſted of the royal crown; every thing was undertaken to ſpread the ſpirit which animated themſelves, and can any man forget the ſituation of Dublin in September, October, and November, 1792, which cauſed apprehenſions in thoſe who were well affected to the government and tranquillity of the country? Can any man forget the ſtate of the nation at this period? her credit was ſhaken, good people ſtood appalled; thoſe loving peace ſtood aſtoniſhed at the languidneſs of government. At length that government came forward which had never ſlept, but had been proceeding with mildneſs, determined not to go forth to action, nor have recourſe to any ſeverer remedies until every man in the ſtate, who had a moment's reflection, muſt ſee the neceſſity of the exertion. The troops are ſummoned to meet, the guards are ſummoned to aſſemble, and the firſt battalion of National Guards were to have paraded, clothed like Frenchmen. The night before, the Lord Lieutenant had ſummoned the council of the kingdom; upon that night, a proclamation iſſued, ſtating that there were intentions to aſſemble men in arms, with ſeditious ſigns, and apprehending danger from their ſo aſſembling; it prohibited their meeting. The proclamation iſſued on a Saturday night, and it produced that ſatisfaction which all good men deſirous of order ſeek to enjoy; and they felt once more the pleaſurable aſſurance that they had a government. Appalled by this proclamation, the corps did not meet on the 8th of December as it was intended, though ſome few were ſeen dreſſed in the National Guard uniform, parading the ſtreets with a mob, crouding at their heels; but however nothing followed. They were ſeen, and bleſſed be God, they were ſeen no more. This proclamation, having for its object the preſervation of the peace of this kingdom and the city in particular, mildly and coolly cautioning all men againſt thoſe meaſures, held out the conſequences that muſt neceſſarily follow, if they did not obey. A proclamation which received the applauſe of the great and good, of the lovers of ſociety, and of every man not loſt to the ſenſe of order and the conſtitution; but odious to every man who was attached to the Society of United Iriſhmen, and whoſe views correſponded with it. While I ſpeak of that Society let me not be underſtood as imputing to every man who is in it, thoſe illegal motives which I impute to the Society in general: there might have been in it no doubt many well meaning perſons, for there were men picked up induſtriouſly to lend their names, in the ſtreets, in the lanes, in the markets, in the highways, and in the fields, even the rich and induſtrious grazier was procured to lend his name. To

C

the

the good, this proclamation gave pleafure and fatisfaction, to the bad it became odious and deteftable; and they accordingly form-ed the intention of bringing the government into difgrace for iffuing that proclamation. A few days after, I am not aware of the particular day, but a few days after the iffuing the pro-clamation, the fociety affembled; the proclamation was upon the 7th, the addrefs I fpeak of was publifhed the 16th of De-cember. The meeting therefore muft have been between the 7th and the 16th of December. The fociety, I fay, affembled, and they agreed upon a certain addrefs to the Volunteers of Ireland, and Dr. *Drennan* is there ftated to have been in the chair, and the traverfer *Secretary.* At that meeting—at that meeting the addrefs to the Volunteers was agreed upon, which is the libel charged againft Mr. *Rowan* as being guilty of pub-lifhing it. Under that addrefs, this was to be done. The volun-teers of Dublin were to be called into action, and thofe papers were to be difperfed among them. For that purpofe the feve-ral volunteer corps at that time exifting in Dublin were fum-moned to affemble in a houfe in Cope-ftreet, belonging to *Par-don*, a fencing-mafter, upon the 16th of December. Accord-ingly upon that day, the feveral corps of volunteers did go with fide arms to this fencing-fchool in Cope-ftreet. The traverfer was, I believe, at the head of one of thefe corps; another very celebrated name was at the head of another of them, *James Napper Tandy.* Who was at the head of the others I am not able to inform you. But in the afternoon of the 16th of December, feveral volunteers, with uniforms and fide arms, affembled in the fencing-fchool. In this fencing-fchool, gentlemen, there was a gallery, and into that gallery there was fuch public accefs that what paffed below may be faid to have paffed in the face of the world; to fuch excefs had thofe perfons carried their defigns as to expofe them to open view, and if I ftate what is not true, there are one hundred perfons in the volunteer corps of the city of Dublin, out of whom a multitude may be called to contradict me. The corps, I fay, affembled in that room. There ftood in the middle of the room a table, and there was a vaft number of printed papers brought in and placed on the table. The dif-ferent corps entered into feveral refolutions, having taken into their wife confideration the proclamation iffued by the Lord Lieutenant and Council; the neceffity for iffuing it is inveftigated, each of the corps took feverally into their confideration the propriety of it, and next day publifhed their different fentiments all expref-five of ftrong difapprobation. So that it is manifeft they were brought publicly together for a ftate purpofe, and to debate a ftate matter. While thefe refolutions were in difcuffion, Mr. *Tandy* and Mr. *Rowan* were feen to take from the table the printed papers that lay upon it, and difperfe them among the feveral volunteers who ftood around them, and to hand them

from

from the lower room to perfons in the gallery, and to perſons not in their confidence; they were handed up promiſcuouſly to any man there, and to many perfons in the ſtreets that evening and the next day; they were flung out of the windows to the mob that ſtood round the room. Theſe, gentlemen, are the circumſtances which preceded the publication of this paper by the traverfer: it will be for you to confider with what view and purpoſe a paper like this was compoſed and thus difperſed. If you believe it was a candid and fair difcuſſion upon conſtitutional ſubjects, or upon grievances real or ſuppoſed, you will not con- fider it as a libel: but if from internal evidence in the paper it- ſelf, and from the circumſtances attending it, you believe it was no ſuch thing, but that it was publiſhed with a view to raiſe difcontents againſt the government—to diſturb the people—to overawe the parliament, or any branch of the ſtate, then you muſt find him guilty. You, gentlemen, will take the paper into your room with you; confider it coolly, and difcharged from all you have heard abroad refpecting it, and determine in your own minds whether it be poſſible to give it any other con- ſtruction than that which the information has afcribed to it. I will ſubmit to you, gentlemen—to you alone I defire to fub- mit the cool examination of that paper, upon the paper itſelf. It is impoſſible with all the ingenuity (and he who comes afcer me on the other ſide has as much ingenuity as any man) to ſhew that it was not written for the purpoſe of overawing the legi- ſlature, or to account for it in any other way. This brings me now to the libel itſelf, and as it has not been read to you in this court, for in open court I wiſh it to be read, I will read it, and make ſuch obfervations as I think neceſſary. " *The Society of* " *United Iriſhmen, at Dublin, to the Volunteers of Ireland. William* " *Drennan, Chairman, Archibald Hamilton Rowan, Secretary. Ci-* " *tizen Soldiers.*" A language, gentlemen, which excites ideas in one's mind that cannot be defcribed. You will perceive in this publication the frippery of the French language as now uſed; and thoſe ideas will be excited, which muſt fill the mind of every man who regards religion, ſociety, or peace, with ter- ror and alarm. " *Citizen Soldiers, you firſt took up arms to pro-* " *tect your country from foreign enemies, and from domeſtic diſtur-* " *bance. For the ſame purpoſes it now becomes neceſſary that you* " *ſhould reſume them.*" The Society of United Iriſhmen, who ſay they are no corporation, yet as if they were a corporation, preſume to tell the armed people of Ireland when it is they ſhould aſſemble: Is that or is it not tending to fedition? Is it or is it not aſſuming a power to overawe the parliament and overturn the government itſelf? " *A proclamation has been iſſued in England for* " *embodying the militia, and a proclamation has been iſſued by the* " *Lord Lieutenant and Council in Ireland, for repreſſing all feditious* " *aſſociations. In conſequence of both theſe proclamations, it is rea-*

C 2   " *ſonable*

" *fonable to apprehend danger from abroad, and danger at home.*
" *For whence but from apprehended danger, are thofe menacing*
" *preparations for war drawn through the ftreets of this capital,*"
(alluding to fome cannon which were drawn through the ftreets
a few days before to protect the inhabitants againft the dangers
apprehended,) " *or whence if not to create that internal commotion*
" *which was not found, to fhake that credit which was not affected,*
" *to blaft that Volunteer honour which was hitherto inviolate.*"
What! did the proclamation forbidding feditious affociations
and affemblies of men, with banners expreffive of difloyalty, violate
the honour of that glorious inftitution, which was,raifed to protect
and fupport that conftitution, that thofe feditious men calling
themfelves volunteers were affembled to deftroy, and this Society of United Irifhmen did wifh to overturn? That is
what is ftated in this, for fo I will call it until you
teach me another language, this abominable feditious libel.
" *Are thofe terrible fuggeft..ns and rumours and whifpers, that meet us*
" *at every corner and agitate at leaft our old men, our women and chil-*
" *dren. Whatever be the motive, or from whatever quarter it arifes,*
" *alarm has arifen; and you,* VOLUNTEERS OF IRELAND,
" *are therefore fummoned to arms at the inftance of government, as*
" *well as by the refponfibility attached to your character, and the*
" *permanent obligations of your inftitution.*" Firft you will
obferve gentlemen, they make the antient volunteers thofe whofe
honor was wounded and blafted by the proclamation, and then
they tell them that the proclamation has fummoned them to affemble in arms—ftrange inconfiftency of rhapfody! With regard to fuch parts as are unintelligible, for there are many parts
the moft bombaftical and abfurd that ever appeared in any publication, I pafs them over, it is not my wifh to criticife upon
them. " *We will not at this day, condefcend to quote authorities*
for the right of having and of ufing arms." Who had called in
queftion the right of the people to carry arms? Is it becaufe the
government faid, that arms fhould not be ufed to the deftruction or
danger of the people, that therefore the legality of carrying them
is queftioned ? " *But we will cry aloud, even amidft the ftorm raifed*
" *by the witchcraft of a proclamation.*" Is that a direct charge
againft government, that they laid a fcheme to raife a ftorm ?
" *That to your formation was owing the peace and protection of this*
" *ifland, to your relaxation has been owing its relapfe into impotence*
" *and infignificance, to your renovation muft be owing its future free-*
" *dom, and its prefent tranquillity. You are therefore fummoned to*
" *arms, in order to preferve your country in that guarded quiet, which*
" *may fecure it from external hoftility, and to maintain that internal*
" *regimen throughout the land, which fuperfeding a notorious police or*
" *a fufpected militia, may preferve the bleffings of peace by a vigilant*
" *preparation for war.*" Now, gentlemen, here you fee a
reflection caft : if they meant to ftate a grievance, or to reafon

upon

upon a point of conſtitution why not do it ?—they had a right.
But does that mark the meaning and intention of the publication ?
Why reflect upon legal eſtabliſhments, and why endeavour to cry
down a body of men, which it was well known to be in the con-
templation of government to raiſe ? They endeavoured to render
odious the militia before it was created, becauſe they foreſaw it
would protect the ſtate againſt the ſchemes which they had
formed.   They next inform theſe men, that they are not em-
bodied as before ſtated, for the protection of their country, but
to reſiſt a body of men about to be conſtituted by government
for the protection and ſafety of the ſtate, but whom they are
pleaſed to deem ſuſpicious ; is not this to raiſe diſturbance ? is
not this to excite tumult ? " *Citizen ſoldiers, to arms ! Take up*
" *the ſhield of freedom and the pledges of peace,—peace the motive and*
" *end of your virtuous inſtitution. War an occaſional duty ought*
" *never to be made an occupation.   Every man ſhould become a ſoldier*
" *in the defence of his rights ; no man ought to continue a ſoldier for*
" *offending the rights of others.   The ſacrifice of life in the ſervice of*
" *our country is a duty much too honourable to be entruſted to merce-*
" *naries, and at this time, when your country has by public authority*
" *been declared in danger, we conjure you by your intereſt, your duty*
" *and your glory, to ſtand to your arms, and in ſpite of a police, in*
" *ſpite of a fencible militia.*"   The police eſtabliſhed in the different
counties are firſt repreſented in an odious light to the volunteers :
a reflection is caſt upon the militia, and now the mercenaries are
ſtigmatized and a diſtinction taken between them and the volunteers of Ireland, thus ſummoned by this corporation of
United Iriſhmen. " *In virtue of two proclamations to maintain good*
" *order in your vicinage, and tranquillity in Ireland.   It is only by*
" *the military array of men in whom they confide, whom they have*
" *been accuſtomed to revere as the guardians of domeſtic peace, the*
" *protectors of their liberties and lives, that the preſent agitation of the*
" *people can be ſtilled, that tumult and licentiouſneſs can be repreſſed,*
" *obedience ſecured to exiſting law, and a calm confidence, diffuſed*
" *through the public mind, in the ſpeedy reſurrection of a free conſtitution,*
" *of liberty and of equality.*"   Here, gentlemen, let me call your
attention, what meaning can be given to theſe words by the
plaineſt man in the hall of theſe courts ? What ! was our free
conſtitution dead.   Do the gentlemen intend by way of argument to excuſe this as the conſideration of a grievance ? They
tell the people they have no conſtitution, that they might look
for another ; is this a cool diſquiſition upon a matter that every
man has a right to enquire into ? is not this to excite tumult ?
Liberty and Equality ! Words, gentlemen, that it would be painful to me to obſerve upon to the extent to which they go, words
that ſuggeſt but too much to every good and reaſonable mind ;
there is no man in this kingdom who would not lay down his
life to preſerve true liberty and equality ; but theſe are but conceptions

ceptions to cajole the ignorant : the vulgar abuse of a conſtitutioa which we poſſeſs to the envy of the world. " *Liberty and* " *equality, words which we uſe for an opportunity of repelling calumny* " *and of ſaying, that by liberty we never underſtood unlimited freedom,* " *nor by equality, the levelling of property or the deſtruction of ſub-* " *ordination. This is a calumny invented by that faction, or that* " *gang, which miſrepreſents the king to the people, and the people to* " *the king, traduces one half of the nation to cajole the other, and by* " *keeping up diſtruſt and diviſion, wiſhes to continue the proud arbi-* " *trators of the fortune and fate of Ireland*". Is not this traducing the government ? But attend, gentlemen, to their definition of liberty. " *Liberty is the exerciſe of all our rights, natural and* " *political, ſecured to us and our poſterity by a real repreſentation of* " *the people ; and equality is the extenſion of the conſtituent, to the ful-* " *leſt dimenſions of the conſtitution, of the elective franchiſe to the* " *whole body of the people, to the end that government, which is col-* " *lective power, may be guided by collective will, and that legiſlation* " *may originate from public reaſon, keep pace with public improve-* " *ment, and terminate in public happineſs.*" Certainly, gentlemen, the ſentence is very ſonorous, and agreeable enough to the ear ; but to the mind it conveys nothing but this, that government is to be conducted by the will of every man, high and low, rich and poor, ignorant and learned ; the people are to govern the people, and how they will do ſo, unhappily for mankind, has been learned from experience. Mark this next paſſage gen- tlemen, for I confeſs I do not underſtand it. " *If our conſtitution* " *be imperfect, nothing but a reform in the repreſentation will rectify* " *its abuſes ; if it be perfect, nothing but the ſame reform will per-* " *petuate its bleſſings.*" This is ſomething like *tobacco hic.*—— If our conſtitution be imperfect, nothing but a reform will render it perfect ;—if it be perfect, ſtill the reform is neceſſary to keep it perfect.—In whatever light it is viewed, reform is neceſſary, and a good conſtitution requires amendment as much as a bad one. I do not feel it neceſſary to dwell upon this, becauſe it is ſo unintelligible, that it cannot deſerve notice. But ſee next what endeavours have been uſed to render odious among the people, thoſe forces upon whom our peace and tranquillity de- pend. " *We now addreſs you as citizens, for to be citizens you* " *became ſoldiers, nor can we help wiſhing that all ſoldiers, par-* " *taking the paſſions and intereſts of the people, would remember that* " *they were once citizens, that ſeduction made them ſoldiers, but nature* " *made them men.*" How will my learned friend when he comes to ſpeak of this part of the caſe ſatisfy you, that it was neceſſary in a publication of this ſort, recommending a reform in par- liament, and to be diſſeminated among thouſands, to tell the ſol- diers, the forces of the ſtate, that their profeſſion was diſho- nourable, that they were impoſed upon, that they ſhould not be entruſted with the protection of the ſtate ? Gentlemen, I am

unwilling

unwilling to dwell upon thefe paffages, it is but neceffary to
mention them to fhew their danger, if they deferve confideration
you will give it to them, if not, you will not wafte your attention upon them. " *That nature made them men.*" It required
no authority to fatisfy them of that. " *We addrefs you without*
" *any authority, fave that of reafon, and if we obtain the coin-*
" *cidence of public opinion, it is neither by force nor ftratagem, for*
" *we have no power to terrify, no artifice to cajole, no fund to*
" *feduce. Here we fit without mace or beadle*". What they
allude to, I fuppofe you, gentlemen, apprehend, they feem to
difdain any diftinction in civil inftitutions. " *Neither a myftery,*
" *nor a craft, nor a corporation.—In four words lies all our power,*
" UNIVERSAL EMANCIPATION and REPRESEN-
" TATIVE LEGISLATURE." In thefe four words lies all
the power of the United Irifhmen, according to this publication,
approved of by the traverfer; he himfelf a member of that fociety, and fecretary of the meeting which compofed it. " *Uni-*
" *verfal Emancipation!*" By that I prefume is meant the giving a right of voting to every man in the community. " *And*
" *Reprefentative Legiflature!*" The meaning of thefe words is
but too obvious. The conftitution is often in the mouths of
men, when the deftruction of it is in their hearts. If the plan
of thefe people were carried into effect, where would be the
Houfe of Peers?—for our legiflature, gentlemen, confifts of
King, Lords and Commons. When government is guided by the
will of all the people and their force carried into action, where
will be the Houfe of Peers? Where will be our conftitution?
buried in the anarchy of republican power, formed from the
dregs of the people. A government confifting of all the people,
guided by the will of all the people; what fenfe but this can be
put upon thefe words? If indeed the context of the paper fhews
you, gentlemen, that any thing elfe was meant (than as I interpret the words) you will take it altogether in that fenfe in
which it appears to have been meant. God forbid I fhould
endeavour to wreft any thing to impute guilt to the gentleman who now ftands at your bar that the *whole* of the paper
does not warrant! But if the words bear that meaning which I
give them, who will fay, that guilt fhall not be imputed to him?
You will form your opinion from reading the whole, and com-
paring the feveral parts with each other. Here comes a fentence
which will puzzle you a little, but which with fome comment
may be underftood. " *Yet we are confident that on the pivot of this*
" *principle, a convention, lefs ftill, a fociety, lefs a fingle man,*
" *will be able firft to move and then to raife the world.*" Here
is an open declaration of their wifh to raife the people, net
only of this country but of the whole world; a proof of peaceable
" intent. *We therefore wifh for Catholic emancipation without any*
" *modification, but ftill we confider this neceffary enfranchifement as*

4

" *merely*

" merely the portal to the temple of national freedom; wide as
" this entrance is—wide enough to admit three millions—it is nar-
" row when compared to the capacity and comprehension of our
" beloved principle, which takes in every individual of the
" Irish nation, casts an equal eye over the whole island, em-
" braces all that think, and feels for all that suffer. The Catholic
" cause is subordinate to our cause, and included in it; for, as
" United Irishmen, we adhere to no sect but to society—to no
" creed but Christianity—to no party but to the whole people.
" In the sincerity of our souls do we desire Catholic emancipation;
" but were it obtained to-morrow, to-morrow would we go on, as
" we do to-day, in the pursuit of that reform, which would
" still be wanting to ratify their liberties as well as our own.
    " For both these purposes it appears necessary that provincial
" conventions should assemble preparatory to the convention of the
" Protestant people. The delegates of the Catholic body are not
" justified in communicating with individuals, or even bodies
" of inferior authority, and therefore an assembly of a similar
" nature and organization,' (French language still occurring
with French ideas) " is necessary to establish an intercourse of
" sentiment, an uniformity of conduct, an united cause and an
" united nation. If a convention on the one part does not soon fol-
" low, and is not soon connected with that on the other, the com-
" mon cause will split into the partial interest; the people
" relax into inattention and inertness; the union of affection and
" exertion will dissolve; and too probably some local insurrections,
" instigated by the malignity of our common enemy, may com-
" mit the character and risque the tranquillity of the island."
" Gentlemen, the paper mentions here the common enemy, as to
who is meant by the expression, you will judge; did they
mean those who were about to defeat their machinations, and
who would not commit the tranquillity of the island to the convention to be assembled? it says " an assembly of a similar na-
" ture and organization is necessary." These are Gallic sen-
tences and suited only to the soil of France. " And risque the
" tranquility of the island, which can be obviated only by the
" influence of an assembly arising from, assimilated with the
" people, and whose spirit may be, as it were, knit with the
" soul of the nation, unless the sense of the Protestant people be,
" on their part, as fairly collected and as judiciously directed; un-
" less individual exertion consolidates into collective strength; un-
" less the particles unite into one mass, we may perhaps serve
" some person or some party for a little, but the public not at
" all. The nation is neither insolent, nor rebellious, nor sedi-
" tious. While it knows its rights, it is unwilling to mani-
" fest its powers; it would rather supplicate administration
" to anticipate revolution by a well-timed reform, and to
" save their country in mercy to themselves."——An address

drefs to the volunteers to obtain univerfal emancipation !—holding
out, that this kind of remonftrance fhould be attended to, before the power of the nation fhould be exerted. What meaning does a common underftanding annex to thefe words ?—Was
it not a threat ?—Was it not to fpirit up the minds of the
people againft the members of parliament ?—Was it neceffary
for the purpofe of cool inveftigation, or to obtain conftitutional
redrefs, that the people fhould exert their power ? and to
threaten parliament, by telling them there was a force to be
raifed againft them ? Unlefs a reafonable account is given why
this language was inferted, and what the meaning of it was, I
muft prefume, it was for the purpofe I mention. " *The fifteenth*
" *of February approaches, a day ever memorable in the annals of*
" *this country as the birth-day of new Ireland ; let parochial meet-*
" *ings be held as foon as poffible,*—[here you have an exact deli-
" neation of the French government]—*let each parifh return de-*
" *legates, let the fenfe of Ulfter be again declared from Dungannon on*
" *a day aufpicious to union, peace and freedom, and the fpirit of the*
" *North will again become the fpirit of the nation.*" Now, gentlemen of the jury, you will mark this next fentence, and it will
be a clue to the whole. " *The civil affembly ought to claim the atten-*
" *dance of the military affociations, and we have addreffed you, citizen*
" *foldiers, on this fubject, from the belief, that your body uniting con-*
" *viction with zeal, and zeal with activity, may have much influence*
" *over your countrymen, your relations and friends.*" The nation
is in danger from foreign foes and from domeftic enemies—fo
they ftate. The proclamation calls forth the forces of the ftate.
The United Irifhmen raife their audible voice, and call the people
to arms. For what ? Is it to affift the government to repel the
foreign enemy and feditious foe ? But how ?—A convention is
to be affembled, and they are to call around them the national
forces. The convention was to meet at Dungannon—there affembled, were thefe forces to reprefs foreign foes and domeftic
fedition ? Gentlemen, it is but too obvious for what purpofe
this was intended : this fentence fpeaks the language of the whole
of this paper—and if it had been drawn with more art than it
is, here is the clue to the whole :—the force of the nation was
to be affembled under the controul of the convention affembled
under the *great feal* of the *United Irifhmen,* who fay they are not
a corporation ; but who have a corporation feal :—For what
purpofe ? to obtain *univerfal emancipation* and *reprefentative legifla-*
ture ! They are held up as fuch a force and controuling power
as muft produce that effect upon the king, lords and commons.
—An effect which they profefs to have defigned for the good
of their country—if they did, they fhould feek its accomplifhment by reafon and by argument. But to publifh a call to arms
to that power and authority which for years this country has

D   refpected,

refpected, and from which, certainly, fince 1784 every bleffing in fociety has been derived (and every man who looks for thofe bleffings of life otherwife than by a due regard to all ranks of men, blafphemes the God which made us all)—I fay, to call upon the whole body of the people to rife in arms and be their own rulers, is a fpecies of government, which, when it comes, will be an equal misfortune to the poor and the rich.—The rich would loofe that which they enjoy, and more—the power of contributing to the neceffities of the poor—Induftry will no longer continue to have the motives to labour and thofe habits of œconomy which the protection of a mild conftitution encourages, but the people will be turned out to a fyftem of plunder, robbery and murder, fuch as we find prevailing in another country. The paper goes on and recites, " *We offer* " *only a general outline to the public, and meaning to addrefs Ireland,* " *we prefume not at prefent to fill up the plan or pre-occupy the mode* " *of its execution, we have thought it our duty to fpeak.—Anfwer* " *us by actions.*[An open invitation to force and violence]— " *You have taken time for confideration. Fourteen long years are* " *elapfed fince the rife of your affociations ; and in* 1792 *did you ima-* " *gine that in* 1792 *this nation would ftill remain unreprefented ?*" Thefe volunteers of 1782 had not all thefe fchemes in view—but this Society here exprefsly tells the people, with arms in their hands, that they remain unreprefented ; and adds, " *How many* " *nations, in this interval, have gotten the ftart of Ireland ? How* " *many of our countrymen have funk into the grave ?*"—What is meant by nations having got the ftart of Ireland ? is it the revolution in France ; they indeed have gotten the ftart of Ireland in calamity and diftrefs, long may they hold their diftance, and long, long may be the period before we fhall overtake them, is my moft fincere and earneft wifh.

Such is this paper—I have read it accurately. Gentlemen of the jury, it is for you to confider the whole of it, and determine whether it was publifhed by Mr. *Rowan*, and whether it be a libel or not ?—If you fhould be of opinion that Mr. *Rowan* is guilty of pub-lifhing this paper, then you are to confider whether it is a libel or not ?—Gentlemen, it is the peculiar felicity of this country, the great bleffing of our conftitution, that we have a trial by jury ; in France it is polluted ; but it is the boaft of our conftitution that we have a trial by jury, and the great prefervative of that blef-fing and of the conftitution itfelf, is the liberty of the prefs ; that is the great bulwark of our free conftitution, we have a trial by jury, and of the freedom of the prefs you are the guardians. You, gentlemen, are by the conftitution appointed to decide upon all thefe queftions touching the freedom of the prefs. The freedom of the prefs cannot be deftroyed but in two ways, firft, by the overweening power of the crown, 2dly, by its own licen-tioufnefs corrupting the minds of the people ; and when it is de-

I

ftroyed

ftroyed, then will our conftitution be at an end. While the
prefs is left open to cool and fair difcuffion upon legal and public topics of grievance and conftitution, fo long will the freedom
of our conftitution endure, and whenever an attempt is made
to controul it, you will ftep in and guard and protect it as you
would guard your property, your lives, and your liberties; you
will fecure it from licentioufnefs. Where its licentioufnefs is not
punifhed through the weaknefs or timidity of a jury, its freedom
can no longer exift. What does the paper which is the fubject of
the prefent queftion purport to be? it looks for a reform of parliament, it calls to arms the citizens under pretence of fupport-
ing the government by refifting it, by fpeaking of grievances
which cannot be endured, it is overawing the parliament. If
fuch licentioufnefs be tolerated, then the freedom of the prefs
will be deftroyed. You, gentlemen, will confider whether this
paper contains in itfelf internal evidence to fhew that the motives of its publication were not for the purpofe of reafoning
with the people, or for the neceffary correction of any evil in the
conftitution, but to excite fedition and tumult. If in that cafe you
believe that Mr. *Rowan* publifhed it, then you muft find him
guilty. If, on the other hand, you are of opinion, that this
was a cool and difpaffionate paper, reafoning with the people in
a becoming manner, acknowledging the authority of the law,
then you will acquit him. Further, let the tendency of the
paper be what it may, if you are of opinion, he did not publifh
it, then you muft acquit him. We will produce a witnefs to
fhew he publifhed an individual paper—we will prove that he
took feveral others and difperfed them abroad—if you believe
the evidence, it will be impoffible but that you muft be fatif-
fied he is guilty. Thus ftands the evidence. I have ftated that
the traverfer was Secretary to the *United Irifhmen*. It will be
proved thus:—he publifhed that paper; if he did, he acknowledged the contents of it to be true, and the paper ftates him to
be fecretary of the fociety. Gentlemen, fuch is the cafe as it
appears to me on the part of the crown. I will not pretend to
anticipate what may be offered by the gentlemen on the other
fide. Two topics, however, have occurred as likely to be introduced:—one is, the cafe of the volunteers—the other, the
functions of a jury under the late act of parliament. Upon the
firft, I have faid abundance to fatisfy you. I will fuppofe however,
that this paper was addreffed to the old volunteers: what then?
The tendency of the paper was to excite thofe volunteers to
commit actions that would tarnifh the honour acquired by
their previous conduct. Let them fhew that the proclamation
(againft which this was a counter-proclamation) went againft
the old volunteers—it meant no fuch thing—it defcribes them fo
and fo. But there were among the old volunteers men actuated
by new principles and new motives, that it became the duty

of

of government to fupprefs them. For your fake they did fo—
no government fhould be influenced but by the profperity of
the whole ftate. But in what refpect did thefe men refemble
the old volunteers? Not in a fingle feature: thefe men were affembled by the call of the *United Irifhmen* in Back-lane; the
ancient volunteers were affembled by the call of government and
the Lord Lieutenant, who diftributed arms among them from the
arfenal, for the public defence; they added to thefe out of their
own pockets whatever they thought neceffary; they were collected to fupport that conftitution which is now fought to be
overturned. Were thefe new volunteers of that defcription?
Were they fo formed? How were they equipped? The green
cockade was adopted in the place of the black. I have no neceffity for this; but fearful that men will have recourfe to fuch
topics to cajole you, I think it neceffary to take notice of them.
Secondly, as to the act of parliament within this kingdom, I
am not aware that it operates here; but even by it, as it now
ftands, and I told you fo before, you have a right to enter
into the guilt or innocence of intention upon this occafion, as
you would upon the trial of any other offence. Gentlemen, to
you, and moft willingly, I commit this cafe; I defire no more
than that you will by your verdict vindicate the freedom of the
prefs and punifh the licentioufnefs of it.

Firft witnefs for the Profecution.

JOHN LYSTER. Examined by the *Prime Serjeant.*

Q. Do you recollect the 16th of December, 1792?
A. I do.
Q. Do you recollect having been at any place that day?
A. I do.
Q. Where?
A. At one *Pardon's* houfe in Cope-ftreet.
Q. Were there many people affembled there?
A. There were to the amount of 150 or 200, with fide-arms
and uniforms, there was a table in the room.
Q. Did any perfon, and who, fit at that table?
A. There was Mr. *Hamilton Rowan* and Mr. *Napper Tandy* at
it, and a good many others.
(Q. By the court—What do you mean by uniforms?
A. Regimental uniforms—fcarlet with different facings.)
Q. Do you know the perfon of Mr. *Rowan?*
A. I do.
Q. (By the court—Do you know him now?
A. He is juft oppofite to me.)
Q. Was he fitting at the table?
A. At one time he was—at another time he was ftanding.
Q. What

Q. What brought you there ?

A. Merely curiofity.

Q. How was it excited ?

A. I happened to pafs through Cope-ftreet, and faw a great croud—I afked what it was—they faid it was a meeting of the *United Irifhmen.* My brother was with me, and we w●nt into the room ; we were in coloured clothes, and to the beft of my recollection, Mr. *Rowan* faid, no gentleman with coloured clothes could be there ; but mentioned, that there was a gallery to which we might go.

Q. Did you perceive any perfon perform any particular part in that affembly?

A. I perceived Mr. *Rowan* about the table very bufy—he had papers in his hand, and there was pen and ink on the table ; he walked about the room, with the papers in his hand.—*Napper Tandy* came up to him, read part of one of the papers—they were handed about—fome were handed up to the gallery—I got one of them, and fo did my brother, and feveral others in the gallery along with me.

Q. Look at that paper—is that the one ?

A. This is the paper I got there.

Q. Was it one of the papers handed up to the gallery ?

A. It was one of the papers handed by Mr. *Rowan* to fome of the people about him, and by them handed up to the gallery.

Q. Your brother alfo got one ?

A. He did.

Q. Was there a number diftributed ?

A. About 30 were thrown up to the gallery.

Q. Have you any reafon to afcertain that to be the particular paper?

A. I have, becaufe it has my own hand-writing upon it.

Q. You made that memorandum upon it ?

A. I did.

Q. Read it.

A. " *I got this paper at a meeting of the United Irifhmen in Cope-ftreet, the* 16*th of December—it came through the hands of* ARCHI‑ BALD HAMILTON ROWAN.*"

Q. (*By the court*—You fay one of thefe papers was read by Mr. *Rowan,* how do you know that ?

A. Becaufe I attended to the words he read, and they agreed with what are in this paper.

Q. Can you fwear that one of thefe very papers was read by him ?

A. I can fwear that part of the words were read, I cannot fwear to the whole.)

Crofs

Crofs examined by the RECORDER.

Q. At what hour was this?

A. To the beft of my knowledge it was between one and two.

Q. Was this upon the 16th of December?

A. It was upon the 16th of December, 1792.

Q. It was upon a Sunday?

A. I believe it was.

Q. How long did you remain there?

A. For about three quarters of an hour.

Q. There were about one or two hundred volunteers below ftairs?

A. There were.

Q. Were they dreffed in the uniforms which you had feen the old volunteers wear?

A. I cannot exactly fay as to the facings of the uniforms— fome of them were green.

Q. Had not fome of the old volunteers green uniforms?

A. They had, and there were fome of the old volunteers in the room.

Q. Were not the old volunteer uniforms fcarlet faced with different colours?

A. They were.

Q. Were all thefe men fitting down, or walking up and down?

A. They were walking—there were very few forms or chairs in the room.

Q. Were they converfing?

A. They were chatting and talking.

Q. Did you fee many of them go up to this table where the papers were?

A. I faw a good many of them go up to it in the courfe of their walking back and forward.

Q. Did you fee many take papers off the table?

A. I did not fee very many of them—I faw four or five or fix of them.

Q. They read them and handed them about?

A. Yes, I faw them do fo.

Q. Did you not fee them hand them about from one to another?

A. I did.

Q. By virtue of your oath, did you ever fee that paper in your hand, in the hands of Mr. *Rowan.*

A. I fwear it was among the parcel upon the table, fome of which were handed up to the gallery—I cannot fay it was touched by his fingers.

Q. (By

Q. *(By the court*—You fay it was among the parcel handed to the gallery ?

A. Yes.

Q. By whom ?

A. It was in the bundle handed by Mr. *Rowan* to feveral there, and by them handed up to the gallery.)

Q. Did that bundle of papers pafs through the hands of more volunteers than one before it came to the gallery ?

A. I believe it did.

Q. Did he hand feveral parcels ?

A. I only faw him hand one to a volunteer who gave it to another.

Q. Then it went through the hands of feveral before it got to the gallery ?

A. It did, through four or five.

Q. Can you tell the name of any man through whofe hands it paffed ?

A. I cannot—I was not fo well acquainted with the gentlemen.

Q. When this bundle of papers was handed up, do you know who in the gallery received it ?

A. They were broken and feparated, I held out my hand and got one of them—my brother another, and other people got fome.

Q. Were there many in the gallery ?

A. There were a great many ?

Q. Did every man there get one ?

A. I cannot fay—every one that chofe to take one might ?

Q. Did they hand them about in the gallery ?

A. The next man faw what his neighbour got, they gave them about, but I never parted with mine till yefterday.

Q. Did you know any other volunteers below ftairs befides Mr. *Rowan ?*

A. I did, Mr. *Tandy ;* and to the beft of my recollection, there was a Mr. *Kenny* whom I knew before.

Q. Did feveral of the volunteers below ftairs hand up papers to the gallery or not ?

A. I dare fay feveral of them did.

Q. Did not feveral men take papers from the table ?

A. I fuppofe they did—I did not obferve whether they did or not. Several, as they paffed back and forward, went to the table and might take them off.

Q. Do you not know that feveral did take papers off ?

A. Several of them did.

Q. You faw thofe papers paffed through the hands of four or five volunteers before they came to the gallery ?

A. A parcel of the papers among which this was came up.

Q. How came you to pitch upon that paper fo accurately ?

A. I

A. I was the firſt who put out my hand.

Q. Did you watch this particular paper?

A. Not that particular paper, but the bundle in which it was.

Q. Will you fwear there were no other papers handed up?

A. To the beſt of my knowledge there were not.

Q. When did you put that memorandum upon it?

A. The very day I got it.

Q. Where?

A. In my lodging.

Q. Did any body advife you to make a *memorandum?*

A. No one did :—I generally, when I get an improper paper make ſuch memorandum.

Q. For what purpofe?

A. Juſt a *fancy* of my own.

Q. Did you make that memorandum in order to enable you to prove it upon a profecution?

A. I did not.

Q. To whom did you firſt communicate your having this paper and the memorandum?

A. I ſhall tell you. There was a brother of mine who did buſineſs for the late Mr. *Adderley*—there were different accounts between them—my brother went to the Caſtle to Mr. *Hobart* to ſhew the accounts—Mr. now Lord *Hobart*, defired my brother to call upon Mr. *Pollock*, the agent for young Mr. *Adderley.*— Mr. *Pollock* faid he had heard that I and my brother were prefent at the meeting in Cope-ſtreet, and that he underſtood it was a very improper meeting.

Q. How long was this after the meeting?

A. I cannot fay.

Q. Was it a week or a month?

A. I cannot recollect. Mr. *Pollock* faid, " You have been there I underſtand." I faid, we were, and that we faw fuch things going forward. I had one of the papers in my pocket and ſhewed it to him. He faid, Mr. *Hobart* heard I was there, and that I ſould give information of it as it was againſt the king and conſtitution. I faid I would not encourage any thing againſt the king, but would do what was proper. Mr. *Kemmis* came to my lodging next day—the circumſtances were talked over—we faid we would make no delay in making any information concerning it, and it was in that manner they came to a knowledge of it.

Q. *(By the court)* What Mr. *Kemmis?*

A. The Crown Solicitor.

Q. Were you of any profeſſion at the time you attended this meeting?

A. I was not.

Q. You are in the army now?

A. I have that honour.

Q. What

Q. What commiffion?

A. An enfign's commiffion.

Q. How long fince did you obta'n it?

A. I have been gazetted fince the 27th of Ju e laf.

Q. In what regiment?

A. In the 4oth.

Q. You fay you heard fome of that paper read?

A. I do, Sir, the greater part of it.

Q. Was this while all the volunteers were walking about?

A. Some were walking about, others gathered about the place while the paper was reading by Mr. *Rowan.*

Q. Can you point out any part of the paper you heard read?

A. I can.

Q. Shew fuch part as you heard?

A. He began, " The Society of United Irifhmen," and fo on.

Q. He did not read it all?

A. He read the greater part.

Q. Can you fay where he ftopped?

A. I cannot.

Q. Did you obtain your commiffion by purchafe?

A. No, I did not:—I got it through the intereft of a lady I have the honour of being related to—Lady *Hobart.*

Q. Pray, were you ever a witnefs to a bond or two bonds executed by your father to one of your brothers?

A. I was.

Q. To your younger brother?

A. Yes.

Q. Was there ever any fuit or iffue directed to try whether the bond was genuine or a forgery?

A. There was an iffue to try whether it was my father's bond or not. I do not fay it was to try whether it was a forgery.

Q. Was it not alledged by your father and your elder brother that it was a forgery?

A. My elder brother thought to keep my younger brother out of the property, and I fuppofe he alledged it was a forgery. I am forry to mention thefe matters here. My father filed a bill againft us, alledging the bonds to be forgeries, and Mr. *Simon Butler* *, a very honourable gentleman, to whom I am under many obligations, undertook the bufinefs, and we recovered the money. I fee the defendant has brought parchments into court this day. I faw Mr. *Blake* who is to give evidence againft me here. If I was aware of thefe things being mentioned, I fhould have the gentleman here who could prove them—I fpeak of the bonds for 5ool.

Q. Was there not an iffue to try them?

A. There was an order to have it tried in the country.

Q. Were you not examined in the country upon that trial?

* An intimate friend of Mr. Rowan.

E

A. I

A. I believe I was.

Q. You are not fure?

A. I am fure.

Q. Did you fwear to the due execution of thefe bonds?

A. To the beft of my knowledge I was examined—I was wit-nefs to the bond.

Q. Can you fwear whether you were examined or not?

A. I cannot fay pofitively whether I was or not—one of my brothers was examined—My elder brother, I believe, cried out to the jury, that he would leave it to a reference.

Q. You cannot fwear pofitively whether you were examined or not?

A. I cannot.

Q. Do you not believe you were examined?

A. I cannot fwear pofitively I was: I do believe to the beft of my recollection I was—but I cannot fwear pofitively.

Q. How long is this ago?

A. It is a good while—I cannot exactly fay.

Q. Is it three years ago?

A. I believe it is.

Q. Only three years ago and you cannot fay pofitively whe-ther you were examined or not?

A. I know I was to be examined, but I cannot fay whether I was or not.

Q. Were you not examined to the beft of your belief?

A. To the beft of my recollection I was: but I cannot fwear pofitively.

Q. Do you recollect the judge before whom that iffue was tried?

A. I do.

Q. Before whom was it?

A. Before one of their lordfhips on the bench (Judge *Boyd*).

Q. Were there not more witneffes than one examined to fhew it was not your father's hand writing?

A. I do not know, I believe there were many examined, but they did not fay pofitively it was not my father's hand-writing.

Q. What verdict was there?

A. There was no verdict at all.

Q. Was it not becaufe the jury could not agree?

A. No, it was not.

Q. Will you fwear to that?

A. I will not; but I think my elder brother called out, perceiving himfelf wrong, and faid, he would leave it to a re-ference.

Q. Was it ever left to the reference?

A. It was.

Q. What was done?

A. I

A. I cannot fay, I was not there ; but moſt people imagined the referees were wrong in doing as.they did.

Q. Did they give the amount of the bonds ?

A. They did not.

Q. What was the amount of the bonds ?

A. One was 500*l.* the other 300*l.* it is not yet decided, my brother intends to bring it into the courts to.ſet aſide the award.

Q. *(By the court.* Do you know what they allowed ?

A. I know not.

Q. Did you ever hear ?

A. Some hundreds.)

Q. Did you hear it was 200*l.* ?

A. I did not.

Q. Two hundred are ſome hundreds ?

A. They are, but as I was not to get any of the money, I believe nothing about it.

Q. Did not a gentleman of the name of *Walter Lambert.* file a bill againſt you ?

A. He did.

Q. Was he executor of *Peter Hamilton* ?

A. He was.

Q. Why did he file a bill ?

A. It is a very unjuſt bill. *Peter Hamilton* had married my fiſter, he became inſane and I went to ſtay with him in a mad-houſe in England ; I had no ſupport from my father at that time, and I thought Mr. *Hamilton*'s relations ſhould pay my expences and ſupport me ; a Mr. *Nagle* recommended me to bring Mr. *Hamilton* home ; I did by force put him on board a ſhip and brought him to Cork, and from thence home to Galway ; he had intervals of reaſon, and he gave me a bond for 150*l.* part of which was paid. I went to Judge *Kelly*, a relation of his, to interfere ; in ſome time I got a note for the money, and after his death the executor filed a bill againſt me.

Q. Did he not charge the note not to be the hand-writing of *Peter Hamilton* ?

A. No : the note was in my hand-writing with Mr. *Hamilton*'s name ſigned by himſelf.

Q. Did you ever recover any part of it ?

A. No, it is not yet determined.

Q. Is there an injunction againſt you ?

A. No : I believe not ; I was nonſuited by the neglect of Mr. *Morton*, my attorney, who left the papers in town, when the trial came on in the country.

Q. After you drew this note, Mr. *Peter Hamilton* put his name to it ?

A. Yes.

Q. And you ſued for it and did not recover ?

A. He

A. He was perfectly in his senses when he put his name to it as I am: he transacted his own business as if he had not been mad.

Q. Did he not live many years after this?

A. No, he did not: he might have lived many years if he had not shot himself.

Q. (By Juror, Mr. *Minchin.* Did you see many more of the papers handed up?

A. I did.

Q. Were there any of another tendency?

A. There were not.)

Second Witness, Mr. *William Morton.*

Examined by the Solicitor General.

Q. Do you remember being at Cope-street, Dublin, on the 16th of December, 1792?

A. I do.

Q. Do you recollect to have seen any thing there, or to have got admission into any place there?

A. I do: I saw a number of men assembled there, for what purpose I cannot say: they were arrayed in military dress.

Q. What were they doing?

A. They drew up a form of resolutions at a table.

Q. Do you recollect to have seen any particular person there?

A. I recollect to have seen Mr. *Hamilton Rowan* and Mr. *Napper Tandy.*

Q. (By the court. Do you know Mr. *Rowan?*

A. I do.

Q. Did you know him before that day?

A. I have seen, but was not acquainted with him.

Q. Do you know him now?

A. I do; he is there, (pointing to him.)

Q. Did or did not Mr. *Rowan* appear to take an active part in that meeting?

A. He did.

Q. Do you recollect any thing about papers of any description?

A. I shall mention what I know: I gained admission into the gallery, there were a number of papers or advertisements brought in, as if wet from the press, and distributed about.

Q. Were they in large or small parcels?

A. There was a large parcel in a man's arm, wet as from the press.

Q. What became of them?

A. They

A. They were laid upon the table, and fome were given to Mr. *Napper Tandy*.

Q. Did you fee any of them?

A. I did.

Q. Had you an opportunity of reading them?

A. I had.

Q. How came you to have that opportunity?

A. I faw fome of them taken up by Mr. *Rowan* and delivered to fome of the members, and by them handed up to the gallery. A gentleman near me received one of them; I immediately took it out of his hand: there were many thrown up; one was read by a gentleman, and I remember while he read it, a number were thrown out of the windows to the mob, who defired more of them, and accordingly they were fent to them.

Q. Was the paper read in a loud manner; did every man know what was doing in the gallery?

A. Every man could hear it, I believe.

Q. Did you keep one of thefe papers?

A. I did.

Q. Where is it?

A. I gave it to a perfon, who, I underftand, has fince miflaid it.

Q. Do you recollect any part of it?

A. The beginning of it: it was from the affociation of United Irifhmen; it began—" To arms citizens, to arms!"

Q. Did you hear it read?

A. I did.

Q. When it was begun, did that paffage make an impreffion upon you that you remember it?

A. It was a young gentleman in the gallery who read it through; the people there called out, read it for the benefit of us all.

Crofs-examined by Mr. FLETCHER.

Q. Are you of any profeffion?

A. I am a gold-beater.

Q. Do you get your livelihood by that?

A. I am an apprentice ferving my time to that bufinefs.

Q. Is your father living?

A. He is not.

Q. How came you to be at this meeting?

A. It was on a Sunday, and I was unemployed. I met a young gentleman who afked me to go to Cope-ftreet. I went from curiofity.

Q. At what hour did you go there?

A. It was in the forenoon, from eleven to one, there were feveral gentlemen in uniform.

Q. What

Q. What was their uniform?

A. Scarlet faced with green; there were some light infantry in their jackets; there were different corps.

Q. Upon your oath, were not all the uniforms you saw, the appropriated uniforms of the old volunteer corps?

A. I cannot say.

Q. Do you not believe they were?

A. I suppose they were; but I had been absent and had not seen them for some time.

Q. You were in the gallery when you saw those bundles of papers?

A. I was.

Q. Were there more than one?

A. Not that I remember; I saw but one.

Q. Did not several persons go up to the table and get these papers?

A. I cannot say; I believe not. I was in the gallery; there was a beam in the middle of the room, and when they went to the upper end of the room, the beam prevented me from seeing them.

Q. You said you saw **Mr.** *Rowan* take one of these papers and hand it to some other person?

A. I did not say one: I saw him take some papers and hand them about.

Q. What papers were they?

A. I cannot say, whether he took them off the table or not. He took part of those that came in: several of the members asked him for some; I suppose he gave them.

Q. Supposition will not do; say upon your oath, what you saw take place with regard to Mr. *Rowan* and these papers?

A. When they came in, Mr. *Rowan* and Mr. *Tandy* took some of them, they delivered them to the volunteers; one of the volunteers threw some up to the gallery, and I got one.

Q. Did you not say there was but one bundle?

A. I did.

Q. Did you say, that from your situation you could not see what passed at the table?

A. Part of the table I could see.

Q. Were you in such a situation as to see every thing which passed at the table?

A. The volunteers were walking up and down, and sometimes I could not see every thing there.

Q. Do you know the names of any of the persons from whom these papers came to the gallery?

A. No. I did not know any one in the room but Mr. *Tandy* and Mr. *Rowan.*

Q. Can you say who the person was who read the paper in the gallery?

A. I cannot. I never saw him before.

Q. Did

Q. Did he read it more than once ?

A. I cannot fay.

Q. Had you any of the papers in your hand when he read it ?

A. I had.

Q. You kept that paper which you received ?

A. I did for fome time.

Q. How long ?

A. I do not recollect : I kept it a week or lefs.

Q. Whom did you give it to ?

A. An acquaintance of mine.

Q. Has he no name ?

[Here the witnefs hefitating in his anfwer, Mr. Sheriff *Gif-fard* called out, that he was the perfon to whom the wit-nefs delivered the paper, upon which the witnefs faid it was to Mr. *Giffard.*]

Q. Why did you refort to him ?

A. I had no reafon : I gave it by accident.

Q. You had no reafon ?

A. None, but that he was the firft perfon I met that I was acquainted with.

Q. Did you not keep it a week ?

A. No.

Q. Did you keep it five days ?

A. No, I believe not one ; for I think I gave it to him the day after I got it.

Q. When you faid you gave it in a week, did you mean the day after ?

A. It was lefs than a week.

Q. Did you mean to convey the idea that you had it but one day, when you faid you had it lefs than a week ?

A. I did.

Q. Upon your oath that was the meaning you intended to convey ?

A. It was.

Q. Upon your oath you fay fo ?

A. I do.

Q. Do you generally fpeak in riddles of that kind ?

A. No.

Q. How long did you keep that paper ?

A. Not one day : on the fame day that I received it, I gave it to Mr. *Giffard.*

Q. This meeting was in the forenoon ?

A. It was.

Q. How long after the paper was diftributed did you con-tinue at this affembly ?

A. I do not remember when it broke up.

Q. Was it before or after dinner ?

A. It was before dinner.

Q. *(By the Court.* Did you ftay till the affembly broke up ?

A. I

A. I did.)

Q. Can you say how long you remained in the place after getting that paper?

A. I cannot say.

Q. What do you believe?

A. Half the time was not elapsed when the papers were distributed, but I do not recollect, there was a young man with me and we were in conversation.

Q. What became of you afterwards?

A. We separated: he went to dinner I suppose.

Q. Where did you go?

A. I went to Mr. *Ryan.*

Q. You dined there?

A. No.

Q. Who is Mr. *Ryan* ?

A. He is a surgeon.

Q. Did you shew the paper to Mr. *Ryan* ?

A. No; but I met Mr. *Giffard* there and I gave it to him.

Q. Did you expect to meet him there?

A. I did not.

Q. Of what business is Mr. *Ryan* ?

A. He is a surgeon.

Q. Does he get money by any other business?

A. I do not know.

Q. There is a paper printed in the house where he lives?

A. There is.

Q. What paper?

A. The *Dublin Journal.*

Q. Does not Mr. *Ryan* superintend the publication of that paper?

A. I believe he does not.

Q. Who is the proprietor of that paper?

A. George *Faulkner.*

Q. Do you believe he conducts that paper now?

A. I am not to know any thing about it.

Q. But can you not form a belief?

A. I cannot form a belief. I do not know.

Q. Did you never hear that Mr. *Giffard* had some interest in that paper?

A. I did hear it.

Q. Do you believe it?

A. I do not. I know not.

Q. What do you believe?

A. I believe he has not.

Q. Did you ever hear it?

A. I did.

Q. Why do you disbelieve it?

A. I heard it from several persons

Q. And

Q. And you do not. believe it ?

A. I do not.

Q. You do not believe that he has any connexion with that paper?

A. I do not believe it.

Q. Have you heard it contradicted ?

A. I have.

Q. By whom ?

A. I do not know?

Q. What relation are you to Mr. *Giffard ?*

A. His nephew by marriage.

Q. And will you, his nephew, fay he has not any intereſt in that paper ?

A. I do.

Q. Is not Mr. *Ryan* a relation of Mr. *Giffard?*

A. He is.

Q. What relation ?

A. I cannot fay.

Q. Who pays the rent of the houfe where Mr. *Ryan* lives?

A. I do not know.

This witnefs retired, and then the paper * produced by Mr. *Lyſter* was read—upon which the cafe for the profecution was reſted.

Lord CLONMELL, *Chief Juſtice,* aſked the counfel for the defendant whether they wiſhed to have the information read, in order to compare it with the publication

Mr. CURRAN.—We have inſtructions not to take any captious objections, and therefore do not think it neceſſary to accept of the offer of the court.

Mr. ATTORNEY GENERAL.—A good reaſon why, Mr. *Curran ;* there is no error in the record.

Evidence for the Defendant.

Francis Blake, Eſq.

Examined by Mr. CURRAN.

Q. You live in Galway?

A. I live now in Dublin, but I did live in the county of Rofcommon.

Q. Do you know a gentleman who was examined here to-day, of the name of *John Lyſter ?*

A. I believe I do.

Q. The fon of *Thomas Lyſter* of Grange?

A. I do know him.

* See the paper at large in the information.

F

Q. Do

Q. Do you think that Mr. *Lyſter* is a perſon who would deſerve credit in what he ſhould ſwear in a court of juſtice?

A. That is a very hard queſtion to anſwer, for I never had any dealing with him, ſo as to ſay from my own knowledge whether he ſhould be believed or not.

Q. I only aſk your opinion: is it your opinion that he deſerves credit upon his oath? Do you believe it?

A. I cannot ſay he is: I might heſitate.

Q. Can you form an opinion?

A. I have made all the anſwer I can—I cannot ſay that he does not deſerve credit—at the ſame time I might have doubts.

Lord CLONMELL.—He only ſays he might heſitate—he has doubts.

Mr. *John Smith.*

Examined by the RECORDER.

Q. Do you know *John Lyſter?*

A. I have ſeen him, I have no acquaintance with him.

Q. Have you ever ſeen him examined as a witneſs?

A. I have.

Q. Where?

A. At Galway ſummer aſſizes, 1791.

Q. Was he the ſon of *Thomas Lyſter* of Grange?

A. I believe he was.

Q. Did you ſee him on the table to-day?

A. I think I did while I was ſtanding upon the ſteps of the Exchequer.

Q. Is it your opinion that he is a perſon to be believed upon his oath in a court of juſtice?

A. I cannot form a general opinion, with regard to the matter upon which he was examined to-day: from what I know of him I would give very little credit to him.

Q. What is his general character?

Mr. ATTORNEY GENERAL.—I objeĉt to that queſtion.

Q. (By the Court.)—You are a man of buſineſs; upon your oath, do you know enough of this man to ſay whether you think he ought to be believed upon his oath?

A. I do not; for I know nothing of him, but what I ſaw at the trial in Galway.

Croſs-examined by Mr. ATTORNEY GENERAL.

Q. Are you a member of the *United Iriſhmen?*

A. I really am not.

3

Mrs.

Mrs. *Mary Hatchell.*

Examined by Mr. FLETCHER.

Q. Do you know Mr. *John Lyſter,* ſon of *Thomas Lyſter* of Grange?
A. I know Mr. *John Lyſter.*
Q. Is he in the army?
A. He is an enſign of the 40th.
Q. Have you known him long?
A. I have known him well for better than a year; by ſight I know him a long time.
Q. From all that you know and have heard of this gentleman, can you form an opinion whether he is a perſon to be credited upon his oath?
A. From my opinion he is not.

Croſs-examined by Mr. SOLICITOR GENERAL.

Q. Pray Madam where do you live?
A. Upper Ormond-quay.
Q. You know a brother of Mr. *Lyſter?*
A. I do well: it calls painful remembrances to my mind by talking of him.
Q. Was there any particular infidelity imputed to this gentleman or his brother?
A. George William Lyſter was married to a daughter of ours (my huſband is living.)
Q. Who is *George William Lyſter?*
A. The younger brother of *John Lyſter.*
Q. Your firſt intercourſe then originated from that connection between *George Lyſter* and your daughter?
A. Yes: *George William Fitzgerald Lyſter* married my daughter.
Q. It was not with your conſent?
A. It was not.
Q. You have not been induced to any painful neceſſity of breaking the marriage?
A. John Lyſter has found means to take away his brother from his wife, inſiſting that he had another wife.
Q. (By the Jury.) How do you know that *John Lyſter* is the perſon who inveigled his brother from your daughter?
A. His elder brother told me ſo.
Q. (By the Court.) Is that the reaſon you do not believe him?
A. It is one of the reaſons.

F 2

Q. What

Q. What other reafons have you?
A. Converfations with his elder brother.

[*Here the cafe was clofed for the defendant.*]

A few moments before the defendant's counfel rofe, a guard of foldiers was brought into the court-houfe by the fheriff.

Mr. CURRAN, for defendant.—Gentlemen of the Jury, when I confider the period at which this profecution is brought forward; when I behold the extraordinary fafeguard of armed foldiers reforted to, no doubt for the prefervation of peace and order: when I catch, as I cannot but do, the throb of public anxiety which beats from one end to the other of this hall; when I reflect on what may be the fate of a man of the moft beloved perfonal character, of one of the moft refpected families of our country; himfelf the only individual of that family, I may almoft fay of that country, who can look to that poffible fate with unconcern? Feeling as I do all thefe impreffions, it is in the honeft fimplicity of my heart I fpeak, when I fay that I never rofe in a court of juftice with fo much embarraffment, as upon this occafion.

If, gentlemen, I could entertain an hope of finding refuge for the difconcertion of my mind, in the perfect compofure of yours; if I could fuppofe that thofe awful viciffitudes of human events, which have been ftated or alluded to, could leave your judgments undifturbed and your hearts at eafe, I know I fhould form a moft erroneous opinion of your character: I entertain no fuch chimerical hope; I form no fuch unworthy opinion; I expect not that your hearts can be more at eafe than my own; I have no right to expect it; but I have a right to call upon you, in the name of your country, in the name of the living God, of whofe eternal juftice you are now adminiftering that portion which dwells with us on this fide of the grave, to difcharge your breafts as far as you are able of every biafs of prejudice or paffion; that, if my client is guilty of the offence charged upon him, you may give tranquility to the public by a firm verdict of conviction; or if he is innocent, by as firm a verdict of acquittal; and that you will do this in defiance of the paltry artifices and fenfelefs clamours that have been reforted to in order to bring him to his trial with anticipated conviction. And, gentlemen, I feel an additional neceffity of thus conjuring you to be upon your guard, from the able and impofing ftatement which you have juft heard on the part of the profecution. I know well the virtues and the talents of the excellent perfon who conducts that profecution; I know how much he would difdain to impofe on you by the trappings of office; but I alfo know how eafily we miftake the lodgement which character and
                                                                eloquence

eloquence can make upon our feelings, for thofe impreffions that
reafon and fact and proof only ought to work upon our under-
ftandings.

 Perhaps, gentlemen, I fhall act not unwifely in waving any
further obfervation of this fort, and giving your minds an opportunity of growing cool and refuming themfelves, by coming to
a calm and uncoloured ftatement of mere facts, premifing only
to you that I have it in ftricteft injunction from my client, to
defend him upon facts and evidence only, and to avail myfelf of
no technical artifice or fubtilty that could withdraw his caufe
from the teft of that enquiry, which it is your province to exercife, and to which only he wifhes to be indebted for an acquittal.

 In the month of December 1792, Mr. Rowan was arrefted on
an information, charging him with the offence for which he is
now on his trial. He was taken before an honourable perfo-
nage now on that bench, and admitted to bail.

He remained a confiderable time in this city, foliciting the
threatened profecution, and offering himfelf to a fair trial by a
jury of his country; but it was not then thought fit to yield to
that folicitation; nor has it now been thought proper to profecute him in the ordinary way, by fending up a bill of indictment to a grand jury. I do not mean by this to fay that informations ex officio are always oppreffive or unjuft; but I cannot
but obferve to you, that when a petty jury is called upon to try
a charge not previoufly found by the grand inqueft, and fupported by the naked affertion only of the king's profecutor, that
the accufation labours under a weaknefs of probability which it
is difficult to affift. If the charge had no caufe of dreading the
light—if it was likely to find the fanction of a grand jury, it is
not eafy to account why it deferted the more ufual, the more
popular, and the more conftitutional mode, and preferred to come
forward in the ungracious form of an ex officio information.

If fuch bill had been fent up and found, Mr. Rowan would
have been tried at the next commiffion; but a fpeedy trial was
not the wifh of his profecutors. An information was filed, and
when he expected to be tried upon it, an error, it feems, was
difcovered in the record. Mr. Rowan offered to wave it, or
confent to any amendment defired. No—that propofal could
not be accepted—a trial muft have followed. That information,
therefore, was withdrawn, and a new one filed, that is in fact a
third profecution was inftituted upon the fame charge. This
laft was filed on the 8th day of laft July. Gentlemen, thefe
facts cannot fail of a due impreffion upon you. You will find a
material part of your inquiry muft be, whether Mr. Rowan is
purfued as a criminal or hunted down as a victim. It is not,
therefore, by infinuation or circuity, but it is boldly and directly
that I affert that oppreffion has been intended and practifed upon
him,

him, and by thofe facts which I have ftated I am warranted in the affertion.

His demand, his intreaty to be tried was refufed, and why? a hue and cry was to be raifed againft him; the fword was to be fufpended over his head—fome time was neceffary for the public mind to become heated by the circulation of artful clamours of anarchy and rebellion; thofe fame clamours which with more probability, but not more fuccefs, had been circulated before through England and Scotland. In this country the caufes and the fwiftnefs of their progrefs were as obvious, as their folly has fince become to every man of the fmalleft obfervation; I have been ftopped myfelf, with, " Good God, Sir, have you heard the news? No Sir, what?—Why one French emiffary was feen travelling through Connaught in a poft chaife, and fcattering from the windows as he paffed little dofes of political poifon, made up in fquare bits of paper—another was actually furprifed in the fact of feducing our good people from their allegiance, by difcourfes upon the indivifibility of French robbery and maffacre, which he preached in the French language to a congregation of Irifh peaants."

Such are the bugbears and fpectres to be raifed to warrant the acrifice of whatever little public fpirit may remain amongft us—but time has alfo detected the impofture of thefe Cock-lane apparitions, and you cannot now, with your eyes open, give a verdict without afking your confciences this queftion; is this a fair and honeft profecution?—Is it brought forward with the fingle view of vindicating public juftice, and promoting public good? And here let me remind you that you are not convened to try the guilt of a libel, affecting the perfonal character of any private man; I know no cafe in which a jury ought to be more fevere than where perfonal calumny is conveyed through a vehicle, which ought to be confecrated to public information; neither, on the other hand, can I conceive any cafe in which the firmnefs and the caution of a jury fhould be more exerted, than when a fubject is profecuted for a libel on the ftate. The peculiarity of the Britifh conftitution, (to which in its fulleft extent we have an undoubted right, however diftant we may be from the actual enjoyment) and in which it furpaffes every known government in Europe, is this; that its only profeffed object is the general good, and its only foundation the general will; hence the people have a right acknowledged from time immemorial, fortified by a pile of ftatutes, and authenticated by a revolution that fpeaks louder than them all, to fee whether abufes have been committed, and whether their properties and their liberties have been attended to as they ought to be. This is a kind of fubject which I feel myfelf overawed when I approach; there are certain fundamental principles which nothing but neceffity fhould expofe to public examination; they are pillars, the depth of
whofe

whose foundation you cannot explore without endangering their strength; but let it be recollected that the discussion of such topics should not be condemned in me, nor visited upon my client. The blame, if any there be, should rest only with those who have forced them into discussion. I say, therefore, it is the right of the people to keep an eternal watch upon the conduct of their rulers; and in order to that, the freedom of the press has been cherished by the law of England. In private defamation let it never be tolerated; in wicked and wanton aspersion upon a good and honest administration let it never be supported, not that a good government can be exposed to danger by groundless accusation, but because a bad government is sure to find in the detected falsehood of a licentious press a security and a credit, which it could never otherwise obtain. I said a good government cannot be endangered; I say so again, for whether it be good or bad can never truly depend upon assertion, the question is decided by simple inspection: to try the tree look at its fruit; to judge of the government look at the people; what is the fruit of good government? The virtue and happiness of the people; do four millions of people in this country gather those fruits from that government to whose injured purity, to whose spotless virtue and violated honour, this seditious and atrocious libeller is to be immolated upon the altar of the constitution? To you, gentlemen of that jury, who are bound by the most sacred obligation to your country and your God, to speak nothing but the truth, I put the question—do they gather those fruits? are they orderly, industrious, religious and contented? do you find them free from bigotry and ignorance, those inseparable concomitants of systematic oppression? or to try them by a test as unerring as any of the former, are they united? The period has now elapsed in which considerations of this extent would have been deemed improper to a jury; happily for these countries, the legislature of each has lately changed, or, perhaps to speak more properly, revived and restored the law respecting trials of this kind. For the space of thirty or forty years a usage had prevailed in Westminster Hall, by which the judges assumed to themselves the decision of the question, whether libel or not; but the learned counsel for the prosecution are now obliged to admit that this is a question for the jury only to decide. You will naturally listen with respect to the opinion of the court, but you will receive it as matter of advice, not as matter of law; and you will give it credit not from any adventitious circumstances of authority, but merely so far as it meets the concurrence of your own understandings.

Give me leave now to state to you the charge, as it stands upon the record:—It is that Mr. Rowan " being a person of a " wicked and turbulent disposition, and maliciously designing " and intending to excite and diffuse amongst the subjects of " this

" this realm of Ireland difcontents, jealoufies and fufpicions of
" our Lord the King and his government, and difaffection and
" difloyalty to the perfon and government of our faid Lord
" the King, and to raife very dangerous feditions and tumults
" within this kingdom of Ireland, and to draw the government
" of this kingdom into great fcandal, infamy and difgrace, and
" to incite the fubjects of our faid Lord the King to attempt,
" by force and violence and with arms, to make alterations in
" the government, ftate and conftitution of this kingdom, and
" to incite his Majefty's faid fubjects to tumult and anarchy, and
" to overturn the eftablifhed conftitution of this kingdom, and
" to overawe and intimidate the legiflature of this kingdom by
" an armed force;" did " malicioufly and feditioufly" publifh
the paper in queftion.

Gentlemen, without any obfervation of mine, you muft fee
that this information contains a direct charge upon Mr. Rowan;
namely, that he did, with the intents fet forth in the information, publifh this paper; fo that here you have in fact two,
or three queftions for your decifion: firft, the matter of fact
of the publication: namely, did Mr. Rowan publifh that paper?
If Mr. Rowan did not in fact publifh that paper, you have no
longer any queftion on which to employ your minds. If you
think that he was in fact the publifher, then and not till then
arifes the great and important fubject to which your judgments
muft be directed. And that comes fhortly and fimply to this,
is the paper a libel? and did he publifh it with the intent charged
in the information? But whatever you may think of the abftract
queftion; whether the paper be libellous or not, and of which
paper it has not even been infinuated that he is the author, thefe
can be no ground for a verdict againft him, unlefs you alfo
are perfuaded that what he did was done with a criminal defign.
I wifh, gentlemen, to fimplify and not to perplex; I therefore fay
again, if thefe three circumftances confpire, that he publifhed it,
that it was a libel, and that it was publifhed with the purpofes
alledged in the information, you ought unqueftionably to find
him guilty; if on the other hand, you do not find that all
thefe circumftances concurred; if you cannot upon your oaths
fay that he publifhed it; if it be not in your opinion a libel,
and if he did not publifh it with the intention alledged: I fay
upon the failure of any one of thefe points, my client is intitled,
in juftice, and upon your oaths, to a verdict of acquittal.

Gentlemen, Mr. Attorney General has thought proper to direct your attention to the ftate and circumftances of public affairs at the time of this tranfaction; let me alfo make a few re-
trofpective obfervations on a period, at which he has but flightly
glanced; I fpeak of the events which took place before the clofe
of the American war. You know gentlemen that France had
efpoufed the caufe of America, and we became thereby engaged
in

in a war with that nation. *Heu nefcia mens hominum futuri!*
Little did that ill-fated monarch know that he was forming the
firft caufes of thofe difaftrous events, that were to end in the
fubverfion of his throne, in the flaughter of his family, and the
deluging of his country with the blood of his people. You cannot but remember that at a time, when we had fcarcely a regular
foldier for our defence; when the old and young were alarmed
and terrified with apprehenfions of defcent upon our coafts; that
Providence feemed to have worked a fort of miracle in our favour. You faw a band of armed men come forth at the great
call of nature, of honour, and their country. You faw men of
the greateft wealth and rank; you faw every clafs of the community give up its members, and fend them armed into the field, to
protect the public and private tranquillity of Ireland. It is impoffible for any man to turn back to that period, without reviv-
ing thofe fentiments of tendernefs and gratitude, which then
beat in the public bofom: to recollect amidft what applaufe,
what tears, what prayers, what benedictions, they walked forth
amongft fpectators, agitated by the mingled fenfations of terror
and reliance, of danger and protection; imploring the bleffings
of Heaven upon their heads, and its conqueft upon their fwords.
That illuftrious and adored, and *abufed* body of men ftood forward and affumed the title, which, I truft, the ingratitude of
their country will never blot from its hiftory, " THE VOLUN-
" TEERS OF IRELAND."
   Give me leave now, with great refpect, to put one queftion to
you: Do you think the affembling of that glorious band of pa-
triots was an infurrection? do you think the invitation to that
affembling would have been fedition? They came under no commiffion but the call of their country; unauthorized and unfanc-
tioned except by public emergency and public danger. I afk was
that meeting infurrection or not? I put another queftion: If any
man then had publifhed a call on that body, and ftated that war
was declared againft the ftate; that the regular troops were withdrawn; that our coafts were hovered round by the fhips of the
enemy; that the moment was approaching when the unprotected
feeblenefs of age and fex; when the fanctity of habitation would
be difregarded and prophaned by the brutal ferocity of a rude in-
vader; if any man had then faid to them " leave your induftry
" for a while, that you may return to it again, and come forth
" in arms for the public defence." I put the queftion boldly
to you gentlemen? It is not the cafe of the volunteers of that
day; it is the cafe of my client, at this hour, which I put to you.
Would that call have been then pronounced in a court of juftice, or
by a jury on their oaths, a criminal and feditious invitation to infurrection? If it would not have been fo then, upon what principle
can it be fo now? What is the force and perfection of the law?
It is the permanency of the law; it is that whenever the fact is

G   the

the fame, the law is alfo the fame; it is that the law remains a written, monumented and recorded letter to pronounce the fame decifion, upon the fame facts whenever they fhall arife. I will not affect to conceal it : you know there has been an artful, ungrateful, and blafphemous clamour raifed againſt thefe illuftrious characters, the faviours of the kingdom of Ireland. Having mentioned this, let me read a few words of the paper alledged to be criminal : " You firft took up arms to protect your country " from foreign enemies, and from domeftic difturbance. For the " fame purpofes it now becomes neceffary that you fhould re- " fume them."

I fhould be the laft in the world to impute any want of can- dour to the right honourable gentleman, who has ftated the cafe on behalf of the profecution : but he has certainly fallen into a miſtake, which, if not explained, might be highly injurious to my client. He fuppofed that this publication was not addreffed to thofe ancient volunteers, but to new combinations of them, formed upon new principles, and actuated by different mo- tives. You have the words to which this conftruction is imputed upon the record ; the meaning of his mind can be collected only from thofe words which he has made ufe of to convey it. The guilt imputable to him can only be inferred from the meaning afcribable to thofe words. Let his meaning then be fairly collected by reforting to them. Is there a foundation to fuppofe that this addrefs was directed to any fuch body of men, as has been called a banditti, with what juftice it is unneceffary to in- quire, and not to the old volunteers? As to the fneer at the words *Citizen Soldiers,* I fhould feel that I was treating a very re- fpected friend with an infidious and unmerited unkindnefs, if I affected to expofe it by any gravity of refutation. I may, how- ever, be permitted to obferve, that thofe who are fuppofed to have difgraced this expreffion by adopting it, have taken it from the idea of the Britifh conftitution, " that no man in becoming a " foldier ceafes to be a citizen." Would to God, all enemies as they are, that that unfortunate people had borrowed more from that facred fource of liberty and virtue ; and would to God, for the fake of humanity, that they had preferved even the little they did borrow. If even there could be an objection to that ap- pellation, it muft have been ftrongeft when it was firft affumed. * To that period the writer manifeftly alludes ; he addreffes " thofe " who firft took up arms :" you firft took up arms to protect your country from foreign enemies and from domeftic difturbance. For the fame purpofes it now becomes neceffary that you fhould

---

* Whoever will take the trouble of reading the refolutions and ad- dreffes of the old volunteers, at and prior to 1783, will find the terms *Citizen Soldiers,* and *Citizen Soldiery,* to have been no uncommon appella- tions to that body.

refume

refume them. Is this applicable to thofe who had never taken
up arms before? " A proclamation," fays this paper, " has been
" iffued in England for embodying the militia, and a proclama-
" tion has been iffued by the lord lieutenant and council in Ire-
" land, for repreffing all feditious affociations. In confequence
" of both thefe proclamations, it is reafonable to apprehend dan-
" ger from abroad, and danger at home." God help us, from
the fituation of Europe at that time, we were threatened with
too probable danger from abroad, and I am afraid it was not
without foundation we were told of our having fomething to dread
at home. I find much abufe has been lavifhed on the difrefpect
with which the proclamation is treated, in that part of the paper
alledged to be a libel. To that my anfwer for my client is fhort;
I do conceive it competent to a Britifh fubject—if he thinks
that a proclamation has iffued for the purpofe of raifing falfe ter-
rors, I hold it to be not only the privilege, but the duty of a citizen, to fet his countrymen right, with refpect to fuch mifrepre-
fented danger; and until a proclamation, in this country, fhall
have the force of law, the reafon and grounds of it are furely at leaft
queftionable by the people. Nay, I will go farther, if an actual
law had paffed receiving the fanction of the three eftates, if it be
exceptionable in any matter, it is warrantable to any man in the
community to ftate, in a becoming manner, his ideas upon it.
And I fhould be at a lofs to know, if the pofitive laws of Great
Britain are thus queftionable, upon what ground the proclamation of an Irifh government fhould not be open to the animadverfion of Irifh fubjects.

" Whatever be the motive, or from whatever quarter it arifes,"
fays this paper, " alarm has arifen." Gentlemen, do you not
know that to be the fact? It has been ftated by the Attorney
General, and moft truly, that the moft gloomy apprehenfions
were entertained by the whole country. " You volunteers of
" Ireland are therefore fummoned to arms at the inftance of go-
" vernment, as well as by the refponfibility attached to your
" character, and the permanent obligations of your inftitution."
I am free to confefs if any man affuming the liberty of a Britifh
fubject, to queftion public topics, fhould under the mafk of that
privilege publifh a proclamation inviting the profligate and feditious, thofe in want and thofe in defpair to rife up in arms to
overawe the legiflature, to rob us of whatever portion of the
bleffings of a free government we poffefs; I know of no offence
involving greater enormity. But that, gentlemen, is the queftion you are to try. If my client acted with an honeft mind and
fair intention, and having, as he believed, the authority of government to fupport him in the idea that danger was to be apprehended, did apply to that body of fo known and fo revered
character, calling upon them by their former honour, the principle of their glorious inftitution, and the great ftake they poffeffed

G 2   in

in their country. If he interpofed not upon a fictitious pretext, but ~~~~al belief of actual and imminent danger, and that their ar~~~~ at that critical moment was neceffary to the fafety of their country; his intention was not only innocent, but highly meritorious. It is a queftion, gentlemen, upon which you only can decide; it is for you to fay whether it was criminal in the defendant to be fo mifled, and whether he is to fall a facrifice to the profecution of that government by which he was fo deceived. I fay again, gentlemen, you can look only to his own words as the interpreter of his meaning; and to the ftate and circumftances of his country, as he was made to believe them, as the clue to his intention. The cafe then, gentlemen, is fhortly and fimply this : a man of the firft family and fortune, and character and property among you, reads a proclamation ftating the country to be in danger from abroad and at home, and thus alarmed— thus upon authority of the profecutor, alarmed, applies to that auguft body, before whofe awful prefence fedition muft vanifh, and infurrection difappear. You muft furrender, I hefitate not to fay it, your oaths to unfounded affertion, if you can fubmit to fay that fuch an act, of fuch a man, fo warranted, is a wicked and feditious libel. If he was a dupe, let me afk you, who was the impoftor? I blufh and I fhrink with fhame and deteftation from that meannefs of dupery and fervile complaifance, which could make that dupe a victim to the accufation of that impoftor.

You perceive, gentlemen, that I am going into the merits of this publication, before I apply myfelf to the queftion which is firft in order of time, namely, whether the publication, in point of fact, is to be afcribed to Mr. Rowan or not. I have been unintentionally led into this violation of order. I fhould effect no purpofe of either brevity or clearnefs, by returning to the more methodical courfe of obfervation. I have been naturally drawn from it by the fuperior importance of the topic I am upon, namely, the merit of the publication in queftion.

This publication, if afcribable at all to Mr. Rowan, contains four diftinct fubjects: the firft the invitation to the volunteers to arm : upon that I have already obferved ; but thofe that remain are furely of much importance, and no doubt are profecuted as equally criminal. The paper next ftates the neceffity of a reform in parliament ; it ftates, thirdly, the neceffity of an emancipation of the Catholic inhabitants of Ireland ; and as neceffary to the atchievement of all thefe objects, does, fourthly, ftate the neceffity of a general delegated convention of the people.

It has been alledged that Mr. Rowan intended by this publication to excite the fubjects of this country to effect an alteration in the form of your conftitution. And here, gentlemen, perhaps, you may not be unwilling to follow a little farther than Mr. Attorney General has done, the idea of a late profecution in Great Britain upon the fubject of a public libel. It is with

peculiar

peculiar fondnefs I look to that country for folid principles of conftitutional liberty and judicial example. You have been prefled in no fmall degree with the manner in which this publication marks the different orders of our conftitution, and comments upon them. Let me fhew you what boldnefs of animadverfion on fuch topics is thought juftifiable in the Britifh nation, and by a Britifh jury. I have in my hand the report of the trial of the printers of the Morning Chronicle, for a fuppofed libel againft the ftate, and of their acquittal: let me read to you fome paffages from that publication, which a jury of Englifhmen were in vain called upon to brand with the name of libel.

" *Claiming it as our indefeafible right to affociate together, in a peaceable and friendly manner, for the communication of thoughts, the formation of opinions, and to promote the general happinefs, we think it unneceffary to offer any apology for inviting you to join us in this manly and benevolent purfuit; the neceffity of the inhabitants of every community endeavouring to procure a true knowledge of their rights, their duties, and their interefts, will not be denied, except by thofe who are the flaves of prejudice, or the interefted in the continuation of abufes. As men who wifh to afpire to the title of freemen, we totally deny the wifdom and the humanity of the advice, to approach the defects of government with " pious awe and trembling folicitude." What better doctrine could the pope or the tyrants of Europe defire? We think, therefore, that the caufe of truth and juftice can never be hurt by temperate and honeft difcuffions; and that caufe which will not bear fuch a fcrutiny, muft be fyftematically or practically bad. We are fenfible that thofe who are not friends to the general good, have attempted to inflame the public mind with the cry of " Danger," whenever men have affociated for difcuffing the principles of government; and we have little doubt but fuch conduct will be purfued in this place; we would therefore caution every honeft man, who has really the welfare of the nation at heart, to avoid being led away by the proftituted clamours of thofe who live on the fources of corruption. We pity the fears of the timorous, and we are totally unconcerned refpecting the falfe alarms of the venal."*——

——" *We view with concern the frequency of wars.—We are perfuaded that the interefts of the poor can never be promoted by acceffion of territory, when bought at the expence of their labour and blood; and we muft fay, in the language of a celebrated author—* " *We, who are only the people, but who pay for wars with our fubftance and our blood, will not ceafe to tell kings,*" *or governments,* " *that to them alone wars are profitable: that the true and juft conquefts are thofe which each makes at home, by comforting the peafantry, by promoting agriculture and manufactories: by multiplying men, and the other productions of nature, that then it is that kings may call themfelves the image of God, whofe will is perpetually directed to the creation of new beings. If they continue to make us fight and kill one another, in uniform, we will continue to write and*

I

fpeak,

speak, until nations shall be cured of this folly."—We are certain our present heavy burthens are owing, in a great measure to cruel and impolitic wars, and therefore we will do all on our part, as peaceable citizens who have the good of the community at heart, to enlighten each other, and protest against them.

" The present state of the representation of the people, calls for the particular attention of every man who has humanity sufficient to feel for the honour and happiness of his country; to the defects and corruptions of which we are inclined to attribute unnecessary wars, &c. &c. We think it a deplorable case when the poor must support a corruption which is calculated to oppress them; when the labourer must give his money to afford the means of preventing him having a voice in its disposal; when the lower classes may say,—" We give you our money, for which we have toiled and sweat, and which would save our families from cold and hunger; but we think it more hard that there is nobody whom we have delegated, to see that it is not improperly and wickedly spent; we have none to watch over our interests; the rich only are represented."——

——" An equal and uncorrupt representation would, we are persuaded, save us from heavy expences, and deliver us from many oppressions, we will therefore do our duty to procure this reform, which appears to us of the utmost importance."

" In short we see with the most lively concern, an army of placemen, pensioners, &c. fighting in the cause of corruption and prejudice, and spreading the contagion far and wide."

——" We see with equal sensibility the present outcry against reforms, and a proclamation (tending to cramp the liberty of the press, and discredit the true friends of the people) receiving the support of numbers of our countrymen."——

——" We see burdens multiplied—the lower classes sinking into poverty, disgrace, and excesses, and the means of these shocking abuses increased for the purposes of revenue."——

——" We ask ourselves—" Are we in England?"—Have our forefathers fought, bled, and conquered for liberty? And did they not think that the fruits of their patriotism would be more abundant in peace, plenty, and happiness?"——

——" Is the condition of the poor never to be improved? Great Britain must have arrived at the highest degree of national happiness and prosperity, and our situation must be too good to be mended, or the present outcry against reforms and improvements is inhuman and criminal. But we hope our condition will be speedily improved, and to obtain so desirable a good is the object of our present association; an union founded on principles of benevolence and humanity; disclaiming all connection with riots and disorder, but firm in our purpose, and warm in our affections for liberty.

" Lastly—We invite the friends of freedom throughout Great Britain to form similar societies, and to act with unanimity and firmness, till
the

the people be too wife to be impofed upon ; and their influence in the go-
vernment be commenfurate with their dignity and importance.

" THEN SHALL WE BE FREE AND HAPPY."

Such, gentlemen, is the language, which a fubject of Great
Britain thinks himfelf warranted to hold, and upon fuch language
has the corroborating fanction of a Britifh jury been ftamped by
a verdict of acquittal. Such was the honeft and manly freedom
of publication, in a country too where the complaint of abufes
has not half the foundation it has here. I faid I loved to look
to England for principles of judicial example, I cannot but fay
to you that it depends on your fpirit whether I fhall look to it
hereafter with fympathy or with fhame. Be pleafed now, gentlemen, to confider whether the ftatement of the imperfection in
your reprefentation, has been made with a defire of inflaming an
attack upon the public tranquillity, or with an honeft purpofe of
procuring a remedy for an actually exifting grievance.

It is impoffible not to revert to the fituation of the times, and
let me remind you that whatever obfervations of this kind I am
compelled thus to make in a court of juftice, the uttering of them
in this place is not imputable to my client, but to the neceffity
of defence impofed upon him by this extraordinary profecution.

Gentlemen, the reprefentation of your people is the vital principle of their political exiftence, without it they are dead, or they
live only to fervitude ; without it there are two eftates acting-upon
and againft the third, inftead of acting in co-operation with it ;
without it, if the people are oppreffed by their judges, where is the
tribunal to which their judges can be amenable ? Without it, if
they are trampled upon and plundered by a minifter, where is
the tribunal to which the offender fhall be amenable ? Without it,
where is the ear to hear, or the heart to feel, or the hand to redrefs
their fufferings ? Shall they be found, let me afk you, in the accurf-
ed band of imps and minions that bafk in their difgrace, and fatten
upon their fpoils, and flourifh upon their ruin ? But let me not put
this to you as a merely fpeculative queftion. It is a plain queftion of fact : rely upon it, phyfical man is every where the fame,
it is only the various operation of moral caufes that gives variety
to the focial or individual character and condition. How hap-
pens it that modern flavery looks quietly at the defpot, on the
very fpot where Leonidas expired ? The anfwer is eafy, Sparta
has not changed her climate, but fhe has loft that government
which her liberty could not furvive.

I call you, therefore, to the plain queftion of fact ; this paper
recommends a reform in parliament ; I put that queftion to your
confciences, do you think it needs that reform ? I put it boldly
and fairly to you, do you think the people of Ireland are reprefented as they ought to be ? Do you hefitate for an anfwer ? If
you

you do, let me remind you that until the laſt year three millions
of your countrymen have by the expreſs letter of the law been
excluded from the reality of actual, and even from the phantom
of virtual repreſentation. Shall we then be told that this is only
the affirmation of a wicked and ſeditious incendiary? If you do
not feel the mockery of ſuch a charge, look at your country, in
what ſtate do you find it? Is it in a ſtate of tranquillity and general ſatisfaction? Theſe are traces by which good is ever to be
diſtinguiſhed from bad government. Without any very minute
enquiry or ſpeculative refinement; do you feel that a veneration
for the law, a pious and humble attachment to the conſtitution,
form the political morality of your people? Do you find that
comfort and competency among your people, which are always
to be found where a government is mild and moderate; where
taxes are impoſed by a body who have an intereſt in treating the
poorer orders with compaſſion, and preventing the weight of tax-
ation from preſſing ſore upon them?

Gentlemen, I mean not to impeach the ſtate of your repreſen-
tion, I am not ſaying that it is defective, or that it ought to be al-
tered or amended, nor is this a place for me to ſay, whether I
think that three millions of the inhabitants of a country whoſe
whole number is but four, ought to be admitted to any efficient
ſituation in the ſtate; it may be ſaid and truly, theſe are not queftions for either of us directly to decide; but you cannot refuſe
them ſome paſſing conſideration at leaſt, when you remember
that on this ſubject the real queſtion for your deciſion is, whether
the allegation of a defect in your conſtitution is ſo utterly unfounded and falſe, that you can aſcribe it only to the malice and
perverſeneſs of a wicked mind, and not to the innocent miſtake of
an ordinary underſtanding;—whether it cannot be miſtake; whether it can be only ſedition.

And here, gentlemen, I own I cannot but regret, that one of
our countrymen ſhould be criminally purſued for aſſerting the neceſſity of a reform, at the moment when that neceſſity ſeems admitted by the parliament itſelf; that this unhappy reform ſhall
at the ſame moment be a ſubject of legiſlative diſcuſſion, and criminal proſecution; far am I from imputing any ſiniſter deſign
to the virtue or wiſdom of our government, but who can avoid
feeling the deplorable impreſſion that muſt be made on the public
mind, when the demand for that reform is anſwered by a criminal
information?

I am the more forcibly impreſſed by this concern, when I conſider that when this information was firſt put upon the file, the
ſubject was tranſiently mentioned in the Houſe of Commons.
Some circumſtances retarded the progreſs of the inquiry there;
and the progreſs of the information was equally retarded here.
The firſt day of this ſeſſion you all know, that ſubject was again
brought forward in the Houſe of Commons, and as if they had
ſlept

flept together, this profecution was alfo revived in the Court of
King's Bench ; and that before a jury, taken from a pannel partly
compofed of thofe very members of parliament, who, in the Houfe
of Commons, muft debate upon this fubject as a meafure of public
advantage, which they might have here to confider as a public
crime. *

This paper, gentlemen, infifts upon the neceffity of emancipating the Catholics of Ireland, and that is charged as part of the
libel. If they had waited another year, if they had kept this
profecution impending for another year, how much would remain
for a jury to decide upon, I fhould be at a lofs to difcover. It feems
a if the progrefs of public reformation was eating away the ground
of the profecution. Since the commencement of the profecution,
this part of the libel has unluckily received the fanction of the
legiflature.   In that interval our Catholic brethren have obtained that admiffion, which it feems it was a libel to propofe :
in what way to account for this, I am really at a lofs. Have any
alarms been occafioned by the emancipation of our Catholic brethren? Has the bigotted malignity of any individuals been
crufhed? Or has the ftability of the government, or has that of
the country been weakened? Or is one million of fubjects ftronger
than four millions? Do you think that the benefit they received
fhould be poifoned by the fting of vengeance ? If you think fo, you
muft fay to them, " you have demanded emancipation and you
" have got it ; but we abhor your perfons, we are outraged at your
" fuccefs ; and we will ftigmatize by a criminal profecution the
" relief which you have obtained from the voice of your country."
I afk you, gentlemen, do you think as honeft men, anxious for the
public tranquillity, confcious that there are wounds not yet com-
pletely cicatrized, that you ought to fpeak this language at
this time, to men who are too much difpofed to think that in this
very emancipation they have been faved from their own parliament by the humanity of their fovereign ? Or do you wifh to
prepare them for the revocation of thefe improvident conceffions ?
Do you think it wife or humane at this moment to infult them,
by fticking up in a pillory the man who dared to ftand forth
their advocate ? I put it to your oaths, do you think, that a
bleffing of that kind, that a victory obtained by juftice over bigotry and oppreffion, fhould have a ftigma caft upon it by an ig-
nominious fentence upon men bold and honeft enough to propofe
that meafure ? To propofe the redeeming of religion from the
abufes of the church, the reclaiming of three millions of men
from bondage, and giving liberty to all who had a right to de-

* Among the names on the pannel were right hon. J. Cuffe, M. P.
—Right hon. D. Latouche, M. P.—Sir W. G. Newcomen, Bart. M. P.—
J. Maxwell, M. P.—C. H. Coote, M. P —Henry Bruen, M. P.—
H. V. Brooke, M. P.—J. Reilly, M. P.—J. Pomeroy, M. P.

mand

mand it ; giving, I fay, in the fo much cenfured words of this paper, giving " UNIVERSAL EMANCIPATION !" I fpeak in the fpirit of the Britifh law, which makes liberty commenfurate with and infeparable from Britifh foil; which proclaims even to the ftranger and the fojourner, the moment he fets his foot upon Britifh earth, that the ground on which he treads is holy, and confecrated by the Genius of UNIVERSAL EMANCIPATION. No matter in what language his doom may have been pronounced;—no matter what complexion incompatible with freedom, an Indian or an African fun may have burnt upon him;—no matter in what difaftrous battle his liberty may have been cloven down ;—no matter with what folemnities he may have been devoted upon the altar of flavery ; the firft moment he touches the facred foil of Britain, the altar and the god fink together in the duft ; his foul walks abroad in her own majefty ; his body fwells beyond the meafure of his chains, that burft from around him, and he ftands redeemed, regenerated, and difenthralled, by the irrefiftible Genius of UNIVERSAL EMANCIPATION.

[Here Mr. Curran was interrupted by a fudden burft of applaufe from the court and hall, filence however was reftored after fome minutes, by the interpofition of Lord Clonmel, who declared the great pleafure he felt himfelf, at the exertion of profeffional talents, but difapproved any intemperate expreffion of applaufe in a court of juftice.]

Mr. Curran then proceeded—Gentlemen, I am not fuch a fool, as to afcribe any effufion of this fort, to any merit of mine. It is the mighty theme, and not the inconfiderable advocate, that can excite intereft in the hearer! What you hear is but the teftimony which nature bears to her own charaĉter; it is the effufion of her gratitude to that power, which ftampt that charaĉter upon her.

And, gentlemen, permit me to fay, that if my client had occafion to defend his caufe by any mad or drunken appeals to extravagance or licentioufnefs, I truft in God I ftand in that fituation, that humble as I am, he would not have reforted to me to be his advocate. I was not recommended to his choice by any connection of principle or party, or even private friendfhip, and faying this I cannot but add, that I confider not to be acquainted with fuch a man as Mr. Rowan, a want of perfonal good fortune.

Gentlemen, upon this great fubjeĉt of reform and emancipation, there is a latitude and boldnefs of remark, juftifiable in the people, and neceffary to the defence of Mr. Rowan, for which the habits of profeffional ftudies, and technical adherence to eftablifhed forms, have rendered me unfit. It is however my duty, ftanding here as his advocate, to make fome few obfervations to you, which I conceive to be material.

Gentlemen,

Gentlemen, you are fitting in a country, which has a right to the Britifh conftitution, and which is bound by an indiffoluble union with the Britifh nation. If you were now even at liberty to debate upon that fubject; if you even were not by the moft folemn compacts, founded upon the authority of your anceftors and of yourfelves, bound to that alliance, and had an election now to make ; in the prefent unhappy ftate of Europe, if you had been heretofore a ftranger to Great Britain, you would now fay, we will enter into fociety and union with you;

Una falus ambobus erit, commune periclum ;

But to accomplifh that union let me tell you, you muft learn to become like the Englifh people ; it is vain to fay, you will protect their freedom if you abandon your own. The pillar whofe bafe has no foundation, can give no fupport to the dome under which its head is placed, and if you profefs to give England that affiftance which you refufe to yourfelves, fhe will laugh at your folly, and defpife your meannefs and infincerity. Let us follow this a little further, I know you will interpret what I fay with the candour in which it is fpoken. England is marked by a natural avarice of freedom, which fhe is ftudious to engrofs and accumulate, but moft unwilling to impart, whether from any neceffity of her policy, or from her weaknefs, or from her pride, I will not prefume to fay, but that fo is the fact, you need not look to the Eaft, or to the Weft, you need only look to yourfelves.

In order to confirm that obfervation, I would appeal to what fell from the learned counfel for the crown, that notwithftanding the alliance fubfifting for two centuries paft, between the two countries, the date of liberty in one goes no further back than the year 1784.

If it required additional confirmation, I fhould ftate the cafe of the invaded American, and the fubjugated Indian, to prove that the policy of England has ever been to govern her connexions more as colonies, than as allies ; and it muft be owing to the great fpirit indeed of Ireland if fhe fhall continue free. Rely upon it fhe will ever have to hold her courfe againft an adverfe current ; rely upon it if the popular fpring does not continue ftrong and elaftic, rely upon it; a fhort interval of debilitated nerve and broken force will fend you down the ftream again, and reconfign you to the condition of a province.

If fuch fhould become the fate of your conftitution, afk yourfelves what muft be the motive of your government ? It is eafier to govern a province by a faction, than to govern a co-ordinate country by co-ordinate means. I do not fay it is now, but it will be always thought eafieft by the managers of the day, to govern the Irifh nation by the agency of fuch a faction, as long as this country fhall be found willing to let her connexion with Great Britain be preferved only by her own degradation. In fuch a

precarious

precarious and wretched state of things, if it shall ever be found
to exist, the true friend of Irish liberty, and British connexion,
will see, that the only means of saving both must be, as Lord
Chatham expressed it, the infusion of new health and blood into
the constitution. He will see how deep a stake each country has
in the liberty of the other; he will see what a bulwark he adds
to the common cause, by giving England a co-ordinate, and co-in-
terested ally, instead of an oppressed, enfeebled and suspected de-
pendant; he will see how grossly the credulity of Britain is
abused by those, who make her believe that her solid interest is promoted by our depression; he will see the desperate precipice to
which she approaches by such a conduct, and with an animated
and generous piety he will labour to avert her danger. But,
gentlemen of the jury, what is likely to be his fate? The interest
of the sovereign must be for ever the interest of his people, because his interest lives beyond his life, it must live in his fame,
it must live in the tenderness of his solicitude for an unborn posterity; it must live in that heart attaching bond by which millions
of men have united the destinies of themselves and their children
with his, and call him by the endearing appellation of king and
father of his people.

But what can be the interest of such a government as I have
described? Not the interest of the king, not the interest of the
people, but the sordid interest of the hour; the interest in de-
ceiving the one, and in oppressing and deforming the other: the
interest of unpunished rapine and unmerited favour: that odious and
abject interest, that prompts them to extinguish public spirit
in punishment or in bribe; and to pursue every man, even to
death, who has sense to see, and integrity and firmness enough to
abhor and to oppose them. What therefore I say, gentlemen, will
be the fate of the man, who embarks in an enterprize of so much
difficulty and danger? I will not answer it. Upon that hazard
has my client put every thing that can be dear to man;—his fame,
his fortune, his person, his liberty and his children; but with what
event your verdict only can answer, and to that I refer your
country.

Gentlemen, there is a fourth point remaining. Says this paper,
" For both these purposes, it appears necessary that provincial
" conventions should assemble preparatory to the convention of
" the Protestant people. The delegates of the Catholic body
" are not justified in communicating with individuals, or even
" bodies of inferior authority, and therefore an assembly of a similar
" nature and organization, is necessary to establish an intercourse
" of sentiment, an uniformity of conduct, an united cause and an
" united nation. If a convention on the one part does not soon
" follow, and is not soon connected with that on the other, the
" common cause will split into the partial interest; the people will
" relax into inattention and inertness; the union of affection
                                                    " and

" and exertion will diffolve, and too probably fome local infur-
" rection, inftigated by the malignity of our common enemy,
" may commit the character and rifque the tranquillity of the
" ifland, which can be obviated only by the influence of an
" affembly arifing from, affimilated with the people, and whofe
" fpirit may be, as it were, knit with the foul of the nation,
" unlefs the fenfe of the Proteftant people be on their part as
" fairly collected and as judicioufly directed, unlefs individual ex-
" ertion confolidates into collective ftrength, unlefs the particles
" unite into mafs, we may perhaps ferve fome perfon or
" fome party for a little, but the public not at all; the nation is
" neither infolent, nor rebellious, nor feditious ; while it knows
" its rights, it is unwilling to manifeft its powers; it would ra-
" ther fupplicate adminiftration to anticipate revolution by well-
" timed reform, and to fave their country in mercy to them-
" felves.''

Gentlemen, it is with fomething more than common reverence,
it is with a fpecies of terror that I am obliged to tread this
ground.—But what is the idea put in the ftrongeft point of view.
—We are willing not to manifeft our powers, but to fupplicate
adminiftration, to anticipate revolution, that the legiflature may
fave the country in mercy to itfelf.

Let me fuggeft to you gentlemen, that there are fome circumftances which have happened in the hiftory of this country,
that may better ferve as a comment upon this part of the cafe
than any I can make. I am not bound to defend Mr. Rowan as
to the truth or wifdom of the opinions he may have formed. But
if he did really conceive the fituation of the country fuch as that
the not redreffing her grievances might lead to a convulfion, and
of fuch an opinion not even Mr. Rowan is anfwerable here for
the wifdom, much lefs fhall I infinuate any idea of my own upon
fo aweful a fubject, but if he did fo conceive the fact to be, and
acted from the fair and honeft fuggeftion of a mind anxious
for the public good, I muft confefs, gentlemen, I do not know in
what part of the Britifh conftitution to find the principle of his
criminality.

But, gentlemen, be pleafed further to confider, that he cannot
be underftood to put the fact on which he argues on the authority of his affertion. The condition of Ireland was as open to
the obfervation of every other man as to that of Mr. Rowan;
what then does this part of the publication amount to? In my
mind, fimply to this : ' the nature of oppreffion in all countries
' is fuch that although it may be borne to a certain degree, it
' cannot be borne beyond that degree; you find it exemplified in
' Great Britain ; you find the people of England patient to a
' certain point, but patient no longer. That infatuated monarch,
' James II. experienced this ; the time did come, when the mea-
' fure of popular fuffering and popular patience was full; when
' a fingle

' a fingle drop was fufficient to make the waters of bitternefs to
' overflow. I think this meafure in Ireland is brimful at pre-
' fent ; I think the ftate of reprefentation of the people in par-
' liament is a grievance, I think the utter exclufion of three mil-
' lions of people is a grievance of that kind that the people are
' not likely long to endure, and the continuation of which may
' plunge the country into that ftate of defpair which wrongs ex-
' afperated by perfeverance never fail to produce.' But to whom
is even this language addreffed? Not to the body of the people,
on whofe temper and moderation if once excited, perhaps not
much confidence could be placed; but to that authoritative
body whofe influence and power would have reftrained the ex-
ceffes of the irritable and tumultuous; and for that purpofe exprefsly does this publication addrefs the volunteers. ' We are
' told that we are in danger ;—I call upon you, the great con-
' ftitutional faviours of Ireland, defend the country to which you
' have given political exiftence, and ufe whatever fanction your
' great name, your facred character, and the weight you have in
' the community, muft give you to reprefs wicked defigns, if any
' there are.
' We feel ourfelves ftrong, the people are always ftrong, the
' public chains can only be rivetted by the public hands ; look to
' thofe devoted regions of Southern defpotifm, behold the ex-
' piring victim on his knees, prefenting the javelin reeking with
' his blood to the ferocious monfter who returns it into his heart.
' Call not that monfter the tyrant, he is no more than the execu-
' tioner of that inhuman tyranny which the people practice upon
' themfelves, and of which he is only referved to be a later
' victim than the wretch he has fent before. Look to a nearer coun-
' try, where the fanguinary characters are more legible ; whence
' you almoft hear the groans of death and torture. Do you
' afcribe the rapine and murder of France to the few names that
' we are execrating here? or do you not fee that it is the phrenzy
' of an infuriated multitude abufing its own ftrength, and prac-
' tifing thofe hideous abominations upon itfelf. Againft the vio-
' lence of this ftrength let your virtue and influence be our fafe-
' guard." What criminality, gentlemen of the jury, can you
find in this? what at any time? But I afk you, peculiarly at this
momentous period, what guilt can you find in it? My client faw
the fcene of horror and blood which covers almoft the face of
Europe : he feared that caufes, which he thought fimilar, might
produce fimilar effects, and he feeks to avert thofe dangers by
calling the united virtue and tried moderation of the country into a ftate of ftrength and vigilance. Yet this is the conduct
which the profecution of this day feeks to punifh and ftigmatize.
And this is the language for which this paper is reprobated to-
day, as tending to turn the hearts of the people againft their fovereign, and inviting them to overturn the conftitution. Let us
now

now, gentlemen, confider the concluding part of this publication: it recommends a meeting of the people to deliberate on conftitutional methods of redreffing grievances. Upon this fubject I am inclined to fufpect that I have in my youth taken up crude ideas, not founded, perhaps, in law; but I did imagine that when the bill of rights reftored the right of petitioning for the redrefs of grievances, it was underftood that the people might boldly ftate among themfelves that grievances did exift; that they might lawfully affemble themfelves in fuch manner as they might deem moft orderly and decorous. I thought I had collected it from the greateft luminaries of the law. The power of petitioning feemed to me to imply the right of affembling for the purpofe of deliberation. The law requiring a petition to be prefented by a limited number, feemed to me to admit that the petition might be prepared by any number whatever, provided, in doing fo, they did not commit any breach or violation of the public peace. I know that there has been a law paffed in the Irifh parliament of laft year, which may bring my former opinion into a merited want of authority. That law declares that no body of men may delegate a power to any fmaller number, to act, think or petition for them. If that law had not paffed I fhould have thought that the affembling by a delegated convention was recommended, in order to avoid the tumult and diforder of a promifcuous affembly of the whole mafs of the people. I fhould have conceived before that act that any law to abridge the orderly appointment of the few to confult for the intereft of the many, and thus force the many to confult by themfelves or not at all, would in fact be a law not to reftrain but to promote infurrection, but that law has fpoken and my error muft ftand corrected. Of this, however, let me remind you, you are to try this part of the publication by what the law was then, not by what it is now. How was it underftood until laft feffion of parliament? You had both in England and Ireland, for the laft ten years, thefe delegated meetings. The volunteers of Ireland, in 1782, met by delegation; they framed a plan of parliamentary reform; they prefented it to the reprefentative wifdom of the nation; it was not received, but no man ever dreamed that it was not the undoubted right of the fubject to affemble in that manner. They affembled by delegation at Dungannon, and to fhew the idea then entertained of the legality of their public conduct, that fame body of volunteers was thanked by both houfes of parliament, and their delegates moft gracioufly received at the throne. The other day, you had delegated reprefentatives of the Catholics of Ireland, publicly elected by the members of that perfuafion, and fitting in convention in the heart of your capital, carrying on an actual treaty with the exifting government, and under the eye of your own parliament, which was then affembled; you have feen the delegates from that convention, carry the complaints of their

grievances

(56)

grievances to the foot of the throne; from whence they brought back to that convention, the aufpicious tidings of that redrefs which they had been refufed at home.

Such gentlemen, have been the means of popular communication and difcuffion, which until the laft feffion have been deemed legal in this country; as happily for the fifter kingdom, they are yet confidered there.

I do not complain of this act as any infraction of popular liberty; I fhould not think it becoming in me to exprefs any complaint againft a law, when once become fuch. I obferve only, that one mode of popular deliberation is thereby taken utterly away, and you are reduced to a fituation in which you never ftood before. You are living in a country, where the conftitution is rightly ftated to be only ten years old; where the people have not the ordinary rudiments of education. It is a melancholy ftory, that the lower orders of the people here have lefs means of being enlightened than the fame clafs of people in any other country. If there be no means left by which public meafures can be canvaffed, what will be the confequence? Where the prefs is free, and difcuffion unreftrained, the mind by the collifion of intercourfe, gets rid of its own afperities, a fort of infenfible perfpiration takes place, by which thofe acrimonies, which would otherwife fefter and inflame, are quietly diffolved and diffipated. But now, if any aggregate affembly fhall meet, they are cenfured; if a printer publifhes their refolutions he is punifhed; rightly to be fure in both cafes, for it has been lately done. If the people fay, let us not create tumult, but meet in delegation, they cannot do it; if they are anxious to promote parliamentary reform, in that way, they cannot do it; the law of the laft feffion has for the firft time declared fuch meetings to be a crime. What then remains? Only the liberty of the prefs, that facred palladium, which no influence, no power, no minifter, no government, which nothing but the depravity, or folly, or corruption of a jury, can ever deftroy. And what calamity are the people faved from, by having public communication left open to them? I will tell you, gentlemen, what they are faved from, and what the government is faved from; i will tell you alfo, to what both are expofed by fhutting up that communication; in one cafe fedition fpeaks aloud, and walks abroad; the demagogue goes forth, and the public eye is upon him, he frets his bufy hour upon the ftage, but foon either wearinefs, or bribe, or punifhment, or difappointment bear him down, or drive him off, and he appears no more; in the other cafe, how does the work of fedition go forward? Night after night the muffled rebel fteals forth in the dark, and cafts another and another brand upon the pile, to which, when the hour of fatal maturity fhall arrive, he will apply the flame. If you doubt of the horrid confequences of fuppreffing the effufion even of individual difcontent, look to thofe enflaved countries where the protection

of

of defpotifm is fuppofed to be fecured by fuch reftraints, even the perfon of the defpot there is never in fafety. Neither the fears of the defpot, nor the machinations of the flave have any flumber, the one anticipating the moment of peril, the other watching the opportunity of aggreflion. The fatal crifis is equally a furprize upon both; the decifive inftant is precipitated without warning, by folly on the one fide or by frenzy on the other, and there is no notice of the treafon till the traitor acts. In thofe unfortunate countries (one cannot read it without horror) there are officers whofe province it is, to have the water, which is to be drank by their rulers, fealed up in bottles, left fome wretched mifcreant fhould throw poifon into the draught.

But, gentlemen, if you wifh for a nearer and more interefting example, you have it in the hiftory of your own revolution ; you have it at that memorable period, when the monarch found a fervile acquiefcence in the minifters of his folly, when the liberty of the prefs was trodden under foot, when venal fheriffs returned packed juries to carry into effect thofe fatal confpiracies of the few againft the many ; when the devoted benches of public juftice were filled by fome of thofe Foundlings of Fortune, who, overwhelmed in the torrent of corruption at an early period, lay at the bottom like drowned bodies, while foundnefs or fanity remained in them ; but at length becoming buoyant by putrefaction, they rofe as they rotted, and floated to the furface of the polluted ftream, where they were drifted along, the objects of terror, and contagion, and abomination.

In that awful moment of a nation's travail, of the laft gafp of tyranny, and the firft breath of freedom, how pregnant is the example ? The prefs extinguifhed, the people enflaved, and the prince undone.

As the advocate of fociety, therefore, of peace, of domeftic liberty, and the lafting union of the two countries, I conjure you to guard the liberty of the prefs, that great centinel of the ftate, that grand detector of public impofture : guard it, becaufe when it finks, there finks with it, in one common grave, the liberty of the fubject and the fecurity of the crown.

Gentlemen, I am glad that this queftion has not been brought forward earlier ; I rejoice for the fake of the court, of the jury, and of the public repofe, that this queftion has not been brought forward till now. In Great Britain analogous circumftances have taken place. At the commencement of that unfortunate war which has deluged Europe with blood, the fpirit of the Englifh people was tremblingly alive to the terror of French principles ; at that moment of general paroxyfm, to accufe was to convict. The danger loomed larger to the public eye, from the mifty medium through which it was furveyed. We meafure inacceffible heights by the fhadows which they project ; where the lownefs and the diftance of the light form the length of the fhade.

l

There

There is a fort of afpiring and adventurous credulity, which difdains affenting to obvious truths, and delights in catching at the improbability of circumftances, as its beft ground of faith. To what other cause, gentlemen, can you afcribe that in the wife, the reflecting and the philofophic nation of Great Britain, a printer has been gravely found guilty of a libel, for publifhing thofe refolutions, to which the prefent minifter of that kingdom had actually fubfcribed his name? To what other caufe can you afcribe, what in my mind is ftill more aftonifhing, in fuch a country as Scotland, a nation caft in the happy medium between the fpiritlefs acquiefcence of fubmiffive poverty, and the fturdy credulity of pampered wealth; cool and ardent, adventurous and perfevering; winning her eagle flight againft the blaze of every fcience, with an eye that never winks, and a wing that never tires; crowned as fhe is with the fpoils of every art, and decked with the wreath of every mufe; from the deep and fcrutinizing refearches of her Humes, to the fweet and fimple, but not lefs fublime and pathetic morality of her Burns—how from the bofom of a country like that, genius and character, and talents, fhould be banifhed to a diftant barbarous foil; condemned to pine under the horrid communion of vulgar vice and bafe-born profligacy, for twice the period that ordinary calculation gives to the continuance of human life? But I will not further prefs any idea that is painful to me, and I am fure muft be painful to you: I will only fay, you have now an example, of which neither England nor Scotland had the advantage; you have the example of the panic, the infatuation and the contrition of both. It is now for you to decide whether you will profit by their experience of idle panic and idle regret, or whether you meanly prefer to palliate a fervile imitation of their frailty, by a paltry affectation of their repentance. It is now for you to fhew that you are not carried away by the fame hectic delufions, to acts, of which no tears can wafh away the fatal confequences, or the indelible reproach.

Gentlemen, I have been warning you by inftances of public intellect fufpended or obfcured; let me rather excite you by the example of that intellect recovered and reftored. In that cafe which Mr. Attorney General has cited himfelf, I mean that of the trial of Lambert in England, is there a topic of invective againft conftituted authorities; is there a topic of abufe againft every department of Britifh government, that you do not find in the moft glowing and unqualified terms in that publication, for which the printer of it was profecuted, and acquitted by an Englifh jury? See too what a difference there is between the cafe of a man publifhing his own opinion of facts, thinking that he is bound by duty to hazard the promulgation of them, and without the remoteft hope of any perfonal advantage, and that of a man who makes publication his trade. And faying this, let me not be

be mifunderſtood; it is not my province to enter into any ab-
ſtract defence of the opinions of any man upon public ſubjects.
I do not affirmatively ſtate to you that theſe grievances, which this
paper ſuppoſes, do in fact exiſt; yet I cannot but fay, that the
movers of this profecution have forced that queſtion upon you.
Their motives and their merits, like thoſe of all accuſers, are put in
iſſue before you; and I need no' tell you how ſtrongly the motive
and merits of any informer ought to influence the fate of his accuſation.

I agree moſt implicitly with Mr. Attorney General, that
nothing can be more criminal than an attempt to work a change
in the government by armed force; and I entreat that the court
will not ſuffer any expreſſion of mine to be conſidered as giving encouragement or defence to any deſign to excite diſaffection, to
overawe or to overturn the government; but I put my client's
caſe upon another ground—if he was led into an opinion of grievances where there were none, if he thought there ought to be
a reform where none was neceſſary, he is anſwerable only for
his intention. He can be anſwerable to you in the ſame way
only that he is anſwerable to that God before whom the accuſer,
the accuſed, and the judge muſt appear together, that is, not
for the clearneſs of his underſtanding, but for the purity of his
heart.

Gentlemen, Mr. Attorney General has faid, that Mr. Rowan did
by this publication (ſuppoſing it to be his) recommend, under the
name of equality, a general indiſcriminate aſſumption of public
rule by every the meaneſt perſon in the ſtate. Low as we are in
point of public information, there is not, I believe, any man,
who thinks for a moment, that does not know, that all which
the great body of the people, of any country, can have from any
government, is a fair encouragement to their induſtry, and protection for the fruits of their labour. And there is ſcarcely any
man, I believe, who does not know, that if a people could become ſo filly as to abandon their ſtations in ſociety, under pretence of governing themſelves, they would become the dupes
and the victims of their own folly. But does this publication
recommend any ſuch infatuated abandonment, or any ſuch deſ-
perate aſſumption? I will read the words which relate to that
ſubject, " By liberty we never underſtood unlimited freedom,
" nor by equality the levelling of property or the deſtruction of
" ſubordination." I aſk you with what juſtice, upon what principle of common ſenſe, you can charge a man with the publication of ſentiments, the very reverſe of what his words avow?
and that, when there is no collateral evidence, where there is no
foundation whatever, ſave thoſe very words, by which his meaning can be aſcertained? or if you do adopt an arbitrary principle of imputing to him *your* meaning inſtead of his own, what
publication can be guiltleſs or ſafe? It is a ſort of accuſation

that

that I am afhamed and forry to fee introduced in a court acting
on the principles of the Britifh conftitution.

In the bitternefs of reproach it was faid, ' out of thine own
' mouth will I condemn thee ;' from the feverity of juftice I demand no more. See if in the words that have been fpoken, you
can find matter to acquit, or to condemn. " By liberty we
" never underftood unlimited freedom, nor by equality the le-
" velling of property, or the deftruction of fubordination.—
" This is a calumny invented by that faction or that gang,
" which mifreprefents the king to the people, and the people
" to the king, traduces one half of the nation to cajole the
" other, and, by keeping up diftruft and divifion, wifhes to
" continue the proud arbitrators of the fortune and fate of Ire-
" land." Here you find that meaning difclaimed as a calumny, which is artfully imputed as a crime.

I fay therefore, gentlemen of the jury, as to the four parts
into which the publication muft be divided, I anfwer thus: it
calls upon the volunteers. Confider the time, the danger, the
authority of the profecutors themfelves for believing that danger
to exift, the high character, the known moderation, the approved
loyalty of that venerable inftitution, the fimilarity of the circumftances between the period at which they were fummoned to take
arms, and that in which they have been called upon to reaffume
them. Upon this fimple ground, gentlemen, you will decide,
whether this part of the publication was libellous and criminal
or not.

As to reform, I could wifh to have faid nothing upon it, I
believe I have faid enough ; if he thought the ftate required it,
he acted like an honeft man ; for the rectitude of the opinion he
was not anfwerable, he difcharged his duty in telling the country that he thought fo.

As to the emancipation of the Catholics, I cannot but fay
that Mr. Attorney General did very wifely in keeping clear of
that. Yet gentlemen, I need not tell you how important a
figure it was intended to make upon the fcene, though from un-
lucky accidents, it has become neceffary to expunge it during the
rehearfal.

Of the concluding part of this publication, the convention
which it recommends, I have fpoken already. I wifh not to
trouble you with faying more upon it. I feel that I have already trefpaffed much upon your patience. In truth, upon a fubject embracing fuch a variety of topics, a rigid obfervance either
of concifenefs or arrangement could perhaps fcarcely be expected. It is however with pleafure I feel I am drawing to a clofe,
and that only one queftion remains, to which I would beg your
attention.

Whatever, gentlemen, may be your opinion of the meaning
of this publication, there yet remains a great point for you
to

to decide upon : namely, whether, in point of fact' this publication be imputable to Mr. Rowan or not? Whether he did
publifh it or not? And two witneffes are called to that fact,
one of the name of Lyfter, and the other of the name of
Morton. You muft have obferved that Morton gave no evidence
upon which that paper could have even been read ; he produced
no paper, he identified no paper, he faid that he got fome paper,
but that he had given it away. So that, in point of law, there
was no evidence given by him, on which it could have gone to a
jury, and, therefore, it turns entirely upon the evidence of the
other witnefs. He has ftated that he went to a public meeting,
in a place where there was a gallery crowded with fpectators;
and that he there got a printed paper, the fame which has been
read to you. I know you are well acquainted with the fact, that
the credit of every witnefs muft be confidered by, and reft with
the jury. They are the fovereign judges of that, and I will
not infult your feelings, by infifting on the caution with which
you fhould watch the teftimony of a witnefs that feeks to affect the liberty, or property, or character of your fellow citizens. Under what circumftances does this evidence come before you? The witnefs fays he has got a commiffion in the army
by the intereft of a lady, from a perfon then high in adminiftration. He told you that he made a memorandum upon the back
of that paper, it being his general cuftom, when he got fuch
papers, to make an indorfement upon them ; that he did this from
mere fancy ; that he had no intention of giving any evidence on
the fubject ; he "took it with no fuch view." There is fomething whimfical enough in this curious ftory. Put his credit
upon the pofitive evidence adduced to his character. Who he
is I know not, I know not the man ; but his credit is impeached. Mr. Blake was called, he faid he knew him. I afked him,
" do you think, Sir, that Mr. Lyfter is or is not a man deferving credit upon his oath ?" If you find a verdict of conviction,
it can be only upon the credit of Mr. Lyfter. What faid Mr.
Blake ? Did he tell you that he believed he was a man to be
believed upon his oath ? He did not attempt to fay that he was.
The beft he could fay was, that he would hefitate. Do you
believe Blake ? Have you the fame opinion of Lyfter's teftimony
that Mr. Blake has ? Do you know Lyfter, if you do know
him, and know that he is credible, your knowledge fhould not
be fhaken by the doubts of any man. But if you do not know
him, you muft take his credit from an unimpeached witnefs,
fwearing that he would hefitate to believe him. In my mind
there is a circumftance of the ftrongeft nature that came out
from Lyfter on the table. I am aware that a moft refpectable
man, if impeached by furprize, may not be prepared to repel a
wanton calumny by contrary teftimony. But was Lyfter unap-
prized of this attack upon him ? What faid he ? ' I knew that

' you

' you had Blake to examine againſt me, you have brought him
' here for that purpoſe.' He knew the very witneſs that was to
be produced againſt him, he knew that his credit was impeached,
and yet he produced no perſon to ſupport that credit. What ſaid
Mr. Smyth, " From my knowledge of him I would not believe
" him upon his oath."

Mr. ATTORNEY GENERAL.—I beg pardon, but I muſt ſet Mr.
Curran right. Mr. Lyſter ſaid he had heard Blake would be
here, but not in time to prepare himſelf.

Mr. CURRAN.—But what ſaid Mrs. Hatehell? Was the pro-
duction of that witneſs a ſurprize upon Mr. Lyſter? Her croſs
examination ſhews the fact to be the contrary. The learned
counſel, you ſee, was perfectly apprized of a chain of private circumſtances, to which he pointed his queſtions. Did he know
theſe circumſtances, by inſpiration? No; they could come only
from Lyſter himſelf. I inſiſt, therefore, the gentleman knew
his character was to be impeached, his counſel knew it, and not
a ſingle witneſs has been produced to ſupport it; then conſider,
gentlemen, upon what ground you can find a verdict of conviction againſt my client, when the only witneſs produced to the
fact of publication is impeached, without even an attempt to defend his character. Many hundreds, he ſaid, were at that meeting, why not produce one of them to ſwear to the fact of ſuch
a meeting? One he has ventured to name, but he was certainly
very ſafe in naming a perſon, who he has told you is not in the
kingdom, and could not therefore be called to confront him.

Gentlemen, let me ſuggeſt another obſervation or two. If
ſtill you have any doubt as to the guilt or innocence of the defendant, give me leave to ſuggeſt to you what circumſtances
you ought to conſider, in order to found your verdict: You
ſhould conſider the character of the perſon accuſed, and in this
your taſk is eaſy. I will venture to ſay, there is not a man
in this nation, more known than the gentleman who is the ſubject of this proſecution, not only by the part he has taken in
public concerns, and which he has taken in common with
many, but ſtill more ſo, by that extraordinary ſympathy for
human affliction, which, I am ſorry to think, he ſhares with ſo
ſmall a number. There is not a day that you hear the cries of
your ſtarving manufacturers in your ſtreets, that you do not
alſo ſee the advocate of their ſufferings—that you do not ſee
his honeſt and manly figure, with uncovered head, ſoliciting for
their relief, ſearching the frozen heart of charity, for every
ſtring that can be touched by compaſſion, and urging the force
of every argument and every motive, ſave that which his mo-
deſty ſuppreſſes—the authority of his own generous example.
Or if you ſee him not there, you may trace his ſteps to the pri-

I   vate

vate abode of difeafe and famine and defpair, the meffenger of
heaven, bearing with him food and medicine and confolation.
Are thefe the materials, of which you fuppofe anarchy and public rapine to be formed? Is this the man, on whom to faften the
abominable charge of goading on a frantic populace to mutiny
and bloodfhed? Is this the man likely to apoftatize from every
principle that can bind him to the ftate; his birth, his property, his education, his charaƈter and his children? Let me
tell you, gentlemen of the jury, if you agree with his profecutors, in thinking that there ought to be a facrifice of fuch a
man, on fuch an occafion; and upon the credit of fuch evidence,
you are to conviƈt him—never did you, never can you give a
fentence, configning any man to public punifhment with lefs
danger to his perfon or to his fame: For where could the hireling be found to fling contumely or ingratitude at his head,
whofe private diftreffes he had not laboured to alleviate, or whofe
public condition he had not laboured to improve.

I cannot, however, avoid adverting to a circumftance that dif-
tinguifhes the cafe of Mr. Rowan, from that of a late facrifice
in a neighbouring kingdom.

The feverer law of that country, it feems, and happy for them
that it fhould, enables them to remove from their fight the victim of their infatuation;—the more merciful fpirit of our law
deprives you of that confolation; his fufferings muft remain for
ever before your eyes, a continual call upon your fhame and your
remorfe. But thofe fufferings will do more; they will not reft
fatisfied with your unavailing contrition, they will challenge the
great and paramount inqueft of fociety, the man will be weighed
againft the charge, the witnefs and the fentence; and impartial
juftice will demand, why has an Irifh jury done this deed? the
moment he ceafes to be regarded as a criminal, he becomes of
neceffity an accufer; and let me afk you, what can your moft
zealous defenders be prepared to anfwer to fuch a charge?
When your fentence fhall have fent him forth to that ftage, which
guilt alone can render infamous; let me tell you, he will not be
like a little ftatue upon a mighty pedeftal, diminifhing by eleva-
tion; but he will ftand a ftriking and impofing objeƈt upon a
monument, which, if it does not, and it cannot, record the
atrocity of his crime, muft record the atrocity of his conviction. And upon this fubjeƈt, credit me when I fay, that I am
ftill more anxious for you, than I can poffibly be for him. I
cannot but feel the peculiarity of your fituation. Not the jury
of his own choice, which the law of England allows, but which
ours refufes: colleƈted in that box by a perfon, certainly no friend
to Mr. Rowan, certainly not very deeply interefted in giving
him a very impartial jury. Feeling this, as I am perfuaded
you do, you cannot be furprized, however you may be diftreffed
at the mournful prefage, with which an anxious public is led to

fear

fear the worft from your poffible determination. But I will not, for the juftice and honour of our common country, fuffer my mind to be borne away by fuch melancholy anticipation, I will not relinquifh the confidence that this day will be the period of his fufferings; and, however mercilefsly he has been hitherto purfued, that your verdict will fend him home to the arms of his family, and the wifhes of his country. But if, which heaven forbid, it hath ftill been unfortunately determined, that becaufe he has not bent to power and authority, becaufe he would not bow down before the golden calf and worfhip it, he is to be bound and caft into the furnace; I do truft in God, that there is a redeeming fpirit in the conftitution, which will be feen to walk with the fufferer through the flames, and to preferve him unhurt by the conflagration.

[After Mr. *Curran* had concluded, there was another univerfal burft of applaufe through the court and hall, for fome minutes, which was again filenced by the interference of Lord *Clonmell*.]

Mr. ATTORNEY GENERAL.—*My Lords!* It is Mr. Prime Serjeant's duty to fpeak to the evidence, but as Mr. *Curran* has let fall fome things to make an impreffion not barely upon thofe who furround us, I muft be excufed in ftating fome facts known to no human being but myfelf. It has been ftated that this was an oppreffive profecution, and that oppreffion has been intended by the delay. Now, I do aver that the inftructions he has received are falfe; that I received no inftructions of the fort from government, and no government could think of prevailing with me in fuch a meafure. I feel within myfelf, that no man could afk me fuch a thing twice in the office I hold. Let the jury confider the fact as it is, let them confider the evidence, and God forbid! they fhould be influenced by any thing but the evidence. Mr. *Curran* ftates that oppreffion is practifed—I am refponfible to the court for my conduct here, and if I have carried on this profecution with oppreffion, I am refponfible to the country. Let this gentleman, if he thinks he has been oppreffed, call me to punifhment—let me be a difgrace in the eye of the country, and let me be driven from that profeffion, in which I have fo long been honoured. The facts are thefe;—the accufation againft Mr. ROWAN was made in the month of December, 1792, he was arrefted in January following, and brought before Mr. Juftice DOWNES and difcharged upon bail. The information was filed in Hilary term; as foon as it was poffible by the rules of the court, Mr. ROWAN pleaded, and the *venire* iffued, I do proteft with a *bonâ fide* intention to try Mr. ROWAN: After that an error was found in the record, though it had been compared before; the error was this; in the record

record the words were " *We would do*" fo and fo ; in the publication it was " *Would we do*" fo and fo. As foon as that error
was difcovered, notice was given that the trial could not come
forward, and the witneffes were difmiffed. In Trinity term application was made to iffue the *venire*, and it appeared from the
RECORDER, that he was aware of the defects ; I am above con-
cealing any thing, I admit he did offer to waive any objection to
the error and go to trial directly. I afked Mr. *Kemmis*, " are
" the witneffes gone out of town"—" They are gone to Galway."
I was therefore obliged to refufe the offer, and entered a *Noli*
profequi and filed a new information. Mr. ROWAN put his plea
upon the file, and in Michaelmas term I applied for a trial.
There were feveral trials at bar appointed, and the court refufed,
in confequence of the bufinefs before them, to try it in that
term ; and appointed it for this term. Thefe are the facts which
I think it my duty to mention, and have no more to fay upon
the fubject, but will leave the cafe entirely to the jury, whofe
verdict will not be influenced by fuch topics as have been thrown
out.

Mr. CURRAN.—Mr. Attorney, I could not know the circumftance you mention, of your witneffes being gone out of town.

ATTORNEY GENERAL.—It was impoffible you fhould.*.

Mr.

* In the latter end of December, 1792, Mr. Rowan was arrefted by
virtue of Mr. Juftice Downes's warrant, on a charge of diftributing a feditious paper.—Mr. Juftice Downes having affured Mr. Rowan, that the examinations, upon which the warrant was grounded, would be returned to
the Clerk of the Crown, and that they would, he fuppofed, be in courfe by
him laid before the next term grand jury, Mr. Rowan, inftead of going to
jail, in purfuance of his own opinion, followed the advice of his law friends,
and gave bail for his appearance in the King's Bench, to anfwer fuch charges
as fhould be there made againft him. During the fucceeding Hilary term,
Mr. Rowan daily attended in the King's Bench, and on the laft day of that
term, finding that no examinations had been laid before the grand jury
againft him, he applied, by counfel, to the court, that the examinations
fhould be forthwith returned, particularly as Mr. Attorney General had, in
the courfe of the term, filed two informations *ex officio* againft him, the one
for the fame alledged offence of diftributing a feditious paper, and the other
for a feditious confpiracy ; whereupon, Mr. Juftice Downes, who was on
the bench, having afferted that he had on the firft day of the term, returned
the examinations to the Clerk of the Crown, and the Clerk of the Crown
having faid that from the multiplicity of examinations returned to him on
the firft day of the term, in the courfe of the term, and even on that day, he
had not had time to look them over, the court refufed to make any order.
Mr. Rowan daily attended the King's Bench in the following Eafter Term,
until the fame was nearly fpent, and finding that no bills were fent up to the
Grand Jury againft him, he moved the court, by counfel, that the recognizance
entered into by him and his bail, fhould be vacated, and publicly declared
that if this motion was not granted, he would furrender himfelf in difcharge

K

of

Mr. PRIME SERJEANT.—Wearied and exhausted as you, my lords, and gentlemen of the jury, must be at this late hour, I yet feel it my duty to trespass a short time upon you, in a prosecution which the Attorney General has been obliged to institute : Gentlemen, I say *obliged*, because prosecution is painful to him, as well as to those who act with him. The infliction of punishment is disagreeable to the court, but in our public duty these weak-, nesses must give way. There is justice due to the public ; my learned

of his bail. The Attorney General consenting, the motion was granted, and the recognizance was vacated.

[It may not be improper here to state, that the above examinations having charged Mr James Napper Tandy with distributing a seditious paper equally with Mr. Rowan, he likewise gave bail; but not having appeared in court pursuant to his recognizance, it was estreated, green wax process issued against the bail, and the amount of the recognizance levied from them, though no bill of indictment, grounded on these examinations, was ever preferred against him, and though his absence was notoriously on another account.]

In the above mentioned Easter Term, a motion was made, on behalf of Mr. Rowan, to fix certain days for trial of the informations filed *ex officio* against him, and the Attorney General having agreed to the appointment of two days in the ensuing Trinity Term, *viz.* the 3d and 7th days of May, those days were accordingly appointed for the purpose. However, in the Easter vacation, the Attorney General served a notice on Mr. Rowan, that he would not proceed to trial on those days, and would apply to the court to appoint other days, grounded on an affidavit to be filed, of which notice would be given: nothing was done upon this notice, and no affidavit was filed, or motion made thereon, and the *venire*, the process necessary for impannelling juries on the days appointed, having been, after being issued, kept by Mr. Kemmis, the crown solicitor, instead of being delivered to the sheriff, a motion was made, on behalf of Mr. Rowan, in the last Trinity Term, that the *venire* should be delivered to the proper officer, in order, that the trials might be had on the days appointed, in case the court should not grant any motion the Attorney General might make for postponing the trials. This motion was opposed by the Attorney General—he declared, that there was error in the information for distributing a seditious paper. Mr. Rowan offered to agree to an immediate amendment of the Information, or that a fresh one should be filed and pleaded to instanter, or that he would release all errors ;—all these offers were severally refused. The object of the Attorney General appeared to be to postpone the trials, and though only one of the informations was stated to be informal, yet the day appointed for the trial of the other, which was supposed to be formal, passed away without trial, equally with the day appointed for the trial of the one which was stated to be informal. The Attorney General afterwards withdrew the information stated to have been informal, and filed another in the stead thereof. Many of Mr. Rowan's friends suspected, that the motive for postponing the trials was the expectation of having, under the shrievalty of Mr. Gifford, juries more favourable to government prosecutions, than they could entertain any hopes of having during the shrievalty of Mr Hutton. In Michelmas Term last, the Attorney General applied to the court, that a day should be appointed for the trial of the information for distributing a seditious paper ; the court would not appoint a day in that term, but appointed a day for the trial of that information in Hilary
Term

ed friend is the advocate of justice to the public, not of persecution against the defendant. There is no man, who recollects the
period at which this publication came out, too notorious and
shameful to be forgotten, who must not have thought it highly
proper to bring the publisher to a legal trial. To the exertions
of government, at that time, it is to be attributed that the trial
by jury still subsists among us, and that he has not been before
now tried at another court ; that the King's Bench has not been
superseded by a *Revolutionary Tribunal*; and that my learned
friend has not, ere now, made room for the Public Accuser. The
defendant must think it fortunate that he is tried according to established law, and defended by counsel of his own election, and before
a jury, bound by a solemn appeal to God, to find according to the
evidence given to them, notwithstanding that disgraceful situation in which it has been stated they will be held, if they presume to find a verdict of conviction. I feel no danger that this
jury can be intimidated by apprehensions, or influenced by prejudice. My learned friend and I have been represented as instru-
ments of oppression against the gentleman at the bar. I consider
it as the talk of the moment, because his learned counsel little
knows us, if he thinks us capable of acting so abominable a part;
he could not mean it in the extent to which it reaches the common ear. I can consider it only as the splendid effusion of his
talents ; he was anxious to lead you, gentlemen, from that which
was the true object of consideration. You have been told, the
defendant was prosecuted because he published an invitation to
the volunteers, entered into the discussion of a reform and Catholic emancipation, and endeavoured to have a national convention
assembled. I will tell the jury it is not a prosecution upon any
one of these grounds ; but a prosecution, because these subjects
were thrown before the public in a paper crammed with libellous
and seditious matter, calculated to inflame. These measures,
which were sought after, should be procured by the power of
reason and not by an intimidation of the legislature. Little does
the defendant's counsel know me, if he thinks I could prosecute
a man for calling upon the volunteers to suppress domestic tumult
or resist a foreign foe ; these are the subjects to which he calls
your attention, totally evading the offensive matter in the publication. Gentlemen, the questions which you are to try are these :

Term following, *viz.* the 29th January last. After Mr. Rowan had received his sentence, being desirous of having the information for a seditious
conspiracy also tried and disposed of, he instructed his counsel to move for
the appointment of a day for the purpose; and the counsel having mentioned
to the Attorney General such his instruction, the Attorney General said,
that it was not his intention to proceed upon that information, and that he
had been prevented only by a press of business from withdrawing it, but
would without further delay, and accordingly the Attorney General has
since entered a *noli prosequi* as to that information.

Was

Was this matter publifhed? Is it a libel? And was the intention criminal? Can he defire more? If it was not publifhed, if it be not libellous and the intention was not criminal, I agree that the defendant ought to be acquitted; and if the jury acquit him after a fair and candid difcuffion of the cafe, no man will be more fatisfied than I fhall. But if, without fuch a confideration, a jury, in times of diftraction and diforder fhould, acquit the factious, I agree with the gentleman, that the world would bear hard upon a jury, who from fear or favour betrayed that fituation in which the law and the conftitution placed them.

Let me now, gentlemen, take that place which it is my duty to take, and which the gentleman on the other fide, I fuppofe from addrefs, fo lightly touched upon. I fhall reverfe the order he adopted. The firft queftion then is, " Whether the publica-" tion of this libel was by the defendant?" If there be a man, entertaining a doubt after the evidence ftated, it is in vain for me to addrefs him: In fupport of the fact of publication Mr. Lyfter has been examined; he ftates that, upon the day of the publication of the paper, he was paffing through Cope-ftreet, in this city, and feeing a great crowd at the houfe of Mr. Pardon, he went there to know what the object of the meeting was; he fays, that on going to the door he faw Mr. Rowan, who prevented him from going to that part where the affembly was, faying he could not be let in with coloured clothes: afterwards he went up to the gallery : a bundle of papers was brought, fome were thrown upon the table, and fome handed up to the gallery, and this particular paper which he produced was thrown from a parcel which Mr. Hamilton Rowan had in his hand. The witnefs got this paper, which was thus for the firft time put into circulation : he gave an account of the manner in which this matter was communicated to the Crown Solicitor. The witnefs was queftioned much as to family matters, with a view to impeach his character, but it has had a contrary effect, for the matter was fubmitted to reference, and the authenticity of the inftrument under which his brother claimed, has been eftablifhed, and fome hundreds awarded, one fhilling of which would not have been given if they believed the inftrument to be forged. When he was interrogated as to thefe matters, he faid he heard, this day, that Mr. Blake was to be examined to impeach his character, " If I knew it before, faid he; I could have had wit-" neffes from the country to fupport me." But when Mr. Blake was called, did he in any refpect whatever impeach the character of Mr. Lyfter? he would not fay that Mr. Lyfter was not to be believed. What then muft you think, when refort has been had to diftant counties to find witneffes to impeach the character of Mr. Lyfter, and out of the 150 men affembled in Cope-ftreet, no one has been brought forward to deny the fact which has been

fworn

fworn to ? Will the jury believe that if the fact could be contro-
verted, men would not come forward with emulation to acquit
Mr. Rowan ? I there join with his counfel: he is far above
bringing any man forward to fwear that which is not the fact;
he would not purchafe an acquittal by fuch means, and therefore
it is, gentlemen, that you have not witneffes to prove he was
not there, or to prove he was inactive upon the occafion.

The next witnefs, gentlemen, was Mr. *Morton :* he goes in
direct confirmation of every thing fworn to by *Lyfter,* though he
does not prove the fame individual paper ; but he remembered
hearing the words of fuch another paper read, it began with the
words, " *Citizen foldiers, to arms !*" This evidence, though not
decifive of itfelf as to the identity of the paper, is corroborative
of the teftimony of *Lyfter,* and fhews that Mr. Rowan was there.
Thus ftands the evidence as to the publication. Can any man
doubt that this paper was publifhed by Mr. Rowan ? It is not
neceffary for me to tell you what is a publication in point of law,
as to writing or printing ; but putting it into circulation is a publication in law and fact. I forgot to take notice of the other
impotent attempts to impeach the credit of Mr. *Lyfter* by the
evidence of *Smyth,* who could not prove any thing ; and the evidence of an unfortunate woman, between whofe daughter and
Mr. *Lyfter*'s brother there had been fome attachment. But that
I leave as matter of law to your lordfhips to ftate to the jury.
Thus ftands the evidence ; and with regard to the publication, if
I were upon the jury, no earthly confideration could induce me
not to give a verdict of conviction.

I fhall now beg leave to call your attention to the publication
itfelf. It is charged in the information that it was defigned to
overthrow the government, to overawe the legiflature, to create
tumult and diforder ; there are paragraphs in the paper to warrant every charge contained in the information, which is, in point
of law, fufficiently fuftained. If there be a fingle paragraph of
this paper to warrant the jury to draw this conclufion, that it was
intended to throw the government into difgrace, to excite the
fubjects to make alterations in the government by force, to excite
them to tumult, to overawe the legiflature by an armed force;
if, I fay, there is a fingle paragraph in this paper, from which
you can draw that inference, it fufficiently proves the fubject matter of the information. The gentleman concerned for the defendant read, from the account of a trial, what an Englifh jury did
in the cafe of the *Morning Chronicle,* as an example for an Irifh
jury, as if that was to bind you upon your oaths ; and yet what
was the cafe ? The jury thought that a printer, endeavouring to
get his bread, was not as guilty as the perfon compofing the libel, and that the former did not diftribute it with any malicious
view.

view. But suppose 500 juries found such a verdict, are you to follow their example? I am wishing to take up the distinction made by the defendant's counsel and my learned friend in the prosecution. If this paper had rested with the invitation of the volunteers to arms, he never would have instituted this prosecution upon that account. As in the case in England, Lord KENYON said, "there may be much innocent matter in the publication, "but *latet anguis in herbâ*, there may be much to censure." But here is a publication teeming with faction, tumult, and sedition; it is impossible to suppose it was intended for the old volunteers, it comes from the Society of *United Irishmen*. The first words have been passed over by the defendant's counsel, but they shew at once the wicked adoption of French principles and French language. Is there any man who does not know that at that period, the French revolutionists universally adopted the expression of "*Citizens.*" This paper begins, "*Citizen soldiers, "you first took up arms to protect your country from foreign "enemies and domestic disturbance; for the same purposes it now "becomes necessary that you should resume them.*" It is not confined to summoning the volunteers to protect their country, it calls them to political discussion: was this a period for such proceedings? "*A proclamation has been issued in England for "embodying the Militia, and a proclamation has been issued by "the Lord Lieutenant and Council in Ireland, for repressing all "seditious associations; in consequence of both these proclamations "it is reasonable to apprehend danger from abroad and danger "at home. For whence but from apprehended danger are those "menacing preparations for war drawn through the streets of "this capital? or whence if not to create that internal commo- "tion which was not found, to shake that credit which was not "affected, to blast that volunteer honour which was hitherto "inviolate.*" Gentlemen, was public credit affected or not? Was there a man at that time who could reckon upon the security of his house for a night? "*Are those terrible suggestions and "rumours and whispers that meet us at every corner, and agitate "at least our old men, our women, and our children. Whatever be "the motive, or from whatever quarter it arises, alarm has "arisen; and you volunteers of Ireland are therefore summoned "to arms at the instance of government, as well as by the respon- "sibility attached to your character, and the permanent obligations "of your institution.*" If this were a real invitation to the volunteers, it would endeavour to reconcile them to government. They were called upon to defend, to stand or fall with the constitution, which they had, so much to their honour, exerted themselves to establish. But here follows a direct insinuation calculated to excite jealousy between the government and them. "*We will not at this day condescend to quote authorities for the "right of having and of using arms, but we will cry aloud, "even amidst the storm raised by the witch-craft of a procla-*
"*mation;*"

" *mation.*" Is that a peaceable invitation to the volunteers?
" *that to your formation was owing the peace and protection of*
" *this island, to your relaxation has been owing its relapse into*
" *impotence and insignificance*"; here the country is reprefented
to be in fuch a ftate, that every man is called upon to refcue
it from infignificance; " *to your renovation muft be owing its*
" *future freedom and its prefent tranquility; you are there-*
" *fore fummoned to arms, in order to preferve your country in*
" *that guarded quiet which may fecure it from external hofti-*
" *lity, and to maintain that internal regimen throughout the land*
" *which, fuperfeding a notorious police or a fufpected militia,*
" *may preferve the bleffings of peace by a vigilant preparation for*
" *war.*"— This is a peaceable, quiet invitation to the Volunteers,
fetting them againft the legalized eftablifhments of the country,
and againft that meafure which was in agitation.

It is called a *fufpected* militia. The eftablifhment of a great
conftitutional force, a militia, will be foon experienced to be of advantage to the kingdom, and not an oppreffion; but too fatal
have been the confequences of decrying it; oppofition was given
to the militia law, and numbers have fallen facrifices to their
error. It is nothing lefs than an order to the army to difband;
that body of men to whom we owe the fafety of the ftate, are
told they are not to be entrufted.—" *Citizen foldiers, to arms,*
" *take up the fhield of freedom and the pledges of peace—peace,*
" *the motive and end of your virtuous inftitution—war, an occa-*
" *fional duty, ought never to be made an occupation; every man*
" *fhould become a foldier in the defence of his rights; no man*
" *ought to continue a foldier for offending the rights of others;*
" *the facrifice of life in the fervice of our country is a duty*
" *much too honourable to be intrufted to mercenaries.*" In
another paragraph it fays, " *By liberty we never underftood un-*
" *limited freedom, nor by equality the levelling of property or*
" *the deftruction of fubordination; this is a calumny invented by*
" *that faction, or that gang, which mifreprefents the King to*
" *the people, and the people to the King.*" What is the
meaning of this paragraph? it was unintelligible to me, until I heard the argument of the counfel; he did fairly avow it to
be the government of this country, that a gang was formed to
preferve themfelves in power; otherwife indeed it is the moft
rank nonfenfe and ribaldry that ever fell from the pen of
man; it feems to be a French idea, to excite tumult in the
whole body of the people. The publication goes on and fays—
" *Here we fit without mace or beadle, neither a myftery nor a*
" *craft, nor a corporation—in four words lies all our power,*
" UNIVERSAL EMANCIPATION AND REPRESEN-
" TATIVE LEGISLATURE; *yet we are confident that on*
" *the pivot of this principle, a convention, ftill lefs a fociety,*
" *lefs ftill a fingle man, will be able firft to move and then to raife the*
" *world. We therefore wifh for Catholic emancipation, without any*
" *modification,*

" *modification, but still we consider this necessary enfranchisement as*
" *merely the portal to the temple of national freedom; wide as*
" *this entrance is—wide enough to admit three millions—it is nar-*
" *row when compared to the capacity and comprehension of our*
" *beloved principle, which takes in every individual of the*
" *Irish nation, casts an equal eye over the whole island, em-*
" *braces all that think, and feels for all that suffer. The Catholic*
" *cause is subordinate to our cause, and included in it; for, as*
" *United Irishmen, we adhere to no sect but to society—to no*
" *creed but Christianity—to no party but the whole people.*
" *In the sincerity of our souls do we desire Catholic emancipation;*
" *but were it obtained to-morrow, to-morrow would we go on, as*
" *we do to-day, in the pursuit of that reform, which would*
" *still be wanting to ratify their liberties as well as our own.*
Here the libel recommends an emancipation to the Catholics,
as a colourable pretence for accomplishing their other schemes.
" *For both these purposes,*" says it, " *it appears necessary that*
" *provincial conventions should assemble preparatory to the conven-*
" *tion of the Protestant people.* The delegates of the Catholic
" *body are not justified in communicating with individuals, or*
" *even bodies of inferior authority, and therefore an assembly*
" *of a similar nature and organization,*" Here the very terms
made use of by the French revolutionists are again adopted in
this publication—he says, "*organization is necessary to establish*
" *an intercourse of sentiment, an uniformity of conduct, an united*
" *cause and an united nation.*"
In the subsequent paragraph, the author inforces the necessity
of the speedy meeting of conventions.— " *If,*" says he, " *a*
" *convention on the one part does not soon follow, and is not soon*
" *connected with that on the other, the common cause will split into*
" *the partial interest; the people will relax into inattention and*
" *inertness; the union of affection and exertion will dissolve; and*
" *too probably some local insurrections, instigated by the malignity*
" *of our common enemy, may commit the character and risque*
" *the tranquility of the island, which can be obviated only by*
" *the influence of an assembly arising from, assimilated with the*
" *people, and whose spirit may be, as it were, knit with the*
" *soul of the nation—unless the sense of the Protestant people be,*
" *on their part, as fairly collected and as judiciously directed; un-*
" *less individual exertion consolidates into collective strength; un-*
" *less the particles unite into mass, we may perhaps serve*
" *some person or some party for a little, but the public not at all.*"
Does this mean to give the fullest dominion to the whole body of
the people, to overawe the governing executive power? Gentlemen, the *mass* of the people is to be collected after the French
manner, and bear down all before them. French doctrines were to
be carried into execution. Are those the innocent examination
of claims and the discussion of great political subjects? To what
part of the discussion was it necessary to tell the army, that

" *seduction*

" *feduction made them foldiers ?*" Was it neceffary for the deliberation of that great queftion, the emancipation of the Catholics of Ireland, to fay to the army, " *feduction made them foldiers,* " *but nature made them men ?*" The words are, " *We now address* " *you as citizens, for to be citizens you became foldiers, nor can* " *we help wishing that all foldiers partaking the paffions and* " *intereft of the people would remember, that they were once citizens,* " *that feduction made them foldiers, but ' Nature made them men.'* I fay gentlemen, where was the neceffity of telling the army, that feduction made them foldiers? Was it neceffary to detach them from their duty, for the purpofes which this publication intended to accomplifh? You are told that their whole creed, their whole fyftem " *lay in four words,* UNIVERSAL EMAN- " CIPATION AND REPRESENTATIVE LEGISLA- " TURE." I fay, without univerfal flavery there cannot be univerfal emancipation, and without the ruin of that conftitution, the panegyric upon which produced fuch a burft of applaufe in favour of the learned counfel, there cannot be a reprefentative legiflature. The legiflative authority confifts of King, Lords and Commons. —But they muft have an elected king, and elected nobles to anfwer their ideas of reprefentative legiflature. I am unwilling to ftate the feditioufnefs of this libel farther : but there is another paragraph that deferves to be confidered, it fays, " *The nation is neither in-* " *folent, nor rebellious, nor feditious ; while it knows its rights, it is* " *unwilling to manifeft its powers ; it would rather fupplicate ad-* " *miniftration to anticipate revolution by a well-timed reform, and to* " *fave their country in mercy to themfelves.*" Here the government of this country was called upon to yield to this reform, to anticipate revolution, and fave this country in mercy to themfelves. The peaceable language of difcuffion! Can you read this publication and fay it was not the intention of the publifher to intimidate and overawe the government of this country? The people are invited to arms to catch a revolution by force, and then the government is called upon to anticipate the revolution by a reform. Is this the peaceable difcuffion for which the counfel contend? Or is this the freedom of the prefs, for which I would go as far as any man. Here the libel appoints a particular day for the convention to meet ; it fays " *The 15th of February ap-* " *proaches—a day ever-memorable in the annals of this country, as the* " *birth day of New Ireland ; let parochial meetings be held as foon as* " *poffible; let each parifh return delegates ; let the fenfe of Ulfter be* " *again declared from Dungannon, on a day aufpicious to union, peace* " *and freedom, and the fpirit of the North will again become the* " *fpirit of the nation. The civil offembly ought to claim the attendance* " *of the military affociations.*" Here the military affociations were particularly called on to attend the civil affembly at Dungannon: Was it for the purpofe of giving weight to their refolutions? Was it for the purpofe of fending their refolutions to parliament, backed by the people in arms? It was a national convention to be attended by a national guard. This was the object of this publication as it strikes me; the very able manner in which it was gone through by my learned friend, makes it unneceffary for me to dwell upon it, leaft I fhould weaken the force of his remarks. If you are fatisfied of the fact that Mr. Rowan did publifh the inftrument in queftion, then you will confider whether that publication, was likely to produce the effects mentioned in the information, and you will decide whether the publication was an innocent or a criminal one? I will agree it is matter for your confideration what was the immediate effect of publifhing this libel? Immediately after it was read, fome copies of it were thrown out to the mob in the ftreet, who called out for more of them, and more of them were thrown out. Here is a fact, which if you believe, is of confiderable weight. Gentlemen, in this cafe there has been no juftification, nothing has been faid to palliate the publication. You will decide on the matter of this libel, and whether it was publifhed with an innocent intention, or with that feditious view charged in the information.

Gentlemen of the jury, in any cafe where a man kills another, it is *prima facie* evidence of malice, but it admits of proof to fhew the manner in which it was done, and whether the party accufed killed the perfon with a felonious intent, or whether the killing was by accident, and not done with any intention of taking away the life of the party. The allufion comes home; here is a libel, and unlefs it is fhewn by excufe or juftification, that it can be qualified, the law will fay it is libellous.

In the prefent cafe, the learned counfel on the part of the defendant has endeavoured to fet your hearts and paffions againft your confciences and judgments, by reprefenting that the liberty of the prefs would be deftroyed by a verdict againft the defendant; but I appeal to the authority to which he appealed to fhew what the liberty of the prefs is, " It is employed as the centinel " to alarm us; we fhould take care it is not abufed and convert- " ed into a traitor; the inftant it degenerates into licentioufnefs " it muft be punifhed." That is an opinion to which every man muft fubfcribe, and which fhould be as lafting as the conftitution itfelf. Gentlemen, I have trefpaffed too long upon your patience; if you can reconcile it to your oaths, that Mr ROWAN did not publifh this paper, or that it does not contain any matter libellous, no man will be better pleafed at an acquittal than I fhall. But on the other hand, I conjure you by your oaths, that uninfluenced by power or prejudice, favour or affection, you difcharge your duty to God, your country, and yourfelves.

Earl CLONMELL, *Lord Chief Juftice.*—Gentlemen of the Jury. At this late hour, it is fome relief to the bench and myfelf that
the

the learned gentlemen of the bar, on both fides, have fo ably fpoken in this cafe, that it is not now neceffary for me to be very pro- lix or voluminous in my obfervations. I fhall therefore, for your convenience and that of the bench, contract my obfervations with- in as fhort a fpace as, in the difcharge of my duty, I think I ought to do. Before I go into the particulars or give any opinion upon the publication, I think it my duty to ftate and fully ap- prize you of a ftatute which paffed the laft feffion of parliament in this kingdom, by which it is declared and enacted, that upon all trials by indictment or information, (which, if it warted it, is an additional folemnization of this mode of trial) where iffue is joined, as in the prefent cafe, for making or publifhing any libel, the jury may give a verdict of guilty or not, upon the whole matter put in iffue, and fhall not be required or directed, by the court, to find guilty merely upon proof of publication, provided the court fhall, according to their difcretion, give their opinion upon the matter in iffue, in like manner as in other criminal cafes. I fhall endeavour, as far as I can, to conform to the fpirit and words of the law. You had the power to do fo before, per- haps you had the right; this act of parliament is a legiflative expofition of that right, and you will exercife it as becomes you. Though the evidence is not long or complicated, yet the paper is both long and complicated, therefore I will adopt that order which has been made by the bar, and clafs my obfervations under four heads, being the leading objects complained of in this information :

1ft. The making the government odious by endeavouring to difparage and degrade it.

2d. To render the people difcontented, not only with the government, but the conftitution.

3d. To folicit the people to take up arms, to intimidate the legiflature.

4th. Endeavouring, by tumult and by force, to make altera- tions in the conftitution and government, and overturn them both.

Gentlemen, every thing which I fhall fay to you, will fall under one of thefe heads. The information, of which I have an abftract in my hand, is that ARCHIBALD HAMILTON ROWAN, malicioufly defigning and intending to excite and diffufe among the fubjects of this realm, difcontents, jealoufies, and fufpicions of our lord the king and his government, and to raife dan- gerous feditions within this kingdom of Ireland, and to draw it into fcandal and difgrace, and to incite the fubjects of our faid lord the king to attempt by force and violence to make altera- tions in the ftate and conftitution, and to excite the fubjects of our faid lord the king to overturn the eftablifhed conftitution of this kingdom, and to intimidate the legiflature of this kingdom

by

by an armed force, on the 16th of December, in the 32d year
of the king, in the county of the city of Dublin, wickedly,
feditioufly, and malicioufly, did publifh a libel of and concerning the government of this kingdom, according to the tenour and
effect following :—" *Society of United Irifhmen to the volunteers of*
" *Ireland*," &c. They ftate themfelves to be a felf-created
body ; they ftate it vauntingly, they fay they have no authority
fave that of reafon, they have no authority in the ftate. I will
therefore confider the language of this paper as that of a body
not known to the conftitution, calling upon the *fubjects* at large,
though they fcorn to call them fo. Let me bring to your minds,
that one gentleman thought the addrefs was to a new created body of volunteers; another gentleman thought it was
addreffed to the original and refpectable volunteers ; take it
either way, if addreffed to the new created volunteers, it was
for the purpofes of fedition, and if to the old original volunteers,
it would be ftill more dangerous if they were to fucceed with them
in altering the conftitution by force. It is ftated, "*William*
" *Drennan, Prefident. Archibald Hamilton Rowan, Secretary.*"
This is a ftrong prefumption that Mr. ROWAN was acquainted
with every part of the paper ; it profeffes upon the face of it
that he was fecretary of this fociety. I fhall come, by and by,
to the queftion of publication ; if he publifhed it, there does
arife a prefumption that he knew what he publifhed : I go no
farther with that obfervation. He fays, " *Citizen foldiers, you*
" *firft took up arms to protect your country from foreign enemies,*
" *and from domeftic difturbances. For the fame purpofes it now*
" *becomes neceffary that you fhould refume them.*" Citizen foldiers,
you firft took up arms, that is, in my judgment, you took them
up originally for thefe two purpofes, it now becomes neceffary
you fhould refume them for thofe purpofes. " *A proclamation*
" *has been iffued in England for embodying the militia, and one in*
" *Ireland for repreffing feditious affociations. In confequence of both*
" *thefe proclamations, it is reafonable to apprehend danger from abroad*
" *and danger at home.*" The printed paper has been proved and
read ; it fays, " *For whence but from apprehended danger, are thofe*
" *menacing preparations for war drawn through the ftreets of this*
" *capital, (inuendo, meaning the city of Dublin) or whence if*
" *not to create that internal commotion which was not found, to*
" *fhake that credit which was not affected, to blaft that volunteer*
" *honour which was hitherto inviolate.*" In my opinion thefe
words fall directly within one of thofe heads I have ftated, as
rendering odious to the king's fubjects the proclamation as in-
fincere and hypocritical, as creating internal commotions, which
it intended to reftrain, and that embarraffment, which was not
found; that it went further to the ruin of the country, fhaking the credit which was not affected, and blafting the volunteer honour which was hitherto inviolate ; as if it was faid to

3   be

be blafted by the executive government. This was, in my mind, a charge of having created diforder, not before exifting, of fhaking the credit of the country contrary to the duty of government; and blafting that volunteer honour, which until this inftrument appeared never was violated. It is charging them, in my opinion, as infidioufly as the meaneft mind can conceive, in a moft vital part, the peace and the credit of the country. Whether it was calculated to inflame the minds of the fubjects, will be for your confideration, on your oaths. It fays, " *There were* " *rumours and fuggeftions which agitated our old men, our women,* " *and children.*" What is that ? Why, this is all an impofition of government, they wanted to frighten you by a bugbear. " *Whatever be the motive, or from whatever quarter it arifes, alarm* " *has arifen ; and you, Volunteers of Ireland, are therefore fum-* " *moned to arms at the inftance of government, as well as by the refpon-* " *fibility attached to your character, and the permanent obligations of* " *your inftitution.*" Here was another imputation upon government; they have raifed apprehenfions and fummoned thefe perfons to take up arms. It goes on and fays, " *We will not at* " *this day quote authorities for the right of ufing arms ; but* " *we will cry aloud even amidft the ftorm raifed by the witch-* " *craft of a proclamation.*" " *We will cry aloud in the ftorm.*" Where or how was it raifed? It fays, " *By the witch-* " *craft of a proclamation.*" Here was an imputation charged upon the proclamations of government, as raifing a ftorm in the country. It fays, " *To your formation was owing* " *the peace and protection of this ifland, to your relaxation has been* " *owing its relapfe into impotence and infignificance ;*" that is, when you were in arms this ifland was protected and in peace, and appeared to be of confideration ; to your relaxation has been owing its impotence and infignificance, therefore it can only be raifed again into importance by your taking up arms. If that is the impreffion of this paragraph, you will confider whether this is a libel upon the government or not. It was a publication not only to the people of this kingdom, but to all the enemies of this nation, faying that this country was in a ftate of impotence and infignificance. It goes on and fays, " *That to your renovation* " *muft be owing its future freedom and its prefent tranquility. You* " *are therefore fummoned to arms, in order to preferve your coun-* " *try in that guarded quiet, which may fecure it from external* " *hoftility, and to maintain that internal regimen throughout the land,* " *which fuperfeding a notorious police or a fufpected militia, may pre-* " *ferve the bleffings of peace by a vigilant preparation for war.*" It is impoffible in a work of this kind, were it twice as libellous as it is, if it could be fo, that it fhould not be mixed with fome profeffions, fome parts better than others ; it muft profefs fome-thing to be received. But it complains of a police and a militia that is fufpected. It fays, if you do not fuperfede a police

and

and militia, you cannot preferve the bleffings of peace. I fay, therefore, in my opinion, no words can be more inflammatory than thefe are. You are charging the police as an evil fort of an eftablifhment; it is called a " notorious police," and the militia as confifting of perfons proper to be fufpected, not to be confided in. It fays, " *You muft preferve the bleffings of peace by a* " *vigilant preparation for war. Citizen Soldiers, to arms!* " *take up the fhield of freedom and the pledges of peace.*" What does that fay? *Your arms* only are the fhield of freedom and pledges of peace; therefore take up arms. " *Peace* " *the motive and end of your virtuous inflitution. War, an* " *occafional duty, ought never to be made an occupation. Every* " *man fhould become a foldier in defence of his rights.*" Was it neceffary to call them together; if their rights were not attacked, why invite them to collect themfelves to defend that right. It fays, " *No man ought to continue a foldier for offending* " *the rights of others. The facrifice of life in the fervice of our coun-* " *try is a duty much too honourable to be entrufted to mercenaries:* They affume, or endeavour to affume, the power of the fword, and degrading the king's forces from that power with which they are entrufted, it fays, the duty we fuggeft is too honourable for mercenaries: Is not this faying, do not truft to the military, and at that time when by public authority it was declared that the country was in danger. The volunteers, in that paper, were called upon to ftand to their arms. Every expreffion of folicitation and ftimulation is ufed. The volunteers were called upon to refume their arms; the nation was impotent and infignificant without it. Citizens to arms! you are fummoned to arms: take up arms in fpite of a notorious police and a fufpected militia, and in fpite of two proclamations. You are to do your duty to preferve good order in your vicinage, in fpite of a police and fencible militia, for they refift peace, and you are to do your duty in fpite of thofe conftituted authorities, and the phrafe is varied, you are invited by the proclamation, that is, this proclamation has done as much mifchief as thofe men they condemn. " *It is only by the military array of men in whom* " *they confide, whom they have been accuftomed to revere as guar-* " *dians of domeftic peace, the protectors of their liberties and lives,* " *that the prefent agitation of the people can be ftilled, that tumult* " *and licentioufnefs can be repreffed, obedience fecured to exifting* " *law, and a calm confidence diffufed through the public mind,* " *in the fpeedy refurrection of a free conflitution, of liberty and of* " *equality,—words which we ufe for an opportunity of repelling* " *calumny.*" That is, it is only by a military array of men you can have a *Free Conftitution;* that is as much as to fay, *the people of Ireland have not a Free Conftitution.* Whether that be the meaning of the paper, as charged in the information, will be for your confideration. The words Liberty and Equality are introduced

troduced for an opportunity, fay they, of repelling calumny;
Where did it come from? Why did the Society find it neceffary to repel it? How did they repel it? By the words Liberty
and Equality, which they think proper to explain in this way.
" *By liberty we never underflood unlimited freedom, nor by equality,*
" *the levelling of property or the deflruction of fubordination. This*
" *is a calumny invented by that faction, or that gang, which mifre-*
" *prefents the king to the people, and the people to the king; tra-*
" *duces one half of the nation to cajole the other, and by keeping up*
" *diflruft and divifion, wifhes to continue the proud arbitrators of*
" *the fortune and fate of Ireland."* Here. he fays, a *Faction* or
Gang mifreprefents the king to the people. Is not this an af-
perfion, endeavouring to render the governing power odious?
What is this gang which he fays mifreprefents the king to
the people? I leave you to determine. Why is the mifrepre-
fentation? The paper infinuates for the purpofes of power
which they abufe. " *Liberty is the exercife of all our rights,*
" *natural and political, fecured to us and our pofterity by a real*
" *reprefentation of the people;' and equality is the extenfion of the con-*
" *flituent to the fulleft dimenfions of the conflitution, of the elective*
" *franchife to the whole body of the people, to the end that govern-*
" *ment, which is collective power, may be guided by collective will.".*
Thefe are terms, gentlemen, which you may probably underftand,
tho' they are conveyed in an unafcertained and declamatory ftile.
—Gentlemen of the jury, at the time that the qualification of a
voter to give his fuffrage to a candidate for a feat in parliament
was originally afcertained, forty fhillings was equivalent then,
as it is calculated, to forty pounds of our prefent currency;
from the time of Henry I. to Queen Anne, the value of money
had advanced in a ratio of one to twelve; from that time to this
it has been as one to twenty; fo that a man then having an
eftate of twenty fhillings a year was equal to a man's having an
eftate of twenty pounds of our prefent money. The elective
franchife never was in the *whole* body of the people in Great
Britain or Ireland.[*] It fays, " *That legiflation may originate from*
" *public reafon, keep pace with public improvement, and terminate*
" *in public happinefs.—If our conflitution be imperfect, nothing but*
" *a reform in reprefentation will rectify its abufes."* In figurative
abftracted expreffions it is not eafy to afcertain the meaning;
although you have an impreffion of the object. This may be a
very innocent propofition; but to me it may be a very wicked one,
when applied to be obtained in the manner here pointed out:
it fays, " *nothing but a Reform will rectify its abufes—nothing*
" *but a Reform will perpetuate its bleffings;"*—and then it goes
on and fays, " *We now addrefs you as Citizens,"* &c.—Not
a word of *fubjects* from beginning to end—that is a word driven
out of fafhion, at leaft in this publication—" *Seduction made*

[*] Vide Prynne Brev. Parl. rcd. p. 187. & 2 Whitelock p. 90. *contra;*

" *them*

"*them foldiers, but nature made them men.*" What had this charge
to the foldiers to do with a parliamentary reform? I quarrel not
with the compofition, it is not my duty, but in my mind here is a
direct charge upon 'the military, that they were impofed upon,
that feduction had made them foldiers. The fword is put into
the'hands of the fovereign, he is vefted with it by the conftitution, and yet this paper fays, it was made an inftrument of
feduction. "*We addrefs you without any authority, fave that of
"reafon, and if we obtain the coincidence of public opinion, it is
"neither by force nor ftratagem, for we have no power to terrify,
"no artifice to cajole, no fund to feduce—here we fit without mace
"or beadle, neither a myftery, nor a craft, nor a corporation.*" -
Here they acknowledge they had no proper authority to call
the people to arms, which they affume to do by that publication ;
they avow that this fociety did make no corporate body or legal authority. They add "*In four words lies all our power, UNIVER-
"SAL EMANCIPATION and REPRESENTATIVE LE-
"GISLATURE. Yet we are confident that on the pivot of this
"principle, a convention, ftill lefs a fociety, lefs ftill a fingle man, will
"be able firft to move and then to raife the world.*" I reft here a little
to confider what idea this writer muft have of the power of the paper, when a fingle man will be able firft to move and then to raife
the world ; one of the charges is, that this paper intended to ftir
the people to arms, it is an admiffion here, a profeffion, a vaunt,
that the fociety, nay lefs, a fingle man, may move and then raife
the world; the expreffion is not one kingdom, but to raife *the world*.
If any thing like it has happened, it is a miferable confideration.
"*We therefore wifh for Catholic emancipation without any modifica-
"tion, but ftill we confider this neceffary enfranchifement as merely
"the portal to the temple of national freedom ; wide as this entrance
"is—wide enough to admit three millions, it is narrow, when com-
"pared to the capacity and comprehenfion of our beloved principle,
"which takes in every individual of the Irifh nation.*" It is but a
portal to freedom : what, unqualified emancipation !—It is for
you to confider what the beloved principle is. Emancipating three
millions is opening a portal—what portal? one which takes in
every individual of the Irifh nation—where? into power, into
the elective franchife ; it embraces all that think, and feels for
all that fuffer. . "*The Catholic caufe is fubordinate to our caufe,
"and included in it, for as United Irifhmen, we adhere to no fect
"but to fociety, to no creed but chriftianity, to no party but the
"whole people. In the fincerity of our fouls do we defire Catholic
"emancipation : but were it obtained to-morrow, to-morrow would
"we go on, as we do to-day, in the purfuit of that reform which
"would ftill be wanting to ratify their liberties as well as our own.*"
You, Roman Catholics, emancipated to-morrow, will not ftop
us, we will go on, and unlefs you go on with us, it will not be
fufficient to eftablifh your liberty. "*For both thefe purpofes, it
"appears neceffary that provincial conventions fhould affemble prepa-
"ratory*

" ratory to the convention of the Proteſtant people. The delegates
" of the Catholic body are not juſtified in communicating with indi-
" viduals, or even bodies of inferior authority, and therefore an
" aſſembly of a ſimilar nature and organization is neceſſary to eſta-
" bliſh an intercourſe of ſentiment, an uniformity of conduct, an
" united cauſe, and an united nation. If a convention on the
" one part does not ſoon follow, and is not ſoon connected with that
" on the other, the common cauſe will ſplit into the partial intereſt ;
" the people will relax into inattention and inertneſs, the union of
" affection and exertion will diſſolve, and too probably ſome local
" inſurrection, inſtigated by the malignity of our common enemy, may
" commit the character and riſque the tranquility of the iſland,
" which can be obviated only by the influence of an aſſembly ariſing
" from, aſſimilated with the people, and whoſe ſpirit may be, as it
" were, knit with the ſoul of the nation : unleſs the ſenſe of the Pro-
" teſtant people be, on their part, as fairly collected and as judici-
" ouſly directed, unleſs individual exertion conſolidates into collective
" ſtrength, unleſs the particles unite into maſs, we may perhaps ſerve
" ſome perſon, or ſome party for a little, but the public not at all :
" the nation is neither inſolent, nor rebellious, nor ſeditious ; while
" it knows its rights it is unwilling to manifeſt its powers ; it would
" rather ſupplicate adminiſtration to anticipate revolution by a well-
" timed reform, and to ſave their country in mercy to themſelves."
Gentlemen, this laſt paragraph is a menace ; for if the pro-
poſal made is not accepted, a revolution is threatened. The
paper in queſtion proceeds in the following words : " The 15th
" of February approaches, a day ever memorable in the annals of
" this country as the birth-day of New Ireland ; let parochial meet-
" ings be held as ſoon as poſſible ; let each pariſh return delegates.
" Let the ſenſe of Ulſter be again declared from Dungannon, on a
" day auſpicious to union, peace and freedom, and the ſpirit of the
" North will again become the ſpirit of the nation. The civil aſſembly
" ought to claim the attention of the military aſſociations." The civil
aſſembly was to be attended by military forces ; was not the intention to alter the conſtitution ? " We have addreſſed you, citizen ſol-
" diers, on this ſubject, from a belief that your body, uniting conviction
" with zeal, and zeal with activity, may have much influence over
" your countrymen, your relations and friends." Armed citizens
was the favourite object that was to be gained ; it ſays, " We
" preſume not at preſent to fill up the plan or pre-occupy the mode
" of its execution, we have thought it our duty to ſpeak.—Anſwer
" us by actions. You have taken time for conſideration. Four-
" teen long years are elapſed ſince the riſe of your aſſociations."—
This part is very material, it ſays to the people, " take up
" your arms," and it ſays, " anſwer us by actions." What
are the actions of men in arms? Armed aſſociations will ſupport the
different meetings. We have ſpoken out to you ; anſwer us with
your actions. " Fourteen long years are elapſed ſince the riſe of your
M　　　　　　　　" aſſociations ;

" *affociations* ; and in 1782 *did you imagine that in* 1792 *this nation*
" *would still remain unreprefented ?* How *many nations, in this in-*
" *terval, have gotten the ftart of Ireland?*" How far Ireland has
been backward in the number of good fubjects, have they afked ?
No. The queftion here is, how many nations have gotten the
ftart of Ireland ? What is meant by th's ftart ? What nations
are there, that have in fourteen years advanced more than ourfelves in happinefs ? None. What actions of other nations
would that publication recommend to Ireland to follow ? It con-
cludes with this fentence ; " *How many of our countrymen have*
" *funk into the grave ?*" Gentlemen, I have gone through the
paper mentioned in the information, and made fuch obfervations as I thought neceffary. I do, as it is my duty, tell you,
that I think it deferves the appellations given to it by the information. I take it to be a fcandalous and feditious libel ; but
that is my opinion only. Gentlemen of the jury, it is you who
are to decide this queftion, whether you think it is a fcandalous
or feditious libel ? the verdict will be yours, and not mine.

Gentlemen, in order to fupport this profecution, the firft witnefs that was produced is *John Lyfter ;* he told you *(here his*
lordfhip ftated the teftimony of Lyfter, as given upon his direct exa-
mination.) On his crofs examination he gave an account of the
manner in which he communicated this matter to Mr. Kemmis,
the Crown Solicitor ; faid he would communicate to him what
he knew ; produced the paper that was read in part by Mr.
ROWAN. Said he did not know where Mr. ROWAN ftopt reading. Says he, the witnefs, did not purchafe his commiffion as
enfign in the army ; got it through the intereft of Lady HOBART,
his relation. The witnefs attefted two bonds, there was an iffue
directed to try whether thofe bonds were genuine. Was afked
whether he was examined as a witnefs at that trial ; believes he
was examined as a witnefs ; the iffue was tryed before Mr. Juftice BOYD ; there was an award of 200*l.* out of 800*l.* Says
Mr. *Lambert* filed a bill againft him about a note for 147*l.* which
Peter Hamilton paffed to witnefs. Attempts were made to impeach the credit of this witnefs upon three or four grounds :
1ft, He was a witnefs to the bonds which were alledged to have
been forged—an unfair tranfaction. 2d, That he got the note
from a perfon alledged to have been infane. 3d, That he had
got a commiffion. 4th, That it was not probable he made
this memorandum. I can only fay, he has given a rational
account of this bufinefs ; but it is your duty to judge of his
credit ; it is my duty to make obfervations, which it is your
duty to reject if they are not well founded. He fays he is an
enfign in the 40th regiment. He got the commiffion through
the intereft of a relation ; and it appears the arbitrators did
give his brother fince, part of the demand, by which, if it
weighed a feather in the cafe, they thought the bond was not

a forgery

a forgery. Says it was ufual to take memorandums on getting
papers of this kind. Says there was about 150 or 200 volunteers in
the room. Was LYSTER's evidence not fatisfactory to you,
he was the only witnefs to this great part of the cafe. This
obfervation has been made : " What ! 150 perfons prefent, and
not one of them comes forward to atteft the innocence of Mr.
ROWAN !"* * * * * * * * *
* * * * * * * * * *
* * * * * * * * * *

But the next witnefs does, in my apprehenfion, as far as he
goes, confirm every word faid by Lyfter. Morton fays, he faw
numbers of perfons in the room doing fome bufinefs at the
table. Saw Mr. TANDY and Mr. ROWAN in the room. The
witnefs had feen them before that day. He identified Mr.
ROWAN in court. He appeared to take an active part in the
bufinefs. Witnefs got admiffion into the gallery. He faw a
bundle of papers on the table, feveral were diftributed to the
mob in the ftreet, who called out for more. The witnefs
got a paper, which he gave to a perfon who faid he had loft it.
Witnefs faid he heard part of a paper read, containing the
words " Citizen Soldiers, to arms." If it ftood upon this man's
evidence, here was not evidence of publication ; and if it refted upon him alone, you fhould acquit the defendant ; but as
corroborating the teftimony of Lyfter, it is very material. If
the counfel for the defendant intended to difcredit the witneffes
for the profecution, they have failed. A gentleman from Galway, a Mr. Blake, was produced, who fays he now lives in
Dublin, gave his evidence as to Lyfter, which I fhall come to
by-and-by. Morton's credit was not queftioned. Morton, on
his crofs-examination, faid, he was an apprentice to a gold-
beater—Believes the perfons he faw at the room in Cope-
ftreet were in the uniform of the old volunteers—Is fure he
faw Mr. ROWAN there—Some of the perfons wore fcarlet with
different coloured facings—witnefs faid he could fee from the
gallery what was done at the table. He gave the paper, the
day he received it, to a perfon in the houfe where the Dublin
Journal is printed. The paper was then read which I have
ftated to you, and you have heard fo much of. Here the profecution was refted. On the part of the defendant was produced Mr. Francis Blake, to fhew that John Lyfter was a perfon
not to be credited upon his oath. Mr. Blake was afked whether Lyfter was a man to be believed upon his oath ; he anfwered he could not fay he is not to be believed upon his oath ;
but he would hefitate. The witnefs was produced to fhew that

* The editor is here under a neceffity of introducing an hiatus, the
printer having refufed to print this part according to the notes furnifhed to
him by the editor.

Lyſter ſhould not be believed upon his oath, but *Blake* ſaid
no ſuch thing. In a queſtion, whether the oath of one man
ought to be received, where another man ſwears he ought not to
be believed upon his oath ; then you would have one man's
oath againſt another. The credit of *Lyſter* is not affected by
what Mr. *Smith* the ſecond witneſs has ſaid The third witneſs
to this point was Mrs. *Hatchell;* ſhe ſaid ſhe knew *John Lyſter;*
ſhe was aſked whether he was to be believed upon his oath ?
ſhe ſaid, according to her opinion, he was not to be believed
upon his oath—She ſaid the witneſs, *John,* had prevailed on
his brother to quit his wife, and ſaid he was married to another
woman, which was not truth—ſaid ſhe heard declarations from
John's elder brother , and that was one of the reaſons why ſhe
ſaid the witneſs, *John,* ought not to be believed upon his oath.
In the uſual courſe of evidence no proof has been adduced to
prove that the witneſs *Lyſter* ought not to be believed upon
his oath.

Gentlemen of the jury, I think this is the evidence on both
ſides, as correctly as I have been able to take it. As to the fact
of publication, it is my duty to tell you, there is very ſtrong
evidence that Mr. Rowan did publiſh that paper, and did publiſh it knowing what he publiſhed , and as to the other matter,
whether it is a libel, I have told you I thought the matter
libellous—libellous in the extreme ; I now tell you, that is my
opinion. If you, upon the whole matter, believe. upon your
oaths, that Mr. Rowan publiſhed the paper, and with the criminal intention ſtated in the information, and for the purpoſes
aſcribed to him, you ought to find him guilty, for I think
the paper entitled to, and deſerves the appellation annexed to
it—it is a ſeditious libel. If you believe he did not publiſh it ;
if you diſbelieve the evidences which have been uncontradicted ;
if you believe he publiſhed it by *miſtake* or *ignorance,* not meaning to publiſh this paper, which might happen, but of which
there is not a title of evidence in this caſe, you will find him
not guilty. I will ſtate this direction in other words ; if you
find him guilty, it muſt be, becauſe you believe in your con-
ſciences he publiſhed it, and that you believe the innuendos
are true ; meaning, as well as you underſtand this paper, reading it ſeparately or collectively together, that he publiſhed it
with a criminal intention : that is, adopting its ſenſe and meaning.
If you acquit him, it muſt be, becauſe you do not believe he
publiſhed it, or that he did not mean to adopt its ſenſe and
meaning. I muſt tell you, his thinking it not miſchievous, is
not a reaſon why you ſhould acquit him. His thinking he was
doing right, if you believe the intention of the paper was to
raiſe forces to intimidate the legiſlature, which is the great object complained of, though he was thinking he was right to
accompliſh his object by every means, will not be an excuſe;
that

that would lead to the acquittal of every felon upon earth. If a man was accufed of a felony, and he thought he was doing a right thing to murder his neighbour, thinking he was doing a right thing would be no excufe to him. If the defendant's object was merely a reform in parliament, yet if he endeavoured by force, or by illegal means, to obtain it, you ought to find him guilty. I have ftated the facts, and made fuch obfervations as occur to me to be neceffary—I have ftated the point of crimination, and I now leave to you to difpofe of the queftion; and have not the leaft doubt you will do as becomes you. If I have been defective, I fhall be corrected by my brethren, whom you will hear with pleafure and information.

The Honourable Mr. JUSTICE BOYD.—Gentlemen of the Jury. My Lord CLONMELL has fo fully ftated the information, it is not neceffary for me to repeat it. With regard to his obfervations, I adopt them every one in the fame degree of latitude in which he delivered them: I think the paper deferves the appellation in the information; it is a falfe, fcandalous, and malicious libel. My Lord CLONMELL mentioned an act of parliament which was made upon its being thought the judges went too far in former cafes, it gives you power to decide on queftions of this kind, whether libel or not; you are to give your opinion upon the whole of the matter, and therefore you are not bound to find according to our direction. My opinion concurs with Lord CLONMELL's, that the paper is a libel. If you, gentlemen of the jury, are of a different opinion, you are not bound to go by the opinion of the court, in point of law, in a cafe of libel. You have heard the evidence, and the firft queftion which arifes is, whether there was any publication of this paper by Mr. ROWAN? If you are of opinion, that Mr. ROWAN did not publifh the paper in queftion, you muft acquit him. If you think it is not a libel, even though he did publifh it, you ought to acquit him. If he publifhed it by miftake or ignorantly, that is a ground for acquittal. But his own opinion of what he thought right, even in obtaining the emancipation of the Catholics, or a parliamentary reform by force of arms; however laudable he thought himfelf, the intention of the publication was a criminal one, and in that cafe you ought to find him guilty.

The Honourable Mr. JUSTICE DOWNES.—Gentlemen of the Jury. The few words I fhall trouble you with, will be in concurrence with what you have heard from the reft of the court. The fact of publication depends upon the evidence you have heard, and the degree of credit you will give to the witnefs. I agree in the obfervations upon Lyfter's teftimony, no degree of difficulty occurs in contradicting him, if what he faid was falfe. If you do believe that Lyfter deferves credit, the publication of this paper is proved to have been made, induftrioufly, by the defendant

fendant, knowing its contents; and under fuch circumftances as, I fhould not hefitate to fay, adopted its contents. If you believe it was publifhed under thefe circumftances which you have heard, it will be for your confideration to determine, whether it be a libel, and with what intent it was publifhed? I concur in the obfervations upon its contents, and I am unable to read it without being of opinion that the tendency of this paper is to excite to arms the perfons to whom it was addreffed, and for the purpofe of making alterations in the government of this kingdom, as charged in the introductory part of the information. If you believe the account of the mode of publication given by *Lyfter*, and believe the defendant adopted this paper as his act, you are to look for the intent upon the paper itfelf, and on which you are to decide. If you believe that the general tendency of it was to excite tumult in the country, and to call to arms any defcription of men, no doubt can be entertained, that it is libellous, and it muft be imputed to the defendant, he having given no evidence of a contrary intention. To attempt to effect by force any alteration in the conftitution of the country, or to overawe the legiflature by force—any fuch act of force would be High Treafon; and to publifh a paper to excite people to do fuch an act, no man can doubt is a libel. If you do think fuch was the tendency of the paper in queftion, you cannot hefitate to find the defendant guilty. There was no evidence to fhew the tendency of the paper was of a contrary nature. The intentions of the publifher are deducible from the paper itfelf; if it was the purpofe of the publifher of the paper to attain an alteration in the ftate by force, it was a criminal intention, however defirable the alteration might be fuppofed to be, or whether the object fought for was in itfelf right, or not. I will not trouble you any farther. I have given the cafe the beft confideration I am able. You will decide upon it according to your oaths, and I have no doubt the defendant will have every juftice in your hands.

The jury withdrew, taking with them the printed paper which had been read in court, and in about ten minutes returned, and brought in their verdict,

WE FIND ARCHIBALD HAMILTON ROWAN—*GUILTY.* *

Lord CLONMELL.—Do the counfel for the defendant defire four days time to move in arreft of judgment?

* When this verdict was firft brought in, there was a loud clap of approbation commenced in the outer hall, it is prefumed from a mifconception that the jury had acquitted the defendant; for when the verdict was repeated, and the word *guilty*, fufficiently ftreffed, the clap was changed into hootings, and hiffings, and groans, that lafted with very little remiffion, during the remainder of the fitting of the court.

Mr.

Mr. CURRAN.—The only inſtructions I have from my client
are to diſclaim any application of that kind : he does not wiſh
to take advantage of errors in the record, if any there be, but
is now ready to attend to receive what ſentence the court may
be pleaſed to pronounce.

Lord CLONMELL.—(After conferring with the other judges)
We will not pronounce judgment till four days.—Mr. Sheriff,
take care of your priſoner.

The counſel for Mr. *Rowan* here objected, that he was not
a priſoner—he had not been in cuſtody—he had not given bail
upon this information—he was bound in no recognizance—was
ſerved with no proceſs—he had appeared to the information by
attorney ;—he pleaded by attorney—the iſſue was tried after
the manner of a civil action, a word merely of the record being
read, and the defendant was not given in charge to the jury as
the practice is, where he appears in cuſtody. Mr. ROWAN attended the trial, it is true, but the court had no judicial cog-
nizance of him ; the information could have been tried in his
abſence—he attended as a common auditor, and the witneſs
being called upon to point him out at the deſire of the bench,
might have been a ſatisfaction to them to ſee that the witneſſes
were ſpeaking of the ſame perſon, but it was altogether unpre-
cedented in ſuch caſes as the preſent. Mr. ROWAN was ready
for ſentence—he claims no indulgence—does not inſiſt upon the
four day rule ; but if the court, for their own accommodation,
chooſe to defer the ſentence for four days, they have no legal
authority for ſending Mr. ROWAN to priſon, until ſentence pronounced, or the uſual and accuſtomed proceſs iſſued againſt
him.

Lord CLONMELL.—If the Attorney General conſents, I have
no objection.

The Attorney General had left court, and the Solicitor for
the Crown remained ſilent.

Lord CLONMELL.—The defendant is a convict, as ſuch he is *Vid. Nr.*
a priſoner—the law muſt have its courſe. Adjourn the court. *Riggen...*

Accordingly the court was adjourned.

Mr. ROWAN was conveyed to the New Priſon, attended by
both the Sheriffs, and a formidable array of horſe and foot
guards.

MONDAY,

MONDAY, FEBRUARY 3, 1794.

A *Habeas Corpus*, grounded on the affidavit of Mr. Matthew Dowling, Mr. Rowan's Solicitor, was granted to bring up John Coultry, confined in Newgate for debt, to fwear an affidavit; Mr. Rowan was alfo ordered up for the fame purpofe; when their affidavits, together with thofe of William Porter, John William Atkinfon, and Francis Clarke, were fworn.

Mr. RECORDER moved the court to fet afide the verdict obtained on Wednefday laft and grant a new trial in this caufe, purfuant to a notice ferved on Mr. Attorney General, and grounded on thefe affidavits, the contents of which he fet forth.

Mr. ATTORNEY GENERAL, having after fome time come into court, moved the court to appoint a day to have Mr. Rowan brought up for judgment.

Lord CLONMELL appointed to-morrow, and at the fame time acquainted the Attorney General with the Recorder's motion, and the nature of the affidavits.

The ATTORNEY GENERAL then defired to have them read; which they were as follows:

The King, at the profecution of the Right Honourable Arthur Wolfe, his Majefty's Attorney General,

AGAINST

Archibald Hamilton Rowan.

WILLIAM PORTER of the city of Dublin, Printer, maketh oath, that fince the commencement of the profecution in this caufe, and previous to the trial had on Wednefday laft, he this deponent had a converfation with George Perrin, of Caftle-ftreet, in the city of Dublin, Bookfeller, in the courfe of which the faid George Perrin declared to this deponent, that this country and its trade never could flourifh until Napper Tandy and Hamilton Rowan were tranfported or hanged, or words to that effect: and deponent was much aftonifhed and concerned, rycollecting the declaration made, when he difcovered that the faid George Perrin had been one of the jury who tried the faid defendant, and found him guilty of the mifdemeanour in this caufe.

WILLIAM PORTER.

Sworn in court this third day of February, 1794.

CARMICHAEL and BRADSHAW, *D. C. C.*

The

The King, at the profecution of the Right Honourable Arthur Wolfe, his Majefty's Attorney General, AGAINST Archibald Hamilton Rowan. | JOHN WILLIAM ATKINSON, of Skinner-row, in the city of Dublin, Watch-maker, maketh oath, that fome time in the month of Auguft laft paft, as deponent beft recollects the time, on the morning after the night whereon fome illuminations had been made upon the event of the capitulation of Valenciennes, this deponent had fome converfation with George Perrin, of Caftle-ftreet, Bookfeller, refpecting the volunteers of Ireland; in the courfe of which the name of Archibald Hamilton Rowan, the defendant, with feveral others, was frequently mentioned; and the faid George Perrin did, upon that occafion, utter a good deal of acrimonious and difparaging language and obfervations againft the body of volunteers in general, and againft the faid Archibald Hamilton Rowan in particular, with feveral others; and the faid George Perrin did then, upon that occafion, alfo fay that they (meaning as deponent well underftood and is convinced) the faid Archibald Hamilton Rowan, with feveral others, deferved and ought to be hanged. Deponent faith he is credibly informed, and verily believes, that the faid George Perrin was one of the jury who on Wednefday night laft found the faid Archibald Hamilton Rowan guilty of the mifdemeanour in this cafe.

JOHN WILLIAM ATKINSON.

Sworn in court the third day of February, 1794.

CARMICHAEL 2nd BRADSHAW, D. C. C.

The King, at the profecution of the Right Honourable Arthur Wolfe, his Majefty's Attorney General, AGAINST Archibald Hamilton Rowan. | JAMES COULTRY, of the city of Dublin, Gentleman, maketh oath, that he has known John Lyfter, who appeared and gave evidence on the trial in this caufe on Wednefday laft, as deponent is credibly informed and believes, and faith, that from his own knowledge, the faid John Lyfter ought not to be credited upon his oath in a court of juftice; in as much as this deponent faw the faid John Lyfter take a falfe oath upon the holy Evangelifts, ftating that a horfe or mare his property, which was feized for debt, was the property of George William Lyfter, and not the property of any other perfon whatfoever; and deponent faith that he the faid John did perfonate his faid brother George William Lyfter, and impofe himfelf

N

himfelf on a magiftrate of the city of Dublin in that name; and
that under the character and in the name of the faid George he
the faid John did take the faid falfe oath, although the faid
George was then labouring under a wound, unable to leave his
bed; which oath he took in a deliberate, cool manner, notwithftanding deponent had previoufly remonftrated in a particular
manner upon the enormity and danger of his doing fo; and deponent further faith, that fhortly after the time faid John Lyfter
took the faid falfe oath as aforefaid, he received a letter from a
man of reputation, refident in the neighbourhood of the country
where faid John Lyfter and his two brothers, Thomas and
George Lyfter, had lived; by which letter deponent was informed, and which he verily believes to be true, the faid Thomas
Lyfter had made an affidavit in the country, precifely contradicting, upon his oath, the fact fworn to by John in the name of
George, as the faid Thomas fwore faid horfe was his particular
property, fworn to as aforefaid, in Dublin, by the faid John
Lyfter;—and which two affidavits deponent has frequently
feen.

JAMES COULTRY.

Sworn in court the third day of
February, 1794.

A. CARMICHAEL.

The King, at the profecution of | FRANCIS CLARKE, of Den-
the Right Honourable Ar- | mark-ftreet, in the city of Dublin,
thur Wolfe, his Majefty's | Peruke-maker, maketh oath, that
Attorney General, | he is well acquainted with John
| Lyfter, the perfon who, as depo-
AGAINST | nent is credibly informed and be-
Archibald Hamilton Rowan. | lieves, appeared and gave evidence
| on Wednefday laft, in this cafe,
on behalf of the profecutor; and deponent faith that, from his
own knowledge, the faid John Lyfter ought not to be credited
on his oath, in a court of juftice, as this deponent has known the
faid John Lyfter to have perjured himfelf; for deponent faith
that having been well acquainted with the faid John Lyfter for
five or fix years paft, during which time the faid John Lyfter had
been frequently in the houfe and fhop of deponent, and during
which time deponent had conftantly dreffed his hair: about three
years ago, or upwards, upon deponent having caufed the faid
John Lyfter to have been fummoned to the Court of Confcience
for a fmall fum of money due deponent by faid Lyfter, he the
said

faid Lyſter attended in faid court purſuant to faid fummons, and
being fworn on the holy Evangeliſts by Alderman Emerfon, in
preſence of this deponent and feveral others, in a peremptory
manner, faid Lyſter depofed that he never had known, or feen
deponent before, or been in deponent's houſe, and that he did
not know deponent's name, notwithſtanding deponent pofitively
faith the faid John Lyſter had, for near three years previous to
that time, frequently, from time to time, been in the houſe and
ſhop of this deponent, in preſence of many perfons, and ne-
vertheleſs deponent had two or three days previous to faid Lyfter's taking faid oath, met faid John Lyſter paffing over Effex-
bridge, and there talked to him for fome time; and deponent
further faith, that in the courfe of three years laſt paſt, the faid
John Lyſter, as deponent has good reafon to be convinced, has
been guilty of perjury in various other inſtances.

Francis Clarke.

Sworn in court the third day of
February, 1794.

Carmichael and Bradshaw, D. C. C.

The King, at the profecution of the Right Honourable Ar-thur Wolfe, his Majefty's Attorney General,
AGAINST
Archibald Hamilton Rowan.

THE defendant, Archibald Hamilton Rowan, maketh oath that,
fince the trial had on Wednefday
laſt, in this cafe, and after defendant had been pronounced guilty
by the verdict of a jury impannelled
and fworn on the faid trial, depo-
nent has received credible information, which he is convinced is
true, that feveral perfons, who had until after faid trial and verdict been ſtrangers and utterly unknown to deponent, would be
material witneffes, on behalf of deponent, upon faid trial; and
that had the faid witneffes been known and attended thereon,
the teſtimony of John Lyſter, who was the principal evidence on
behalf of the profecution, would have been fully difcredited.
Deponent further faith he has alfo, fince faid trial and verdict,
been credibly informed, and verily believes, fome of the perfons
who were on faid jury have, previous to faid trial, made ufe of
expreffions tending to difapprove of deponent and his conduct,
refpecting the fubject matter of this profecution; and which in-
duces deponent to believe they had, previous to faid trial, been
biaffed againſt, and had formed impreffions in their mind unfavourable to deponent. Deponent further faith, that from the
daily information and accounts which deponent and his friends

have

have received, and are receiving, of the life, conduct and character of said John Lyster, he has no doubt of proving fully and satisfactorily, that the said John Lyster ought not to be believed on his oath.

ARCHIBALD HAMILTON ROWAN.

Sworn in court the third day of
February, 1794.

A. CARMICHAEL.

After Mr. Rowan's affidavit was read, it was deemed adviseable by his counsel, that he should make a further one. The court were accordingly pleased to wait until it was prepared and sworn. It was then read as follows:

The King, at the prosecution of } THE defendant, Archibald Ha-
the Right Honourable Ar- | milton Rowan, maketh oath, that
thur Wolfe, his Majesty's | he hath heard the several affidavits
Attorney General, | of Francis Clarke, James Coultry,
AGAINST | William Porter, and John Willi-
Archibald Hamilton Rowan. | am Atkinson, this day made in
this cause, read in open court, and saith that all and every the matters contained in said affidavits, and every of them, were utterly unknown to this deponent until after the trial and verdict in this cause; and that this deponent had no reason to believe, and never heard until after said trial, that said persons or any of them could have given evidence of the facts sworn to this day by them, or any of them, in their said affidavits mentioned; or any other material evidence upon the trial of the issue in this cause. This deponent further saith that he heard the evidence given by John Lyster and William Morton upon the said trial, charging deponent with having read, distributed and published the paper in the information in this cause mentioned, at Cope-street, in Pardon's fencing-room; and this deponent positively swears that the said testimony was utterly false. Deponent further saith that he heard, and believes, John Giffard, one of the sheriffs, and by whom, or his under-sheriff, the pannel of the jury was arrayed to try this cause, is and has been for some years the conductor or proprietor of a news-paper generally considered a government paper; that the said Giffard has also some lucrative employment in the revenue, and a commission in the Dublin militia; and that he verily believes the said Giffard was, and is, strongly prejudiced against deponent; and that the said Giffard did labour to have a pannel

of

of fuch perfons arrayed, as he knew, or believed, to be unfairly prejudiced againft this deponent.

ARCHIBALD HAMILTON ROWAN.

Sworn in court the third day of
February, 1794.

G. JAMES.

After it was read the court afked the Attorney General, whether he wifhed for time to have thefe affidavits anfwered; to
which he having replied in the negative, the court ordered Mr.
Rowan to be brought up to-morrow; and adjourned.

TUESDAY, FEBRUARY 4, 1794.

Mr. RECORDER faid he was inftructed that there were four
new affidavits, fworn to the fame purpofe as thofe read yefterday,
to prove that others of the jurors had ufed expreffions of enmity
againft Mr. Rowan before the trial, and prayed that they might
be read.

Mr. ATTORNEY GENERAL objected, for that yefterday was
the laft day, in which any affidavits could be made, and now it
was attempted to bring others without any notice; he was
willing that this cafe fhould meet the faireft and fulleft inveftigation, but would not confent that the rules of court fhould be de-
parted from on this, more than on any other occafion.

Mr. RECORDER.—I am very fenfible that in ordinary civil
cafes, where any motion is made to fet afide a verdict, the party
muft apply within four days, and lay a fufficient ground for the
motion; but even then the court would fometimes indulge the
party with another day, to lay before it new materials, in advancement of juftice. The intention of the traverfer, or his
counfel, was not to do any thing by furprife, or to bring thefe
affidavits haftily forward, to prevent the crown from anfwering
them; we are willing to give any reafonable time for that purpofe.
But your lordfhips will confider the circumftances in which this
traverfer ftands; that he is in confinement and not at liberty to
fearch for evidence, or the neceffary materials for his defence;
not ftanding in the fituation of a defendant in any civil action,
but in a fituation which the law regards fo far, as never to impute
laches

4

laches to any man whilst he is in prison. If it is necessary, I
am instructed that affidavits can be made, that the matters, now
brought forward, were only discovered since the rising of the court
yesterday, and there is scarce an hour that further evidence does
not come forward, tending to shew the truth and reality of the
present case. The information now offered to the court has been
so lately brought to light, that the agent has not had time to
brief the affidavits; I have only been informed, on my way into
court, of the purpose for which they are brought forward, and am
still ignorant of their contents; and as the justice of the case may
be advanced, and no inconvenience can result from it, I trust
your lordships will allow these affidavits to be read, and the motion either to go forward now, or to wait till the counsel for the
crown shall have an opportunity of answering them.

Mr. ATTORNEY GENERAL.—The rank, character, or situation of any man standing in this court accused of a crime, I conceive to be a matter of perfect insignificance, when put in com-
petion with the settled rules of distributive justice. There are a
certain number of days given to move in arrest of judgment, or for
a new trial; within which the party is to lay before the court the
ground upon which he means to move: all then that is insisted
upon is that this defendant should be bound by the same rule that
binds every man in the like circumstances: for if a party should be
at liberty from day to day to bring forward new affidavits, there
never would be an end of any prosecution. Mr. Recorder's observation shews the good sense of this rule; he says new materials
are pouring in every hour—I doubt it not; and that new affidavits may come in to-night; and the same arguments used to-day
will be used to-morrow.

Mr. CURRAN.—There was no objection made yesterday to the
reading of affidavits, which were made and sworn in the presence
of the court. Mr. Attorney General has himself said that the
defendant was at liberty yesterday; if so, he is equally within the
rule to-day, for this is only a continuation of the same motion:—
this is a question put, as it were, to the conscience of the court,
viz. do your lordships think that justice has been so done, that it
ought not to be sent to a new enquiry; and shall any rule of practice be suffered to preclude the light, which should inform that conscience?—It would be absurd that no distinction should be made
between ordinary and extraordinary cases; in small matters sum-
mary justice is enforced; but in such a case as this (he would speak
as guardedly as possible) the court will consider that punishment
is not inflicted vindictively, but for example and prevention; and
that nothing gives so much force to the preventive effect of sen-
tences of courts of justice, as all the world being able to say, every fair enquiry has been made, and the sentence has passed in consequence

fequence of an impartial verdict. There is a way known to our
law to fet verdicts afide, where there has been any abufe of juftice;
any fault in the returning officer, the jury, or the witneffes; or any
miftake in the court:—all applications and information for this
purpofe have been received with indulgence; and upon the moft
cool enquiry it has been found that the verdict, upon which the
fentence was had, muft have fatisfied the reafonable, fair, confci-
entious mind of any man;—this it is which gives to the fentence
of the law that good and tranquilifing effect, for which alone it is
intended.

We are now prepared to fhew that more of thefe jurors have
made exprefs declarations of malice, and fhall it lie in the mouth
of the profecutor to fay, there is a rule which operates like a
trap upon the confcience of the court of King's Bench; that
after a certain moment it becomes fo helplefs, that let what will
arife it can do juftice no longer?

I fay the rules are the inftruments, not the tyrants of the
court; as to the point of practice it is conceived that trials at
bar are not within the four day rule; but I go upon a more folid ground, and appeal to this, that the court has a right to receive information, at any time, in furtherance of juftice; if it were
neceffary to cite cafes, there has been a very late one in this court,
where it has exercifed the very fame difcretion.

After the verdict was brought in, not having the leaft idea
that there was any fact exifting, which could impeach the verdict,
the traverfer's counfel ftated, that if it was the pleafure of the
court, he fhould appear to receive fentence; and let me obferve
that he did not at that time conceive that he was in cuftody; he
was not called on to appear; there was no order, and the only
judicial knowledge the court had of his being prefent, was that
a witnefs turned to him, to identify him; if then inftead of being at large, as he ought to have been, he was put into prifon,
where he had not the fame opportunity of procuring evidence,
however univerfally it might exift, can there be a ftronger circumftance to fhew that he is peculiarly entitled to the indulgence
he feeks.

Mr FLETCHER, *on the fame fide.*—When I fee the temper of the
audience which furrounds me, I fhall avoid touching upon public
topics with the fame delicacy, which the gentleman who preceded me has done. If juftice is the object of this profecution,
why ftand upon fuch punctilious points of practice, and *inter
apices juris:* in the cafe alluded to, it was infifted that the four
day rule did apply to trials at bar, but the court decided otherwife, and there is good reafon for the diftinction; in cafes coming from the country this rule is neceffary, to prevent the one
party from keeping the *poftea* in his pocket, until he could furprife the other at a time when he was not, perhaps, fo well prepared

pared to impeach the verdict; it is neceffary, then, that there fhould be a fixed time that no advantage may be fnatched; but there is no analogy to a cafe of this kind, which is entirely in the breaft of the court.

In the Dean of St. Afaph's cafe, a great profecution inftituted, like this, to anfwer the ends of public peace and public policy, the court did exercife its wifdom upon the merits of the bufinefs before it; the rule was not adhered to, but the parties were let in after the four days had expired. As to the objection which has been thrown out, that if this matter is poftponed we may come in to-morrow, and the next day, and fo on; it is anfwered, that we will undertake, if it fhould l'e over till to-morrow, to reft fatisfied, and feek for no more materials.

This is merely a point of practice, and it ftrikes my mind as folly to fay, that fo high a court as this has not its practice with-in its own power.

Lord CLONMEL, *Chief Juftice.*—On the day that Mr. Rowan was convicted, we were called upon for judgment; but we con-ceived, that even if it was not a matter of right upon adjudged cafes, it was ftill proper, that the defendant fhould have four days to queftion the verdict, or move in arreft of judgment: Suppofe, inftead of that, we had then pronounced judgment, all argument would have been concluded, for it would have been abfurd to fay, that he fhould have been fuffered, after that, to unravel the pro-ceedings; then what has paffed fince? A motion has been made and entertained upon affidavits, ftating facts, of which the party has had information fince that day; I mention this to fhew, that there has been no precipitancy in the court, nor poffible hardfhip in what it has done. Yefterday Mr. Rowan made an affidavit, fome others were alfo made; Mr. Rowan defired to make a further one, and the court waited till a late hour, till it was compofed and fworn; the Attorney General was then called upon, who declined to anfwer thefe affidavits; the court then cer-tainly concluded it was to hear no more of the collecting of ma-terials for this motion, but that it fhould go on and be argued like every other of the fame kind.

It is faid the rule of court, with refpect to moving for new trials, does not extend to cafes tried at bar, in the city of Dublin; that does not apply to this cafe, for the reafon before mentioned, that within four days judgment would be pronounced; fo that from the nature of the thing, this motion muft be made within four days.

See what confequences would follow, from the letting in affi-davits pending a motion of this kind; there is not an argument to be ufed by counfel on either fide, that would not lay the foundation for a new affidavit, fo that a motion would never have an end.

We

We are all of opinion, that it would introduce confufion into the practice of the court and be a pernicious precedent, and that the affidavits cannot be read.

[Here there took place fome altercation upon the queftion of practice, who fhould firft go on ; the traverfer's counfel infifting, that the affidavits *primâ facie* entitled them to their motion, and that the ufual practice of giving the laft word to the crown did not extend to a motion of this kind ; but the court upon the authority of the King againft Horne, defired the defendant's counfel to proceed in fupport of the motion.]

Mr. FLETCHER.—This is a profecution highly interefting, not only to that moft refpectable individual, who is the immediate object of it (for fo I fhall continue to call him notwithftanding the verdict) but alfo to the community at large ; it is a great profecution directed upon folemn and deliberate grounds, to attain the ends of public peace and public juftice ; the court will fcrutinize into a verdict that affixes the guilt of a high mifdemeanor on a character fo refpectable; the only end of fuch profecutions muft be to deter others from the commiffion of fimilar crimes, and to fatisfy the public mind, and to convince the world that guilty practices do not go unpunifhed ; it therefore becomes neceffary, that fuch a verdict fhould be free from the fhadow of objection, otherwife fo far from having the falutary effect propofed, it might have a very different one; men will fcan the ground upon which fuch verdicts have been had ; points of practice, and objections *inter apices juris*, amongft the quirks and pranks of the law will then vanifh, and the public will ftamp reprobation on a verdict obtained under circumftances of fufpicion and unfairnefs.

The affidavits, on which we ground our motion, are now to be taken as true as the gofpel, the verity of them cannot be fhaken ; the gentlemen concerned for the profecution have been called on to anfwer them, and have not done it ; thefe affidavits then, furnifh three objections to the verdict.

1*ft*. As to the perfon upon whofe evidence alone (upon the face of your lordfhips notes) the verdict could be fuftained, two or three affidavits go pointedly to fhew that he is utterly deftitute of credit.

2*dly*. There is another clafs of affidavits impeaching one of the jurors for deep malignity conceived againft my client.

3*dly*. There is that of the traverfer himfelf, who fwears that the teftimony of the witneffes was falfe, and further that he has reafon to believe that the perfon, who arrayed the pannel, did it through favour, and purpofely chofe men hoftile to him and to his principles.

Now even if any one of thefe grounds taken feparately, were not fufficient to fhake the verdict, it becomes a matter of high

O   concern

concern to fee whether the refult of the whole does not, at the leaft, furnifh a doubt that *juftice has not been done*; if fo, it brings it within the great principle upon which alone new trials fhould be granted. It cannot be expected that a cafe fhould be found, appofite in every minute particular; the prefent cafe has a good deal of novelty, and I cannot find any accurately agreeing with it; but you have the high authority of that luminary of the law, Lord Mansfield, thus declaring himfelf in the cafe of Bright and Enyon, 1 *Bur.* " If we have reafon to think that " juftice has not been done, we will fend it to *another examina-* " *tion.*" It is upon fuch broad principles that I go, and if that was the opinion of his lordfhip, in a civil action, between man and man, with how much greater reafon fhould it be fo in a trial between the fovereign of the land and fo refpectable a citizen, who is accufed of violating the laws of that land, to which it was his duty to be amenable. Will any man in his right reafon fay, that the great broad liberal principle fhould not be applied *a fortiori* to a cafe of this kind, where the liberty of the fubject is at ftake, with all that he holds dear;—where the public peace, and the opinion the world may entertain of public juftice, are involved.

Taking it then for granted, that this principle applies at leaft as ftrongly to criminal cafes, as to civil, there are abundance of authorities in the books—[Here he apologifed for not being better prepared, having only got his brief on his way to court.] —In *Bac. tit.* New Trials, there is a cafe where new evidence was let in, and it is true, there are in the fame page, cafes where it was refufed; what conclufion is to be drawn from this, but that every cafe of this nature ftands upon its own peculiar foundation, and is not to be ftrictly governed by any decided cafe, becaufe when it is not a queftion of abftract law, but a confideration emanating and flowing from a combination of circumftances, never the fame in any two cafes, it is of all queftions that can come before a court of common law, that moft peculiarly within its own found judicial difcretion, that can be gathered from reporters, differing in attention and ability, in fome broad principles of general analogy: wherever there is any ftrong leading feature in the cafe, it muft be judged of according to its own tendency and effect; it is apparently from the ofcitancy of the reporters, from their being unacquainted with the facts, and for want of more correct and particular notes, that we find fo much feeming contradiction, otherwife we fhould find the opinions of the judges nearly the fame in all fimilar cafes, but varying with the peculiar circumftances of each particular cafe; as in the prefent, the verdict certainly would not be fet afide, unlefs it appeared that the new evidence came to the parties knowledge fince the trial.

But

But there is a circumſtance which, in my opinion, pointedly diſtinguiſhes this from all other cafes, *viz.* that the new evidence is applicable to the credit of the principal witneſs, upon whoſe teſtimony the verdict muſt have been found, and not to any fub-ſtantive matter, making a particular ingredient in the cafe. Nor is it a new fubſtantive defence. For the court has wiſely faid, we will not ſet aſide verdicts on account of evidence, which might reaſonably have come to the knowledge of the party before, for then whenever the point, upon which he reſted, proved inſufficient, he would next ſhift his ground, and try ſome new ſort of de-fence.

Having often ſearched for cafes of this kind, I can fay, upon my recollection, that there is none like the preſent to be found; your lordſhips then have no guide but your own diſcretion, and your own notes to recur to, where you will fee in what point of view this gentleman's evidence appeared.

At the trial, he admitted that two bonds had been ſet up by his younger brother againſt his elder, which he was called to prove, as a fubſcribing witneſs : he admitted, that the genuineneſs of theſe bonds had been the fubject matter of ſuits in courts of juſtice; that both his father in his life-time, and ſince his death, his eldeſt brother, had impeached the authenticity of thcfe bonds, to which he had figned his name, as a witneſs: he admits an iſſue out of Chancery to try their authenticity : that they went down and were the fubject matter of a trial; but that ſome com-promiſe being mentioned, a juror was withdrawn and the matter fubmitted to referees, who gave only 200*l.* inſtead of 800*l.* which was the value of the bonds. He was aſked whether he was ex-amined at the trial, to prove the validity of theſe bonds; his an-ſwer was, I cannot charge my memory with theſe facts ; a pretty extraordinary anſwer from one who, in other reſpects, has been fo accurate. Since the commencement of this buſineſs, he has got a commiſſion by the good offices of a lady, who was his relation, and before that, he had no buſineſs nor profeſſion.

Thus did the teſtimony of this witneſs, who alone attempted to bring the publication home to the traverſer, appear extremely fufpicious, even upon his own examination. It will appear upon your lordſhips notes, that a gentleman from the fame neighbour-hood was afterwards aſked, is ſuch a perſon to be credited upon his oath? he anſwered, it was a very hard matter to fay ; but made uſe of the words, " I might heſitate." Another was examined; what did he fay?—" It is a very hard queſtion—I know but little more than what happened on the trial, where he was examined ; I would for my own part give him very little credit". But being preſſed again, he faid he did not think him-ſelf warranted to fay, he was not to be credited, from any par-ticular knowledge of his own. A very reſpectable witneſs of the other fex was then called, who faid ſhe would not credit

O 2

him

him upon his oath. She was crofs-examined in a manner which plainly fhewed, that the conductors of the profecution were aware that the character and credit of the witnefs was to be impeached, and by whom it was to be impeached, and yet have been able to bring forward nothing to fupport it. This lady was afked, if there was any particular infidelity which fhe had to complain of in the witnefs? fhe anfwered, that he had a brother who was married to her daughter, whom he had endeavoured to feduce from his wife. This however not proving fufficient at the trial to difcredit the witnefs, I truft we fhall now be allowed to bring forward the new matter, which has fince come to our know-ledge, in corroboration, explanation, and illuftration of what paffed there.

The hair-dreffer charges the witnefs with direct perjury; he ftates that he knew him, and dreffed his hair for a length of time, and fued him for the debt thereby incurred, in the Court of Confcience, where the other on his oath, denied that he had ever feen him, or that he ever knew his name, although the hair-dreffer fwears to a converfation that paffed between them that day, upon Effex-bridge; there has been time to anfwer that affidavit, it remains however uncontradicted, therefore I am en-titled to take it as true, and it ought to have as much weight as that of the moft dignified perfon in the ftate. It is the fame thing as if this witnefs had been called upon the table, and gone down without crofs-examination, and then where would have been the evidence to fupport the publication?

There is alfo another witnefs who tells a ftory about a horfe caufe, when Lyfter made an affidavit, and therein perjured him-felf, by perfonating and fwearing in the name of his brother.

It is true, at the trial, the jury would have been judges of the credit of the witneffes, but your lordfhips would not have paffed over the teftimony of thefe two men, and if you had then ftated, that there was not a fingle witnefs but himfelf, to give any legal proof of publication, it is for your lordfhips to judge, whether the jury would have found the verdict they did; and it is enough for me, if I can even raife a doubt, to ufe Lord Mansfield's words, in Bright v. Enyon—whether juftice has been done.

But it does not ftand upon the ground alone, of the impeach-ment of the witnefs, there are two other affidavits impeaching the conduct of one of the jurors. Perhaps it may be argued from public convenience, that when the party has not been fortunate enough to find evidence of this kind before the trial, upon which to challenge the array or the particular jurors, it is better that the individual fhould abide his misfortune, than that confufion and irregularity fhould be introduced into the jurifprudence of the country; but I truft your lordfhips will make that confideration bend to the greater queftion—has juftice been done.

What

I

What is judicial difcretion? It is the found application of judicial knowledge and good judgment to the peculiar circumftances of each individual cafe;—it is the inveftigation of every minute circumftance in a proceeding, to which found fenfe and liberal underftanding can be applied.

But you have alfo the affidavits of that refpectable man, of whom the voice of the kingdom of Ireland will fay, that he would not fully his unfpotted honor by ufing any unworthy artifice for the purpofe of evading any punifhment however great.

This alone ought not to fhake the verdict; but will any man attempt to fay, that an affidavit of that kind, which has been admitted, and has been read, and muft obtain the belief of every man in and out of court, will not have fome weight to induce your lordfhips to fufpect that juftice has not been done.

Mr. FLETCHER then recapitulated the four grounds of the motion.-

1ft. New evidence not difcovered till after the trial.

2d. New evidence to impeach that witnefs without whom (had he been out of the way) there could have been no verdict of conviction.

3d. Evidence to impeach the jury.

4th. The evidence of the traverfer as well to the witneffes as the fheriff.

And concluded, that it would be more becoming the officers of the crown to fay—we will not have fuch a verdict as this to go abroad and be fcrutinifed in every country, where the Englifh language is read. If we cannot have a conviction confiftent with juftice and with decency, we will have none.

Mr. RECORDER, *on the fame fide*, followed Mr. Fletcher, putting the fame arguments in a ftriking and varied point of view; —he obferved, that by fetting afide this verdict and fending the caufe back again to receive a folemn, ferious and deliberate inveftigation, from a fair jury of the country, returned by a returning officer whom the traverfer has no reafon to diftruft, there could not follow the fmalleft mifchief, and then, if upon fair evidence laid before the court on one fide and the other, he fhould happen to be convicted, that conviction would have the effect which was intended; but if this verdict was to ftand after the evidence which had appeared upon the trial, and after the lights which had been thrown upon it fince, there is not a perfon prefent in the court, and believing that teftimony falfe, that would not feel forrow, to fee the judgment of a court of juftice fo founded.

If this gentleman had been indicted in the ordinary way, for a mifdemeanor, he would have had an opportunity of knowing the party profecuting, and the fpecific charge made againft him.

But

But when an information is filed *ex officio*, it is the practice of the officers of the crown to keep the information they receive in their pocket for their own juftification, and the defendant is not authorized to call upon the crown for a copy of the examinations fworn.

Lord CLONMELL, *Chief Juftice.*—When this was mentioned before, it occurred to me, that there had been an examination fworn before a magiftrate, and he was not prevented from applying for it.

Here Mr. ROWAN appealed to Mr. Juftice DOWNES, whether he had not, when before him, requefted to know who the perjured villain was that could have fworn againft him, and whether, for that purpofe, he had not been inclined to refufe the offer of bail, chufing rather to go to prifon, that he might know his accufer and profecute him, (for he had been refufed a copy of the examinations) and faid, that had he gone to gaol then, as he was inclined, he would have been, without doubt, acquitted, when the former fheriffs were in office, and when there was not the fame *felection* of jurors.

DOWNES, *Juftice*—Admitted that the defendant had ftated nothing but what paffed, and that he had got no information from him refpecting the profecutor.

Mr. RECORDER.—The perfon profecuted, *ex officio*, knows nothing more than what appears upon the information filed, which gives him not the fmalleft intimation of the witnefs who is to profecute him.

He then made fome pointed obfervations upon the teftimony of Lyfter, who fwore that there were one or two hundred people walking up and down, having no feats; and yet in the midft of fo much confufion, he was able, from a diftant gallery, to diftinguifh that gentleman's voice, which did not appear very loud, nor very fhrill, nor very remarkably articulate, in reading a paper which he prefumes to fwear was the very paper which is the fubject of this profecution; nor could he remember whether he had been examined fome time within three years, upon fo important a queftion as a forgery imputed by one of his brothers to another, and in which he was himfelf involved.

But even if he could be fuppofed an honeft man, his teftimony was bad, as, to fay the beft, his memory and apprehenfions muft have been very defective.

If thofe circumftances of difcredit had not appeared upon the trial, it might have been improper to admit them now; but in the prefent fituation of things, it would be a favour to
the

the witnefs, if he thinks he has been flandered, to give him an opportunity of fhewing, upon a new trial, that he is not perjured; and as it was faid to be an eafy matter for the defendant to bring a third perfon out of this crowded and promifcuous affembly to contradict him, fo it cannot be difficult for him to bring fome individual out of a private gallery to fupport him.

The evidence of Morton was moft palpably falfe, for he fwore that his uncle Giffard, to his belief, had not any thing to fay to the conduct of the Dublin Journal, nor could he fay any thing of the relationfhip that fubfifted between his coufin Ryan and the fheriff, who was their common uncle.

And he concluded by obferving, refpecting the traverfer, that at all events it would not convict him in the opinion of unprejudiced and moderate men, to have gone further in fuch circumftances than moderate men would go; that the traverfer, whofe affidavit fcarcely any man in the community would doubt, had fworn that the evidence of Lyfter was falfe, and that the jury were prejudiced, and returned by a perfon adverfe and hoftile to him; and that the public could not but feel horror at a fentence pronounced upon fuch a foundation.

He protefted folemnly, that feeling for the dignity and character of the adminiftration of juftice in this country, he was more interefted in the event of the prefent motion, than in that of any other in which he was ever concerned. The King had not in his dominions a fubject more warmly attached to the conftitution in church and ftate than he; but he was, at the fame time, a friend to the civil and religious liberties of the people. The man who goes too far in doing what he thinks may tend to fecure thefe, may be cenfured by moderate men, but he will not, therefore, ceafe to be efteemed by moderate men. Mr. Rowan may, perhaps in fome inftances, have gone too far on this fubject; but his conduct has always been known to originate in the beft and pureft motives, and there was not in fociety a man more refpected, nay, admired—than he.—It was, therefore, effential in the higheft degree, that a verdict, by which fuch a man was fubjected to public and exemplary punifhment, fhould be above all exception.

Mr. Curran, *on the fame fide.*—It was an early idea, that a verdict in a criminal cafe could not be fet afide, *inconfulto rege,* but the law had ftood otherwife without a doubt, to impeach its principle for the laft two reigns.

Common fenfe would fay, that the difcretion of the court fhould go at leaft as far in criminal as in civil cafes, and very often to go no further would be to ftop far fhort of what was right, as in thofe great queftions where the profecution may be confidered either as an attempt to extinguifh liberty, or as

a neceffary

a neceffary meafure for the purpofe of repreffing the virulence
of public licentioufnefs and dangerous faction; where there
can be no alternative between guilt or martyrdom, where the
party profecuted muft either be confidered as a culprit finking
beneath the punifhment of his own crimes, or a victim facri-
ficed to the vices of others. But when it clearly appears that
the party has fallen a prey to a perfecuting combination, there
remains but one melancholy queftion, *how far did that combination
reach?*

There have been two cafes lately decided in this very court,
the King and Pentland, where the motion was made and refufed,
and the King and Bowen, where it was granted; both of which
fhew, that captious fophiftry, and technical pedantry, had here,
as well as in England, given way to liberal and rational enquiry; and that the court would not now, in their difcretion,
refufe a motion of this kind, unlefs they could, at the fame
time, lay their hands upon their hearts, and fay, they believed
in their confciences that juftice had been done; fuch was the
manly language of one of their lordfhips (Mr. Juftice Downes);
and fuch the opinion of the court on a former occafion.

He then cited 7 Modern 57. as referred to in Bacon tit. Trial,
to fhew that where there was good ground of challenge to a juror,
not known at the trial, it was fufficient caufe for fetting afide
the verdict.

In England they have a particular act of parliament, en-
titling the party to ftrike a fpecial jury to try the fact, and
then he has time between the ftriking and the trial, to queftion
the propriety of that jury: here my client had no previous information till the inftant of trial, who his jurors are to be.

There are certain indulgences granted at times, perhaps by
the connivance of humanity, which men, who are not entitled
to demand them in an open court, obtain neverthelefs by fidelong
means, and perhaps the little breach which affords that light to
the mind of the man accufed, is a circumftance which the court
would feel pain, even if called upon, to fay, fhould in all cafes
be prevented; but to overturn principles and authorities, for
the purpofe of oppreffing the fubject, is what this court will never do.

The firft of the affidavits I fhall confider, is that of the traverfer.
I do not recollect whether it ftates the fheriff, in avowed terms, to
be an emiffary or a hireling agent of the Caftle, therefore do not
ftate it from the affidavit; but he fwears, that he does believe that
he did labour to bring into the box a jury full of prejudices,
and of the blackeft impreffions; inftead of having, as they ought,
fair and impartial minds, and fouls like white paper.

This fheriff now ftands in court, he might have denied it if he
would, he had an opportunity of anfwering it; but he has left
it an undenied affertion—he was not certainly obliged to anfwer
it,

it, for no man is bound to convict himself. But there is a part of that charge which amounts, at the least, to this, " Your heart was poisoned against me, and you collected those to be my judges, who, if they could not be under the dominion of bad dispositions, might be at least the dupes of good." The most favourable thing that can be said is this, you sought to bring against me honest prejudices, but you brought against me wicked ones The very general charge, that he sought for persons, who he knew were most likely to bring prejudices with them into the jury box, is a part of the affidavit, that it was incumbent on him to answer if he could.

I do not contend, that what is charged in the affidavit, would have been a ground of principal challenge to the array; but hold it to be the better opinion, that a challenge to the array for favour, does well lie in the mouth of the defendant.

The antient notion was, you shall not challenge the array for favour where the king is a party; the king only can challenge for favour, for the principle was, that every man ought to be favourable to the crown, but thank God, the advancement of legal knowledge and the growing understanding of the age, has dissipated such illiberal and mischievous conceptions.

But I am putting too much stress upon such technical, discarded, and antiquated scruples. The true question has been already stated from the authority of Mr. Justice Downes, and that question is, Has justice been done?

Is it a matter, upon which scarce any understanding would condescend to hesitate, whether a man had been fairly tried, whose triors had been collected together by an avowed enemy, whose conduct had been such, as to leave no doubt that he had purposely brought prejudiced men into the box.

In every country, where freedom obtains, there must subsist parties. In this country and in Great Britain, I trust there never will be a time, when there shall not be men found zealous for the actual government of the day. So, on the other hand, I trust, there will never be a time, when there will not be found men zealous and enthusiastic in the cause of popular freedom and of the public rights. If, therefore, a person in public office suffers his own prejudices, however honestly anxious he may be for a prosecution carried on by those to whom he is attached, to influence him so far as to choose men, to his knowledge, devoted to the principles he espouses, it is an error which a high court of judicature, seeking to do right and justice, will not fail to correct.

A sheriff, in such a case, might not have perceived the partiality of his conduct, because he was surveying it through the medium of prejudice and habitual corruption. But it is impossible to think that this sheriff meant to be impartial, it is an in-

terpretation

terpretation more favourable than his conduct will allow of; if he deferves any credit at all, it is in not anfwering the charge made againft him : At the fame time, that, by not anfwering it, he has left unimpeached the credit of the charge itfelf.

[Here the fheriff tendered fome form of an affidavit, which the court refufed to have fworn or read, for the fame reafon that thofe, fworn and tendered by the defendant's counfel, had been before refufed. Mr. Curran, however, confented to its being fworn and read; but the Attorney General declined it, being unacquainted with the contents, and uninftruded as to its tendency; it therefore was not fworn.]

Mr. Curran—Is this then the way to meet a fair application to the court, to fee whether juftice has been done between the fubject and the crown. I offer it again, let the affidavit be read. And let me remind the court, that the great reafon for fending a caufe back to a jury, is that new light may be fhed upon it; and how muft your lordfhips feel, when you fee that indulgence granted to the confcience of the jury, denied to the court?

Mr. Attorney General.—I am concerned that any lawyer fhould make a propofition in the manner Mr. Curran has done; he propofes to have an affidavit read, provided we confent that others, which the court have already refufed, fhould be now read *. I did not hear it offered; but is it to be prefumed I will confent to have an affidavit read, about which I know nothing. Yefterday, without any communication with a human being, I did fay, that I conceived it unneceffary to anfwer any of the affidavits, thinking that they were not fufficient to ground the application made to the court. And it is prefumed I am fo mad as to confent to the reading of affidavits, which I have not feen.

[Here fome altercation took place, and Lord Clonmell, Chief Juftice, interpofed, faying, that the counfel had certainly a right to argue it upon the ground, that the fheriff was biaffed, and did return a jury prejudiced againft the traverfer.]

Mr. Curran was then proceeding to obferve upon the expreffion of one of the jury, fworn to in another affidavit, " That " there would be no fafety in the country, until the defendant " was either hanged or banifhed." When it was afked by the court, Whether the time of its coming to the knowledge of the traverfer, that the fheriff was biaffed, was ftated in his affidavit?

---

* It may not be improper to obferve, that Mr. Attorney General miftook Mr. Curran's propofal, which was an *unqualified* offer to have Mr. Giffard's affidavit read.

M.

Mr. Curran anfwered, he was in prifon, and could not have the attendance of thofe counfel, whofe affiftance he had in court, and befides, from the nature of the circumftances, it was impoffible he could have been fufficiently apprized of its confequences, for he faw not that pannel till the day of the trial, when he could not have had time to make any enquiry into the characters, difpofitions, or connections of the jury. Mr. Curran then reverted to his argument on the expreffion of the juror.

If triors had been appointed to determine the iffue, favourable or not, what would have been their finding? Could they fay upon their oaths, that he was not unfavourable to that party, againft whom he could make fuch a declaration?

Favour is not caufe of principal challenge, which if put upon a pleading, would conclude the party. Favour is that which makes the man, in vulgar parlance, unfit to try the queftion. And as to the time thefe facts came to his knowledge, he has fworn that he was utterly ignorant of them at the time of his coming into court to take his trial.

I will not glance at the character of any abfent noble perfon, high in office, but let it be remembered, that it is a government profecution, and that the witnefs has, from a low and handicap fituation, fcraped himfelf into preferment, perhaps, for I will put the beft conftruction upon it, by offering himfelf as a man honeftly anxious for the welfare of his country; in fhort, it is too obvious to require any comment, what the nature of the whole tranfaction has been, that he had got his commiffion as a compenfation, *pro labore impendendo*, and came afterwards into court to pay down the ftipulated purchafe.

Had this then been an unbiaffed jury, was there not fomething in all thefe circumftances, that might have afforded more deliberation, than that of one minute per man, for only fo long was the jury out; and had this been a fair witnefs, would he have lain down under a charge, which if true, ought not only to damn this verdict, but his character for ever? What would a corps of brother officers think of a perfon charged, upon oath, with the commiffion of two wilful perjuries, and that charge remaining undenied? Here is an undenied charge, in point of fact, and although I do not call upon the court to fay, that this is a guilty and abominable perfon, yet furely the fufpicion is ftrongly fo, and muft be confidered. This was at leaft a verdict, where the evidence went to the jury under flighter blemifhes than it will if my client has the advantage of another trial, for then he will put out of the power of man to doubt that this witnefs has been perjured. This witnefs, who has had notice, both here and at the trial, of the afperfions on his character, and yet has not called a human being to fay that he entertained a contrary opinion of him.

Was

<

Was he known, any where? Did he crawl unobserved to the castle? Was it without the aid or knowledge of any body, that that gaudy plumage grew on him, in which he appeared in court? If he was known for any thing else than what he is stated to be, it was, upon that day, almost a physical impossibility, in a court-house, which almost contained the country, not to have found some person, to give some sort of testimony respecting his general character. For though no man is bound to be ready at all times to answer particular charges, yet every man is supposed to come with his public attestation of common and general probity. But he has left that character, upon the merits of which my client is convicted, unsupported, even by his own poor corporal swearing. You are called upon, then, to say, whether upon the evidence of a being of this kind, such a man as that is to be convicted, and sentenced to punishment, in a country where humanity is the leading feature, even of the criminal law.

He then observed upon the second witness.—A man coming to support the credit of another collaterally, is himself particularly pledged; then what was his testimony! He did not know whether Mr. Giffard was concerned in the newspaper!!! And now, you have the silence of Giffard himself, in not answering Mr. Rowan's affidavit to contradict that. And next, he did not know whether his own cousin-german was the relation of their common uncle!!! I call upon you, my lords, in the name of sacred justice, and your country, to declare whether the melancholy scenes and murderous plots of the Meal-tub and the Rye-house, are to be acted over again. And whether every Titus Oates that can be found, is to be called into your courts, as the common vouchee of base and perjured accusation.

He then proceeded to another ground, namely, that the direction of the court was not, as he conceived, agreeable to the law of Ireland. The defence of my client (he added) was rested upon this, that there was no evidence of the fact of publication, upon the incredibility of the fact, and the circumstances of discredit in the character of the witness; yet the court made this observation: " gentlemen, it scarcely lies in the mouth of Mr. Rowan " to build a defence upon objections of this kind to the cha-" racters of witnesses, because the fact was public; there were " many there, the room was crowded below; the gallery was " crowded above: and the publicity of the fact enabled him to " produce a number of witnesses to falsify the assertion of the " prosecutor, if in fact it could be falsified!" Is that the principle of criminal law? Is it a part of the British law that the fate of the accused shall abide, not the positive establishment of guilt by the prosecutor, but the negative proof of innocence by himself? Why has it been said in foolish old books, that the law supposes the innocence of every man 'till the contrary is proved? How has it happened that that language has been admired for its

humanity, and not laughed at for its abfurdity, in which the
prayers of the court are addreffed to Heaven for the fafe deliver-
ance of the man accufed ? How comes it that fo much public time
is wafted in going into evidence of guilt, if the bare accufation of
a man did call upon him to go into evidence of his innocence?
The force of the obfervation is this, Mr. Rowan impeaches the
credit of a witnefs, who has fworn that he faw him prefent, and
doing certain acts at a certain meeting; but it is afked has he
fubftantiated that difcredit, by calling all the perfons, who were
prefent, to prove his abfence from that meeting, which is only
ftated to have exifted, by a witnefs whom he alledges to have perjured himfelf? I call upon the example of judicial character;
upon the faith of that high office, which is never fo dignified as
when it fees its errors and corrects them, to fay, that the court
was for a moment led away, fo as to argue from the moft feduc-
tive of all fophifms, that of the *pofitio principii.*

See what meaning is to be gathered from fuch words; we fay
the whole that this man has fworn is a confummate lie; fhew it
to be fo, fays the court, by admitting a part of it to be true. It
is a falfe fwearing; it is a confpiracy of two witneffes againft this
defendant; well then it lies upon him to rebut their teftimony,
by proving a great deal of it to be true! Is conjecture then, in
criminal cafes, to ftand in the place of truth and demonftration?
Why were not fome of thofe—(I will ftrip the cafe of the honour of names which I refpect)—but why were not fome of thofe,
who knew that thefe two perfons were to be brought forward,
and that there were to be objections to their credit—if, as it is
ftated, it happened in the prefence of a public crowd, rufhing in
from motives of curiofity, why were not numbers called on to
eftablifh that fact? On the contrary the court have faid to this
effect: Mr. Rowan, you fay you were not there; produce any
of thofe perfons with whom you were there, to fwear you were
not there! You fay it was a perjury; if fo, produce the people
that he has perjured himfelf in fwearing to have been there! But
as to your own being there you can eafily fhew the contrary of
that, by producing fome man that faw you there! You fay you
were not there? Yes. There were one hundred and fifty perfons there: now produce any one of thofe to fwear they faw you
there!

It is impoffible for the human mind to fuppofe a cafe, in which
infatuation muft have prevailed in a more progreffive degree, than
when a jury are thus, in fact, directed to receive no refutation,
nor proof of the perjury of the witnefs, but only of his truth.
We will permit you to deny the charge by eftablifhing the fact :
we will permit you to prove that they fwore falfely to your being
there, by producing another witnefs to prove to a certainty that
you were there.—[Interrupted by Lord Clonmell.]

Lord

L*rd CLONMELL, *Chief Juſtice.*—The reaſoning of the court
was ſtrong upon that point ; this is a tranſaction ſtated by the
witneſs to have happened in open day, in a crowded aſſembly in
the capital, amidſt a number of perſons dreſſed in the uniform of
Hamilton Rowan. There has been nothing ſuddenly brought
forward to ſurpriſe the traverſer ; yet what has he done, did he
offer as in the common courſe to prove an alibi ? It is ſtated to
be at ſuch a day ; the witneſs ſwears at ſuch an hour—the place
is ſworn to have been full of people, of Mr. Rowan's friends :
but if there was even a partial aſſembly, it would be eaſy ſtill to
produce ſome one of thoſe perſons who were preſent to ſay, that
the fact did not happen which has been ſworn to, or if you ſay
Mr. Rowan was not there, it is eaſier ſtill to prove it by ſhewing
where he was ; as thus : I breakfaſted with him, I dined with him,
I ſupped with him, he was with me, he was not at Pardon's ;
diſprove that aſſertion by proving an affirmation inconſiſtent with
it.

Mr CURRAN.—I beg leave to remind the court of what fell
from it. " He may call" (ſaid the court) " any of thoſe perſons,
" he has not produced one of them ;" upon this, I think, a
moſt material point does hang " He might have called them,
" for they were all of his own party."

Lord CLONMELL.—That is if there were ſuch perſons there ;
or if there was no meeting at all he might have proved that.

Mr. CURRAN.—There was no ſuch idea put to the jury, as
whether there was a meeting or not : it was ſaid they were all of
his party, he might have produced them, and the non-produc-
tion of them was a " volume of evidence" upon that point. No
refinement can avoid this concluſion, that even as your lordſhip
now ſtates the charge, the fate of the man muſt depend upon
proving the negative.

Until the credit of the witneſs was eſtabliſhed he could not be
called upon to bring any contrary evidence. What does the duty
of every counſel dictate to him ; if the caſe is not made out by
his adverſary or proſecutor ? Let it reſt ; the court is bound to
tell the jury ſo, and the jury are bound to find him not guilty.
It is a moſt unſhaken maxim, that *nemo tenetur prodere ſe ipſum.*
And it would indeed be a very inquiſitorial exerciſe of power, to
call upon a man to run the riſque of confirming the charge, under the penalty of being convicted by *nil dicit.* Surely at the criminal ſide of this court, as yet, there has been no ſuch judgment
pronounced. It is only when the party ſtands mute of malice,
that ſuch extremes can be reſorted to. I never before heard an
intimation from any judge to a jury, that bad evidence liable to
any and every exception ought to receive a ſanction from the
ſilence

silence of the party. The substance of the charge was neither more nor less than this: that the falsehood of the evidence shall receive support and credit from the silence of the man accused. With anxiety for the honour and religion of the law, I demand it of you, must not the jury have understood that this silence was evidence to go to them; is the meaning contained in the expression " a volume of evidence" only insinuation! I do not know where any man would be safe. I do not know what any man could do to screen himself from persecution; I know not how he could be sure, even when he was at his prayers before the throne of Heaven, that he was not passing that moment of his life, on which he was to be charged with the commission of some crime, to be expiated to society by the forfeiture of his liberty or of his life. I do not know what shall become of the subject, if a jury are to be told that the silence of the man charged is a " volume " of evidence" that he is guilty of the crime; where is it written? I know there is a place where vulgar frenzy cries out, that the public instrument must be drenched in blood; where defence is gagged, and the devoted wretch must perish. But even there the victim of such tyranny is not made to fill, by voluntary silence, the defects of his accusation, for his tongue is tied, and therefore no advantage is taken of him by construction; it cannot be there said that his not speaking is a volume of evidence to prove his guilt.

But to avoid all misunderstanding, see what is the force of my objection: is it that the charge of the court cannot receive a practicable interpretation, that may not terrify mens minds with ideas such as I have presented? No—I am saying no such thing, I have lived too long and observed too much not to know, that every word in a phrase is one of the feet upon which it runs, and how the shortening or lengthening of one of those feet, will alter the progress or direction of its motion. I am not arguing that the charge of the court cannot by any possibility be reconciled to the principles of law; I am agitating a bigger question; I am putting it to the conscience of the court, whether a jury may not have probably collected the same meaning from it, which I have affixed to it, and whether there ought not to have been a volume of explanation, to do away the fatal consequences of such mistake.

On what sort of a case am I now speaking? on one of that kind, which it is known has been beating the public heart for many months: which, from a single being in society, has scarcely received a cool or tranquil examination. I am making that sort of application, which the expansion of liberal reason and the decay of technical bigotry have made a favoured application.

In earlier times it might have been thought sacrilege to have meddled with a verdict once pronounced; since that the true principles of juſtice have been better underſtood ; ſo that now, the whole wiſdom of the whole court will have an opportunity of looking over that verdict, and ſetting right the miſtake which has occaſioned it.

Mr. Curran made other obſervations, either to corroborate his own, or to anſwer the oppoſite counſel ; of which it is impoſſible to give an exact detail ; and concluded thus : You are ſtanding on the ſcanty iſthmus that divides the great ocean of duration ; on one ſide of the paſt, on the other of the future : a ground, that while you yet hear me, is waſhed from beneath our feet. Let me remind you, my lord, while your determination is yet in your power, *dum verſatur adhuc intra penetralia Veſtæ*, that on that ocean of future you muſt ſet your judgment afloat. And future ages will aſſume the ſame authority, which you have aſſumed ; poſterity feel the ſame emotions which you have felt, when your little hearts have beaten, and your infant eyes have overflowed, at reading the ſad hiſtory of the ſufferings of a Ruſſel or a Sidney.

[The concluſion of Mr. Curran's ſpeech was marked by another burſt of applauſe, ſimilar to thoſe which accompanied his former exertions in this cauſe.]

WEDNESDAY

Mr. ATTORNEY GENERAL, *for the crown.*—My Lords, it is .rny bufinefs to offer fuch arguments as occur to me, to refift what .has been advanced in favour of Mr. ROWAN, upon this motion to .fet afide the verdict and grant ,a new trial. It is to me, my lords, a great happinefs, that it has arrived at this ·ftage, when the fubject will be examined by the rules of legal reafoning, ,without an appeal to the paffions of men, or any attempt to influence the argument by topics deduced from extrinfic matter. .I fhould be forry when I return to my own houfe, that paffion fhould fo far make me forget my reafon. It is the duty of every man, whether profecutor or advocate for the profecuted, to promote the ends of juftice, and obtain decifions upon argument, and argument alone. It is not the duty of counfel to determine the weight of argument: they are to offer the beft arguments they can; when they pafs that, they pafs the bounds of duty.

This, my lords, is faid to be a verdict againft evidence, becaufe .the credit of the principal witnefs was fuch, as that he deferved no credit, and that now, if the verdict be fet afide, new evidence .will be offered, fince come to the knowledge of the party, further to fhew that the witnefs did not deferve credit.—Another ground is this, that the fheriff, who returned the jury, had a prejudice againft the accufed, and laboured to procure a pannel prejudicial againft Mr. ROWAN. Another ground is, that one of the jurors had exprelfed himfelf in a certain way, fhewing he had an ill opinion of Mr. ROWAN upon fome fubject or other. Such, my lords, are the grounds fpecified in the notice. A further objection was made from the bar, of which no notice was given, namely, that one of the judges had mifdirected the jury. If there be any weight in it, the party by ftrict form can derive no advantage from it—but I do not confine myfelf to form, it is my defire that this matter fhould be fairly enquired into according to the rules of law ; therefore I will obferve upon that, and make .fuch anfwer to it as occurs to me, firft calling upon your lordfhips and the gentlemen in this court, for beyond that I defire no attention, to give me an impartial hearing. I appeal to thofe only who have knowledge of law and the rules of cool reafon ; the reft is matter of indifference. My lords, this information was filed a year fince againft Mr. ROWAN ; he was arrefted upon a previous information which was returned to the Crown-office in Hilary Term, 1793 ; a *noli profequi* was entered upon that, by reafon of a miftake in copying one of the words, fo that if ·brought to trial, he muft have been acquitted without entering into the merits. Another information was filed ; that was pleaded .to, and immediately an application was made to have him tried in Michaelmas Term. The court conceived that, confiftent with

Q   the

the difcharge of general duty, it was impoffible to have him tried
then, and this term was appointed. The pannel was returned to
the office in the ufual manner ; I have a right to fay fo, becaufe
there is no fuggeftion to the contrary ; and it was open to any
man who pleafed to look at it. On Wednefday fe'nnight the
record came to be tried. The jury were called at ten o'clock ;
they were called a fecond time, a third time, and a fourth time ;
and it was not till near twelve o'clock that the Jury were fworn.
All that time there was no challenge taken to the array. No application was previoufly made, no fuggeftion filed to have the
venire directed to any other officer than the gentleman who
returned the pannel. But when the jurors were called to the
book, feveral were challenged and a pretty general queftion was
put to feveral, I do not fay to all of them, to declare whether
they had delivered any opinion upon the cafe. To that queftion
I beg attention from every impartial man—They were permitted
to give anfwers, though I rely upon it, that by law, in a criminal cafe, the party had no right to put fuch a queftion. So
that after an hour and half's deliberation, the party knowing
who were to be called, fuch as were thought proper to be queftioned, were examined and permitted to anfwer. But the fair-
nefs with which this profecution was intended to be conducted is
manifefted by another circumftance. A juror of the name of
Dickfon was actually fworn, and afterwards he faid he had given
an opinion—it was defired that he might be difcharged. I in-
ftantly gave my confent. Mr. CURRAN defired not my confent,
but that I fhould move it myfelf ; I did move it, becaufe I
thought it was right to have him difcharged. The jury were
then fworn and the merits were gone into. Two witneffes were
produced, one fwearing to the actual fact of publifhing the very
paper in the record ; another, who though he did not fwear to
the very paper, yet did give fuch evidence as, if he was worthy of credit, muft give every reafonable man conviction, that
it was the very fame libel. Three witneffes were produced and
examined to the credit of *Lyfter*, the witnefs for the crown ;—
one did not fay he was unworthy of credit, but that he would
hefitate : another was not much inclined to give him belief ; and
it is infifted that fuch evidence was direct and pofitive to take
away his credit, and therefore your lordfhips fhould fet afide this
verdict. The crofs-examination by the counfel for Mr. ROWAN
throughout, directly and in terms, admitted that there was a meeting that day at Cope-ftreet; that Mr. ROWAN was there, and that
the Volunteers were there affembled ; the whole crofs-examination went to that fact ; the drefs and uniform of the Old Volunteers, every fact was infifted upon, and it was not until yefterday,
in a kind of joke, that the contrary was infifted upon. Mr.
ROWAN's affidavit does not deny the meeting.—Away, therefore,
with

with the childifh obfervation, that a man could not be called from
a meeting which did not appear to exift.

I will now come to the merits of the cafe upon the objections
made. There was nothing omitted which could be faid for
Mr. Rowan : it is not fit for me to fay that any thing was faid
which ought not to have been faid. But, my lords, fomething
was faid with regard to the right of courts to fet afide verdicts
in criminal cafes, not capital : no man difputed the right, or
queftioned it. Mr. Curran went into the hiftory of that branch
of the law and the doctrine of fetting afide verdicts *rege inconfulto*; how it was with regard to ancient times, I am not fatisfied ; but fure I am, and fo I hope it will remain, that this court
will have a right in favour of the defendant, and in his favour
only, to fet afide a verdict againft him. But the exercife of that
great power, touching the trial by jury, muft be applied according to the known rules of law. Mr. Curran ftated that an
exact inftance was not to be found in the books, and from the
hurry, I fuppofe, in which he had confidered the fubject, he.fell
into the obfervation that the practice is of fo modern a date that
many precedents could not be found : he confined it to the two
laft reigns ; but, my lords, the reports in William III's. time are
full of fuch applications ; the practice prevailed in the reign of
Car. II. how much earlier I cannot fay—there are an infinity of
cafes upon the fubject, and he was right when he faid there was
no fuch cafe as this ; and before your lordfhips make a precedent
of this, I am fure you will give it all the attention it deferves.
I repeat the obfervation, that the confequence of this determination to the public and the adminiftration of criminal juftice,
is of the laft importance ; and that, however right it is, that
Mr. Rowan fhould feek redrefs by thefe means, and that every
poffible exertion fhould be made in favour of a man ftanding a
culprit at your bar ; yet, my lords, the confideration of that man,
or any other, let him be who he may, dwindles to a thing of no
value, when compared to the general juftice of the country.
There can be no diftinction here ; and here alone there is
equality among fubjects, between the higheft man in the ftate,
and the men who fhout in the hall at the names of *Titus Oates
and Algernon Sidney*. The cafe, my Lords, comes then to this,
whether upon the affidavits which have been made you fhould
fet afide this verdict ? They fay thefe affidavits are to be taken
as true—I fay they are not : they were made and produced in
court in my abfence. I was called—I knew no more of them
than the man in Weftminfter-hall. I heard them read, and it
did ftrike me, that they were of fuch a nature, that I ought not
to give an anfwer to them ; I therefore did not confent to a rule
unlefs caufe, but was ready to meet the counfel at the moment.
It is to be taken as true that fuch affidavits are made ; that Mr.
Rowan can find two witneffes fwearing to thofe facts which

have

have been mentioned; but it cannot be taken as true, that thofe, alledged facts are true; it is not for your lordfhips to fay they are true or falfe ; nor if witneffes were found to fay that what has been ftated refpecting *Perrin* was falfe, could you determine that ? but whether you fend it back to fee whether a jury would give them credit or not, that is what you are to determine; you are to fend it back to let in the fame fpecies of evidence which has been already adduced without fuccefs. As to Mr. Rowan's affidavit, he fwears to fomething he heard, and fomething he believes—that muft be taken as true ; that is, that he heard fomething and that he believes it—if that were a ground for a new trial, verdict may be had after verdict. Something has been fpread abroad, that your minds might be influenced by fomething without doors—a thing impoffible. Let the cry be what it may by the feditious and the turbulent, the whole will be thought of rightly on a future day. What has been faid cannot influence you, who will determine according to the rules of law. It is defired, that you will fet afide this verdict, that evidence may be given to fhew *Lyfter* is not worthy of credit. Gentlemen have argued this cafe, certainly of the firft talents and ingenuity, fome of them have had as much experience in thefe matters as any gentleman who has the honour of wearing a bar gown ; but I muft fay fome little things fell from them, which were rather extraordinary; one gentleman faid he had only got his brief the night before ; another faid he had got his on his way to court; but they knew the affidavits were to be made, they heard them read the day before ; fomething was faid of a cafe which had *M. S.* oppofite to it in the margin. I believe there are not many gentlemen who could recollect cafes in the books cited as from manufcript cafes, and quote them as fuch from memory. I have ufed great diligence upon the fubject, and agree with Mr. Curran, there is not one to be found. You are defired to fet afide the verdict, becaufe the witnefs was not to be credited. Who made you judges of that ? Are you the guardians of the lives, the liberties and the properties of the people ? Which of you determines the credit of the witneffes? I have fat at my lamp the moft of the night and have found nothing like this. But I will, for a moment, fuppofe what I do not admit, that it might be a ground for fetting afide the verdict : bring it to the teft of reafon, bring it to the bar of fenfe where it fhould be tried. You are to fet afide a verdict, to let in evidence to the credit of a witnefs, when his credit was impeached ; witneffes were examined to his credit, and fo ftrong fay they was the evidence againft him, that it ought to have deftroyed his credit. The cafe was made, witneffes were examined, and the whole was left to the jury. For, my lords, it is a fad miftake which has been fent abroad, that becaufe one witnefs fays another is not to be believed, that therefore,

fore, what the firft fays is true. Are the jury to give up all
the circumftances? Their own obfervation to the opinion of
another man perhaps as much prejudiced as any? But here
the matter was examined; they were prepared with evidence to
the hiftory of this man's life, and after a verdict is had upon
that, fome men are picked up in the ftreets to give fome
evidence, that is, that they do not believe the witnefs, to eke
out a ground for fetting afide the verdict, in a cafe where the
objection has been already made and already tried. Here in-
cidentally let me obferve upon another part of the cafe. The
verdict is againft evidence, becaufe the witneffes were not to
be believed: there is no man fo young at the bar as not to fee
the futility of fuch an argument: a man may have difcredited
himfelf upon various occafions, and yet may give fuch teftimony, accompanied with other circumftances, as fhall entitle
him to belief, though a thoufand fhould oppofe him. " My
" Good Lord Primate of Armagh, do you know Mr. Lyfter?"
" I do, I have known him concerned in many tranfactions of a
" bafe nature, he is not to be believed." What? if that was
fworn to by that faint upon earth, fhall the pofitive fwearing
difcredit the teftimony though it be accompanied with circumftances which fpeak its truth? Can that be law? I hope not,
for it is not reafon. There are cafes which fay a verdict fhall
not be fet afide, though an incompetent witnefs has been examined, who was not known to be incompetent at the time.
That is a ftronger cafe than the prefent, and applies to the
ground of objection with refpect to the jury. *Turner v. Pearce*,
1 *Durnf. & Eaft.* 717.—*Wright v. Littler.* 3 *Bur.* 1244.—Here
I muft trefpafs upon your lordfhips time to take notice of another obfervation. It is infifted that you ought the rather to let
him in, becaufe this was an information filed *ex officio* by the
Attorney General, by which he was deprived of an opportunity of knowing the witnefs againft him, and confequently that
though in ordinary cafes a new trial ought not to be granted
upon that ground, yet here it ought. The gentleman who
made this obfervation, was here again a little hurried, for if he had
reflected one moment, he would fee that the cafes are precifely the
fame. The party in an indictment has no right to fee the examinations till trial, and fometimes not even then. In an information he has no right to fee them. So that whether it be
an information or an indictment, he is alike forbid to fee the
examination. If he be profecuted by indictment, the examination will be returned to the crown-office. If by information, the
examinations are put into the fame crown-office on the firft day
of the term. It was faid that in the cafe of an indictment,
what was fworn could be known. All that could appear would
be that fome of the grand jury might forget their oaths and difclofe the fecrets of the profecution, though they are fpecially

3   fworn

sworn not to mention what appears upon the examinations. This observation was made without thought, therefore; and could not have been made for any good purpose with respect to this motion; it was made for nothing but to imprefs the people with an idea that there has been severity or oppression in this case, not allowable, and that the subject has been put under difficulties, not occurring in the ordinary course of justice. But upon a cool enquiry it will be found that the manner of proceeding makes no difference in the case. If there be any way by which the informations in the crown-office can be got at (I hope there is not) he might have made use of that; but Mr. Rowan was apprised; he came here with witnesses to trace facts happening at various times; he put his defence on that. Mr. *Lyster's* name was inserted in the papers, and it was notorious for many months that he was the man. But I disclaim that, your lordships have no right to know it, but you know that Mr. Rowan came prepared with witnesses against him. Another observation occurs. I will suppose, what I never will admit till a solemn decision is had, that the objection made on account of the want of credit would be a good ground for setting aside the verdict, even after that credit had been examined to, or provided no witness was found to come forward, yet you cannot entertain this motion, for the knowledge of the existence of the evidence since the trial is not sworn to. Mr. Rowan has made an affidavit that he did not know it; that affidavit is to be taken as true— I believe he did not. But he appeared by attorney, he defended by attorney, and it is not sworn even to his belief, nor has his attorney sworn, nor is there a syllable to tell you that those concerned for him were not apprized of the fact. If these affidavits be admitted, there is nothing to be done but conceal every thing from the party, to keep back that which may eventually serve the motion for a new trial, in case of any thing against him. I feel that if this were an ordinary case, the bare statement of the fact would drive the motion out of court; the fact has been enquired into by the jury; notwithstanding what has been said of the witness, he may have told the truth, and it is impossible it should be otherwise.

The other objection is that one of the jurors did not stand indifferent; a ground of challenge which was not taken, and not having been taken, the verdict shall be set aside and the party have a new trial. The statute law has directed that in treason the party shall have a copy of the pannel a certain number of days; in no other case has the party such a right, he is to take his challenge as the party comes to the book; that is the law of the land, that has been the simple law under which our ancestors lived happy for ages, by which juries have been chosen and formed, who have for ages protected every thing dear to Britons and Irishmen; and now, for the first time, I will be bold

to

to fay, in any criminal or civil cafe, the verdict is to be fet afide
becaufe there lay a challenge to a juror, not known to the party
at the time of the verdict. I will fuppofe that there was a
principal caufe of challenge to this man ; no inftance of fuch a
cafe can be produced where that was a ground for a new trial;
there is no neceffity to examine further into the circumftances ;
there is no caufe of challenge now ftated—What is it ? There
was an illumination in Dublin laft Auguft, when the juror and
Atkinfon fell into converfation of and concerning—What ? the libel
calling the citizens to arms ? No fuch thing—But an illumination takes place for the capture of a town, they fall into a converfation about the Volunteers in general, in which the juror
faid, the country could not profper unlefs *Hamilton Rowan* and
Napper Tandy were hanged or tranfported ; not a fyllable refpecting the matter in hand—Not one word of this matter.
Would that be a caufe of challenge to a juror ? Moft undoubtedly not—and the man who ufed the expreffion, fuppofing he
did ufe it, gave no caufe of challenge, and now, though the
eleven others agreed in that verdict, you are to fend it back to
a new trial—For what ? to have two triors fworn to afcertain
whether Mr. *Perrin* was a perfon to be challenged or not.
The juror gave an opinion of different men upon a political
fubject. What man is there who has not given an opinion
upon fuch a fubject ? If there be, he is cold to the interefts of
his country. But does it apply, that the man ufing fuch expreffions is not competent to meet a queftion of facts upon evidence
before him, though the party may be concerned in a particular
meafure not agreeing with his opinion. I may think the conduct of a man dangerous ; I may fpeak of the confequences of
his conduct as I think. But does it follow that fuch a man
paffing a verdict upon his oath upon the examination of witneffes to a particular fact, is therefore to be unfavourable to the
perfon of whom he had entertained the opinion ? Was there
a fingle allufion to the matter in queftion ? It is not a caufe
of challenge to a man, that he has delivered an opinion upon
the very fubject : he muft have done it through malice and
with an improper view ; and the reafon is, that an honeft man,
may deliver an opinion upon what appears before him, concerning which, when examined, he may have a different opinion ; even upon the fubject itfelf, it muft be clearly fhewn,
that the opinion was unfair or malicious, 2 *Salk.* 589. But
fee what is defired ; fuppofe it a caufe of challenge, fuppofe it
a principal caufe of challenge, then, my lords, I fubmit, that
the verdict fhould not be fet afide ; becaufe, by law the challenge muft be taken, if to the array, before a juror is fworn ;
if to the polls, it muft be as each man comes to the book.—
So very ftrong is it, that after one juror is fworn, the law will
n ot allow a challenge to the array ; and yet where would be
the

the difficulty? but fuch was the fimplicity of our ancient law, that it would not allow it, *Hob.* 235. And now, my lords, after the party has taken all the advantages which he could take, afking queſtions he had no right to aſk, putting afide a juror actually fworn, after having the advantage of every thing which he could defire; you, my lords, and the people, (for they are appealed to upon a judicial trial!) have been told, that this trial was carried on by cruel and unjuſt means, and you are defired to fet afide this verdict, upon matters, fuggeſted in thefe affidavits, refpecting a juror, which was no caufe of challenge, upon a fuppofed converfation, as it feems to me, touching the volunteers, probably over a bowl of punch, and not about the fubject of any trial.

I now come to the third objection, that the ſheriff has been partial: Mr. *Rowan* fwears, as to his belief, that the ſheriff has an office under government—is a militia officer, and conductor of a paper, commonly called a government newfpaper— that the ſheriff is prejudiced againſt him—and that the pannel was returned by Mr. *Giffard*, or his fub-ſheriff, and that he laboured to return a pannel which he either knew or believed to be prejudiced againſt Mr. ROWAN. If the affidavit has any meaning, it means this, that there lay a challenge to the array, for that the ſheriff was partial, and procured a jury for the purpofe of convicting Mr. ROWAN. He is not pleafed to inform your lordſhips when he heard of thefe facts, or when he firſt formed his belief. This was not omitted from want of recollection in himfelf, or thofe who advifed him; becaufe, in his affidavit touching the evidence, he takes care to tell you, that he did not hear of it till after the trial; fo that it does not appear that Mr. ROWAN was not apprized of this when the jury came into the box—when the *venire* iſſued—when the trial at bar was moved for in Michaelmas term, or when he put in his plea—look at the fituation in which your lordſhips ſtand—look at what precedent you are called upon to make—you let the man take his trial, with an objection in his poffeffion that may fet afide all the proceedings, and he declines to make it—the party is to be tried by a jury—he fubmits to the jury, for he made no challenge, he is found guilty, and now he fays, I had a caufe of challenge, I took my chance—fend me to another trial, that I may make it. My lords, I would almoſt aſk, is this decent?—the law protects every man, gives him a right to have a fair jury, the law points him out the way, and he is not to overbound thofe limits, to do that which has not been done fince the days of our Saxon anceſtors. He knew thefe facts, that *Giffard* was ſheriff, that he was an officer in the militia, that he had a place in the revenue—what had he to do? Mr. ROWAN had able counfel, men of the firſt talents and information—his remedy was eafy and without delay or expence
—why

—why not come in here and fuggeft the facts? If he had, the *venire* would have gone to the other fheriff, and *Giffard* could not have meddled. But mayhap the other fheriff is partial—fuggeft that then, and if the objection be well founded, the *venire* will go to the coroner. If the objection would not be fufficient for that purpofe, it cannot be fufficient for this purpofe ; but it is faid he was not aware of this fuggef-tion ; I will not impute it to the counfel—Mr. Rowan muft have been aware of it when they came into the box—why not challenge the array? He forgot to do that, till one of them was fworn ;—then why not challenge for favour? Where are thefe men who have told him thefe ftories? Why do they not make affidavits? Why does he take a chance for a verdict, knowing thefe facts? Having taken his chance, he now calls upon you to fet afide the verdict upon that. Make that example, my lords, and you overfet the criminal law, that which is the guardian of our lives and properties, and you make it depend upon the art, defign and knavifh conduct of thofe concerned. The objection is founded upon the conduct of the fheriff; that conduct was known previous to the trial, therefore I rely upon it, that this verdict ought not to be fet afide ; and if it be, it will be an example big with dangerous confequences. It has been faid, Mr. *Giffard* did not anfwer the affidavits, and there-fore they muft be taken as true—Mr. Rowan believes what he has fworn, but are the facts true ftill? No. He might have produced perfons to prove the facts—*Giffard* has not anfwered the affidavits, it was offered to let him anfwer; but you muft put that out of the cafe ; whether he be ready to anfwer them or not, I do not know, and I do not care. I at once faid to the gentlemen, I meet you on your own ground—*Giffard* could not make an affidavit in this cafe, he may make one extra-judicial-ly if he pleafes.

I come now to the other objection, which they had no right to make—the mifdirection of the judge : the eloquent gentle-man applied it as pleafantly as any ferious fubject could be ap-plied ; the whole was fophiftry or joke.—He imputed this to one of your lordfhips, that the jury were to find againft Mr. Rowan, becaufe he did not fhew that the facts did not happen, where fo many perfons were prefent. Your lordfhips beft know what the obfervations you made were—the trial ftood thus, witneffes were examined for the profecution—witneffes were examined to difcredit thefe, which is always matter for the jury : there was clear evidence of the guilt of Mr. Rowan, if they believed the witneffes ; but witneffes were produced to difcredit the firft. The jury were to confider how far the opinions of thofe perfons were to have weight, and every circumftance was to be taken into confideration. It was taken as true, that there was a meeting, that Mr. Rowan was prefent at the meeting, and the queftion was, Whether he publifhed fuch a paper there? If there

.. R   was

was fuch a meeting and he was there, it muft occur to every
perfon, that if he wanted to difcredit the witneffes, it could
be beft done by fhewing that he did not publifh the paper. It
was a judicial enquiry into a queftion of fact, and it was a proper obfervation, fuggefting itfelf to the mind of any honeft
judge, to fay, you are to confider, here there was a meeting ;
if you believe that there is not a witnefs produced from this
number to contradict the evidence, it was a natural obfervation,
but no direction was given to the jury ; your lordfhips gave
your opinion upon the libel, whether right or wrong is not the
enquiry : there are few reafonable men, who have read or fhall
hereafter read that paper, who will not feel that it was the moft
dangerous and feditious libel, publifhed at the time it was, that
ever came from the prefs. But your lordfhips told the jury,
that notwithftanding what you faid, they were to form their
own opinion ; I do not rely upon the want of notice, but upon
a full and fair difcuffion, let this cafe be decided as the law
admits. One topic more remains, my lords, I fhould never
touch upon it, if fo much had not been faid about it, more
than ever was known to pafs from the lips of counfel—I fpeak of
Mr. ROWAN's own affidavit, and the credit to be given to it.
I am not to fpeak of the credit given to any man, it is not
my province ; but it is the firft time I ever heard, that a man
fwearing to his own innocence fhould affect the determination
of a judge in a criminal cafe. A great prefs was made upon
this :—we were told—I know not what—and what if I did
know, I choofe not to repeat—of the confequences that might
attend a belief of this gentleman's affidavit : I am not appre-
henfive of any confequences from it : the public mind is tranquil upon fubjects, and whatever tumult or noife is made by the
little mob behind me, or any where elfe, for a few hours, or a
few days, the learned and the good will fee, that the cafe has
been determined upon the known rules of law, and that juftice
has been adminiftered to this gentleman, as to every other. But
the fact is not as it has been infinuated ; he has not fworn to his
innocence ; he has not fworn, that if the verdict be fet afide, he
has a good caufe of defence. He fwears generally, that the
teftimony of the witneffes is not true ; not a fyllable with regard to his innocence. I defire to infer nothing from this ; but
I defire that nothing may be inferred from what he has fworn,
to what he has not fworn. It is faid, he is a gentleman of great
worth, I know him not, I dare fay he is ; if he be, it may furnifh fome deduction, that there was fomething which he could
not deny ;—I defire not to prefs it further, that affidavit can
have no weight in the difpofal of this cafe, and I feel fenfible,
that the time will come, when it can have no effect upon the
people. But be their opinion what it may, be the confequence
what it may—*Fiat juftitia—ruat cælum.*

4   Mr.

Mr. Solicitor General, *same side.*—My lords, I was in hopes it would not be neceffary for me to addrefs you. This is the fixth day that th's fubject has taken up the time of the court, it is impoffible not to feel it as trefpaffing much upon your time. The fubject has been magnified into confequence not neceffarily belonging to it ; you have heard this cafe with dignified patience and with dignified attention, with an exemplary degree of temper, not difturbed by the efforts of unbridled eloquence. It is impoffible to efcape your lordfhips wifdom, that by the late act of parliament there was a latitude given to the jury upon the fubject of libels. The learned gentleman who laboured this argument, went into an invetligation of the facts, very briefly. He, in an argument of three hours or more, a few days ago, fcarcely took up ten minutes in the inveftigation of facts : he has faftened the fact of publication " round the neck of his client;" that publication was a calling to 'arms to introduce a reform in the reprefentation of the people, and an emancipation of the Catholics. He faid the prefent publication was the " honeft effufion of a manly mind."—Inftead of difclaiming the publication, the learned counfel has made a " wreath of it to decorate the brows of his client." This motion is to fet afide the verdict. In 3 *Wilf.* 45. *Swaine* v. *Hall.* Lord Chief Juftice Wilmot faid in this cafe, there was a contrariety of evidence on both fides; and although I am ftill of opinion that the weight of evidence was with the plaintiff, yet I difclaim any power to controul this verdict of the jury, who are the legal conftitutional judges of the fact.

My lords, I forbear to follow the learned counfel for the defendant through the vaft variety of matter which he has introduced upon the occafion of the trial, with a degree of *boldnefs* and *freedom*, that was very unufual to my ear, fcarcely admiffible in any affembly, the moft popular known to the country. There was another circumftance, I beg to put to your lordfhips mind ; in the progrefs of the crofs-examinations, it appeared, that at the meeting in Cope-ftreet, there was a new fpecies of men, under the cloak of old volunteers, with new devices and new badges of fedition, as a harp divefted of the royal crown. *** It was moft induftrioufly pointed out, that they were the old antient volunteers. The witnefs faid the men were dreffed in fcarlet turned up with blue, yellow, &c. Here was a declaration of the fact, that there was a meeting : give me leave to afk, was that fact capable of difproof, namely, was there a meeting of volunteers in Cope-ftreet ?—Did that fact reft on the teftimony of an incredible witnefs ?—The fact happened thirteen months ago ; there was full opportunity to collect materials,

* No fuch fact appeared, or was afferted, on the direct or crofs-examination of any of the witneffes.

to

to difprove what was fworn to, with regard to that meetng. Was it not competent to Mr. Rowan to difcredit the man if his evidence was untrue, to prove there was not a meeting on the 16th December, 1792, of volunteers at *Pardcn's?*—That no man appeared there with fide arms, or did wear thofe badges of fedition. Was it capable of difproof?—Not one of the 150 perfons have been brought to difprove the evidence of *Lyfter,* that there was fuch a meeting. There is not an affidavit to prove the innocency of the party accufed, that he did not publifh the paper in queftion. My lords, is this a cafe in which your lordfhips can fay, you are diffatisfied with the verdict? Or that cafe in which the court can fay, that juftice has not been done? It was faid, that it will do no harm to fend this cafe back to anotherinveftigation ; but, my lords, can you fend it back, without deciding upon the credit of witneffes, which it is the province of the jury to decide upon? Give me leave to obferve, upon the concurring evidence of *Morton* ; he does not go to the collateral part of the cafe, he goes to the very principal part, namely, the publication of the paper ; he was able to repeat part of the paper (which he faid was read) by memory, *viz.* " *Citizens foldiers, to arms.*"

This verdict is fought to be fet afide, in order to give the defendant an opportunity of being able to find more witneffes againft the credit of *Lyfter,* when he has already ranfacked the province of Connaught for evidence.

If you do fet afide the verdict, upon the ground of thefe affidavits, you do not give *Lyfter* an opportunity of vindicating his character, which has been depreciated on the prefent occafion.

This verdict is fought to be fet afide upon the ground of the challenge to the jury. I am bold to fay, there is not a fingle authority in the law books to fhew where a verdict has been fet afide for matter of challenge. If the juror was competent at the time, you will not fet the verdict afide for challenge to the jury. There are authorities which do fay, that a challenge for competency is not a ground for granting a new trial. See the *Compleat Juryman,* 261. There the law with refpect to challenges to jurors, is fully laid down, and feveral cafes referred to.

As to the objection, that the fheriff was partial ; a fheriff is the returning officer intrufted by law ; if Mr. Rowan had fuggefted the objection at the time, before any of the jurors was fworn, no doubt your lordfhips would have poftponed the trial, or iffued a *venire* to the coroner; on this ground therefore this motion cannot be fupported.

This is the firft time, in the hiftory of criminal proceedings, where an eloquent character has with unbridled liberty faid, that there were confpiracies formed againft his client, who ftood in the alternative between guilt and martyrdom ;—if, faid he,

he, his client fhould be found guilty, he has been the victim of a
perfecuting combination, it was one queftion how far this combination was to reach. Give me leave to confider this eulogium
to be of a dangerous and feditious tendency, againft the jurifdiction of this country. The folemn and cool inveftigation
of matters criminal, is not driven as yet to appeals to the
people. Much has been faid about the liberty of the prefs;
the beft mode to preferve the freedom of the prefs, is to
curb its licentioufnefs. The moft popular character that ever
exifted in England, Lord CAMDEN, on the decifion of a cafe
mentioned in the 11th volume of the *State Trials* 1122, gave his
opinion on the dangerous confequences of libels; he faid, that
they excited difcontent againft the government, and tended to
deftroy the liberty of the prefs by its licentioufnefs, and faid that
the worft government was better than no government at all.

It has been a fortunate event for this country, that this matter has been brought to trial; if, in confequence of the fummons to arms by the publication of this paper, the people in
arms had by force overawed the government; if the people in
arms had proceeded to act, the gentleman who now ftands at
the bar for publifhing a libel and charged to be a mifdemeanor,
would be accufed of high treafon againft the ftate; if there had
been one act of force committed, by the clamorous rabble,
who fhouted yefterday at your bar, in confequence of this fummons to arms, it would fasten the crime of high treafon upon this
gentleman. It has been a moft fortunate circumftance, that a
proclamation did iffue, it quelled this paper trumpet of fedition.
The gentleman at the bar, in every other department of life, is
an honourable, a good, and a virtuous citizen, the friend of his
country; but he is a miftaken zealot in point of politics; a
mad philanthropift.

The new fcheme of fearching for an *Utopia*, a nation perfect
in every refpect, has driven millions to their graves; is that the
country which has, in the language of the paper in queftion, got
the *ftart* of us?

I do rejoice that this trial was had, for it has faved that
individual character, of whom moft men fpeak good things, and
I am one of thofe, who have the honour of knowing him; but
to let him go on uncontrouled, might be dangerous to himfelf,
he might pull down the building upon himfelf—he lives to
look at the image of his king before him. He has had the
moft patient trial I ever knew in the annals of this country.

Mr. FRANKLAND, *fame fide.*—Every obfervation, every cafe,
and every principle of law, has been fo very fully ftated by Mr.
Attorney General, that I feel it neceffary to comprefs what I
have to fay, into the narroweft compafs; and after fo much has
been faid by the learned gentleman who fpoke laft, I fhall be
very

very brief. The avowed perfonal regards for the gentleman at the bar, which the learned counfel have for him, have called forth the moft fplendid difplay of talents that has been known ; but I confider this cafe merely as a cafe between the king and a common traverfer ; if this motive had not called forth the exertion of the eminent abilities of the learned counfel, this motion ought to have been decided in ten minutes.

Mr. Rowan now applies to the difcretion of this court upon many affidavits, in none of which he has ftated one fubftantive cafe to make upon a new trial. He has made two affidavits himfelf, in neither of which he has ftated, that he is not guilty of the crime charged. Upon thefe affidavits have you ground to fay, firft, that this verdict is contrary to juftice ? That the verdict was found upon falfe evidence, not deferving any credit ?

I will admit that there is an analogy in principle, between criminal and civil cafes ; but I will be bold to fay, there is not a cafe in the books, confidering the circumftances that arife in this cafe, where an application has been made for a new trial. There is no cafe where a new trial has been granted, merely becaufe the witnefs produced had fpoken falfely. However, fuppofing it was a ground for an application, then look to the circumftances attending this cafe. You cannot forget that the traverfer and his counfel came prepared to impeach the character of *Lyfter*. The jury, it muft be prefumed, has weighed the evidence ; they found a verdict. Do you now fend back this cafe to a new trial, becaufe the perfon who has fworn that Mr. Rowan did publifh the paper at fuch a meeting in Cope-ftreet, has fworn falfe ?

In cafes of this kind, your lordfhips will look with eagles eyes. The court will never fet afide a verdict on the ground, that a *witnefs produced* has *fworn falfe.* This *Lyfter* fhould be indicted for perjury, and then thefe two men may bring forward the circumftances ; but it would be abfurd to fet afide the verdict againft Mr. Rowan upon the affidavits of thofe two perfons, who have fworn that *Lyfter* perjured himfelf on fome other particular tranfactions. In every application for a new trial, upon the allegation that evidence has been difcovered which was not known antecedent to the trial ; an affidavit of not only the *party* himfelf, but alfo of his *attorney* is required. Now, give me leave to afk, why thefe grounds are ftated upon this affidavit of Mr. Rowan himfelf, and not of Mr. *Dowling*, his attorney upon record ? If you fhould grant a new trial, when this neceffary ingredient, the affidavit of his attorney, has not been complied with, would not every attorney in the hall, the inftant he was employed to defend a client charging him with a mifdemeanour, fay to him, do you liften to no one ; do not enquire about your defence ; I fhall fhut the mouth of every man to you upon the fubject, and

go

go to trial, and give yourfelf a chance of a verdict of acquittal ; if you fhould happen to be acquitted, it is well, but if the verdict fhould be again't you, then apply to the court to fet afide that verdict, upon the ground of facts which I now tell you of, and which you can fwear has come to your knowledge fince the trial. Let it not be underftood that I mean to apply that there was fuch a fcheme between the prefent parties. No ; but I am adducing a cafe to the court. I would not have it imagined that I impute any thing in the cafe I have fuppofed, to the prefent defendant ; he is a man of honour ; but courts will decide upon eftablifhed general rules, applicable to the cafe of every man.

The notice in this cafe is very generally fhaped : Is he to be granted a new trial upon the ground ftated by thefe affidavits ? Nothing can be more clear than that the defendant had a knowledge that *Lyfter* was to be produced again't him. *Lyfter* was examined, and witneffes were examined to difcredit him. Will it be contended that there was not evidence for the jury to weigh and deliberate upon ? The verdict of the jury fhews they did decide on *Lyfter*'s evidence. To fay, therefore, that this is a verdict again't evidence, is utterly untenable ; it is not a verdict again't evidence ; it comes then to this, is it a verdict again't the weight of evidence ; will your lordfhips eftablifh fuch a rule as this ? You never will interpofe with the province of the jury : the court will not fay it was a verdict again't the weight of evidence, the whole of the evidence did go to the jury, and upon that evidence the jury were competent to decide.

As to the fecond ground, that fome of the jury were prejudiced again't, and at enmity with the traverfer : Upon that ground I was told, that Mr. Curran laid down the pofition from a cafe in 5th *Bacon* which referred to 7th *Modern*, 57. where a challenge for favour is a good caufe of fetting afide a verdict. Suppofing the cafe to be in point, yet in the prefent cafe the facts fet forth in thefe affidavits would not conftitute a good challenge to the poll, or to the array. This appears from the triors oath in *Co. Lit.* to determine whether you are bound to look to the words of this affidavit ; fuppofing, but not admitting, that the juryman did ufe the words mentioned fix months before the trial ; before he was fworn, it was not a good caufe of challenge to the poll. Supofe that fix months ago, the words ufed by a juryman were thefe, " Mr. Rowan has committed " murder," when the juror came to be fworn on the trial four days ago, on a charge for a mifdemeanor, the juror might fay, my mind is now difabufed, I was under an error when I did fpeak the words mentioned, but I never made any declarations upon the matter in iffue. The trior's oath is, " to enquire whether the juror " ftands indifferent as to the matter in iffue between the parties." Give me leave to fay, that by the principles of law, the court will

never

never fend a caufe back to be tried on account of the words fpoken, as charged in this affidavit, unlefs the words fpoken were fuch as in law would be a good legal challenge to favour.

The objection made to the fheriff, as returning officer, is for partiality. I was aftonifhed when the traverfer and the counfel came forward on a motion to fet afide the verdict, becaufe the defendant knew a fact, without ftating when he came to the knowledge of that fact, which would be confidered as a good legal challenge to the array. Is it becaufe a man is proprietor of a newfpaper, has a place in the revenue, and holds a commiffion in the militia, and he returns the jury—is that a good caufe of challenge to the array ? But, if it has any weight, when did Mr. Rowan come to the knowledge of thofe facts ? Mr. Rowan could have made his objections before the trial ; he had a knowledge of thefe facts, he knew that Mr. *Giffard* was proprietor of a newfpaper called a government newfpaper, had a place in the revenue, and held a commiffion in the militia. He could then, by an affidavit, have applied to the court, ftating that he could not have a fair trial. Your lordfhips would no doubt have poftponed the trial. I do not find in the notice, any mention made relative to any mifdirection in the judge. The court was unanimous, the whole matter was left to the jury, who were told that they were to judge of the credit they would give to the witneffes. Mr. Rowan's being at the meeting was a fact admitted ; for on the crofs examination of *Lyfter* it was preffed by the counfel, that the meeting confifted of the old volunteers, that their uniform was fcarlet with different coloured facings. The fact of Mr. Rowan being at that meeting was proved by *Morton*, and he faid he heard part of the paper read, as " *Citizen Soldiers, to* " *arms !*" There were near 200 perfons at that meeting ; that was the fact capable of difproof ; if fo, there has not been a fingle perfon produced to difprove it ; that is as a volume of evidence of the truth. I muft fay I rejoice at hearing this voluntary eulogium on his private character. That has nothing to do with applying to your difcretion to fet afide the verdict, which twelve men on their oaths have found. This motion ought not to have taken up ten minutes of your lordfhips time. I think there is no ground to fet afide the verdict.

Mr. Prime Serjeant, *fame fide.*—My lords, unlefs your lordfhips pleafe, I have no defire to fpeak on this motion.

Court.—As you pleafe—ufe your own difcretion.

Mr. Prime Serjeant.—My lords, I am counfel on the part of the Crown. This cafe is totally different from any cafe in the books. It is unneceffary to go into the detail of the evidence

dence on which your lordſhips have, in faĉt, given your opinion.
This is a motion made to ſet aſide the verdiĉt, where no evidence on the part of the defendant was adduced, but merely to
diſcredit the witneſs produced on the part of the proſecution.
They aſk you to ſtep out of your proper ſphere, to judge of
the credit of the witneſſes, which is the province of the jury only
to do. Where evidence has been adduced on both ſides, the
court may give their opinion to the jury, where the weight of
evidence lies, but the jury are to determine as to the evidence
and the credit they will give to it. I ſhould apprehend there
would be a clamour againſt the court, if your lordſhips were to
ſtep off the bench into the jury box ; becauſe the court has
nothing to ſay to the credit of the witneſſes. Were you to ſet
aſide this verdiĉt, it would be taking away the opinion which
twelve men on their oaths have formed, and which opinion the
jury were bound by the law of the land to entertain. Therefore, on the ground of the verdiĉt being contrary to evidence,
or to the weight of evidence, in a caſe where there was no evidence on one ſide, there is not a man of common underſtanding
that cannot ſay there is no ground for this motion.
. It is ſaid, that a juror was prejudiced againſt the traverſer.
If there was any contrariety of evidence, if there was any point
on which that prejudice was to operate, if there was any ſcruple of evidence on one ſide, and prejudice was to give way to
that ſcruple, there might be ſome weight in the objeĉtion, but
here there was nothing to exerciſe his prejudice upon ; there is
therefore nothing in this objeĉtion as a ground to ſet the verdiĉt aſide. If five hundred witneſſes had come forward to ſay,
that *Lyſter* is not to be believed upon his oath, it is not for the
court to determine, but ſolely for the conſideration of the jurors.
The jury muſt determine whether *Lyſter* was deſerving of credit,
or not; even if this objeĉtion had more weight than it has, the
door is ſhut upon it, as againſt the traverſer. The whole of
the caſe went to the jury, and by their verdiĉt it appears, that
they did give credit to what was ſaid by *Lyſter*.—2 *Atkins* 319.
An iſſue was direĉted to try the validity of a deed, a witneſs
ſwore to the execution of the bond *at a certain time and place*.
Before the trial, the defendant in the aĉtion gave notice, he
would impeach the credit of the witneſs, becauſe he was abroad
at the time of the alledged atteſtation to the deed. The caſe
went to trial; there was a verdiĉt on the evidence intended to
be impeached. The party applied for a new trial, on affidavit,
that the perſon was at a *different place* when the deed was alledged to have been executed. The court ſaid they would not entertain the motion ; he ought to have come prepared at the
trial ; we will not now give you an opportunity of bringing on
your witneſſes at a new trial.

S   With

With refpect to the incredibility of *Lyfter*, three witneffes were examined, and now your lordfhips are called upon to have an examination of *Clarke*, who appears to have been the hair-dreffer of *Lyfter*, and to let in the evidence of Mr. *Coultry* that *Lyfter* does not deferve credit, after the examination of three witneffes to that point at the trial. Is the hefitation of Mr. *Blake* to impeach the character of Mr. *Lyfter?* Or the pofitive affertion of any man? With refpect to the public principles and character of witneffes, are they to be again enquired into, after they had gone through the fiery *ordeal* of a crofs-examination? The court would not permit it, after the witnefs had gone from the table. As to the general character of *Lyfter*, it could not be gone into : evidence did not go to the point that he did deferve cre-dit or not. An objection is made on account of the declaration of the juror ; it was not a declaration of any opinion as to the mat-ter in iffue between the parties ; fuch declarations therefore, could not be the ground of a challenge to the juror. 2 *Hawkins* 589.

If there be objections to a juror for partiality, it would be a ground of challenge, if accompanied with fome particular in-ftances of malice. The law makes ill will in a juror neceffary to fupport the caufe of challenge.

The charge againft the fheriff is that he did impannel perfons prejudiced, and at enmity againft the defendant ; but no particu-lar prejudice is mentioned in the affidavit : Mr. ROWAN does ftate he heard, and believes, that Mr. *Giffard* is conductor of a news-paper, called a government news-paper, &c. It is not faid that *Giffard's* labours were fuccefsful, fo as to have a fingle perfon on the jury who was unfairly prejudiced againft defendant. Mr. ROWAN has not fwore that the pannel was abfolutely com-pofed of perfons prejudiced againft him, and fuch were chofen by the contrivance of Mr. *Giffard;* this was in the nature of a challenge to the array made partially, through the mifconduct of the returning officer.

As to the incompetency, it is no ground to fet afide the ver-dict ; judge GROSE fays, " as to the queftion of competency of " witneffes after trial, on a motion for a new trial, we are bound " to reject fuch teftimony now ;" though a decifion of compe-tency peculiarly belongs to the court, 1 *Durnford and Eaft's Reports,* 717.

Locke fays, that where a tranfaction is done in open day, where there is a poffibility of contradicting it, not contradicting it is an admiffion of the fact. The obfervations mentioned will have a conclufive effect upon the mind of every man that hears me.

Adjourned to Friday, February the 7th, 1794.

FRIDAY,

This day the court proceeded to deliver their opinions, *seriatim*.

Lord Clonmell, *Chief Justice.*—This is a motion made on behalf of the traverser, Archibald Hamilton Rowan, founded on a notice dated the third of February inftant; and it is to fet afide the verdict had againft him in this caufe: firft, as being contrary to the juftice of the cafe; as founded upon falfe evidence, and upon teftimony not deferving of any credit. The fecond ground is, that fome of the jury, who found the verdict, were prejudiced and at enmity with the traverfer, and had declared that opinion before they were fworn upon the jury. The third ground is, becaufe the fheriff who arrayed the pannel was prejudiced againft the defendant, and did array the pannel fo as to have him tried by an unfair jury.

The motion is ftated to be founded upon fix affidavits, (of which I have copies, as have my brothers) ftated to have been filed in this caufe on the third of February, ftating the nature of the cafe, and the reafons to be offered. The motion was called on that day and ordered to ftand for the next day, when another ground of objection was made in the argument of the motion, or fuggefted by counfel, founded upon an obfervation ftated from his memory, and unfupported by any oath; which he argued from, as if ufed by me in my charge to the jury; which I fhall take notice of in its proper place. The affidavits to the firft point in the notice, for I have endeavoured to clafs them fo as to make them intelligible to every perfon; the affidavits, I fay, to the credit of Lyfter, are three:

1ft. *Clarke,* the peruke-maker, who is of opinion that Lyfter is not to be credited, as he believes, becaufe in a fuit in the Court of Confcience he, *Lyfter,* perjured himfelf, by denying any acquaintance with him. The next is *Coultry,* a gentleman, who is of the fame opinion, becaufe, he fays, *Lyfter* perjured himfelf refpecting a horfe, and made a falfe affidavit in the name of his brother, whom he perfonated. Mr. Rowan, in one of his affidavits, for he has made two, alfo fwears to the fame points: that he believes, if thefe two perfons had attended at the trial and been examined, this witnefs, *Lyfter,* would have been totally difcredited. That he fwears is his belief, and I dare fay, that impreffion is made upon his mind. And he adds further, that from what he and his friends are daily hearing, he has no doubt of proving fully, that *Lyfter* is deferving of no credit on his oath. Thefe are to the firft point. Touching the fecond point in the notice, that is, the partiality or prejudice of the jury, or fome of them, *William Atkinfon,* a watch-maker, has made an affidavit, ftating

that

that in Auguft laft, on an occafion of fome illumination, he had a converfation with Mr. *Perrin*, one of the jurors, refpecting the volunteers; and that, with refpect to the body in general, he fpoke with acrimonious language; but particularly with refpect to HAMILTON ROWAN; that he and NAPPER TANDY deferved to be hanged, or the country would never profper, or to that effect; and Mr. *Porter* fwears that, fince the commencement of this profecution, and before the trial, Mr. *Perrin* made ufe of fome other expreffions of the fame fort; and Mr. ROWAN fwears, that he believes that fome of the jurors did, previous to this trial, ufe expreffions tending to afperfe him, therefore they were heated againft him, and had impreffions in their minds unfavourable to him.

With refpect to the third point in the notice, Mr. ROWAN fwears he heard and believes that Sheriff *Giffard*, by whom, or by whofe under-fheriff, the pannel has been arrayed, is the conductor of a paper generally underftood to be a government paper; that he has a lucrative office in the revenue, and is an officer in the Dublin militia; and that he is ftrongly prejudiced againft him, and did labour to have fuch a pannel arrayed, of fuch men as he knew were unfairly prejudiced againft him. Thefe are the affidavits touching the three grounds ftated in the traverfer's notice. And as to the general merits, Mr. ROWAN further ftates, that he was prefent during the trial, and that he heard the evidence given by *Lyfter* and *Morten*, charging him with having read, diftributed and publifhed the paper in *Pardon's* fchool, and he fwears that faid teftimony is utterly falfe. This he pofitively fwears to; but he does not, however, deny any of the particular facts alledged in the information againft him; as to that he is filent, and he undertakes to contradict no fact fworn in the evidence againft him, but that which I have mentioned.

Thus ftand the affidavits upon which this motion is grounded. It may not be amifs to give a fhort hiftory of this cafe, fo far as we have judicial knowledge of it, in order to throw light upon the fituation in which Mr ROWAN ftood when his trial came on. He was arrefted in confequence of the publication in queftion, above a year ago, and gave bail to that arreft, before Hilary 1793, *viz.* on the 20th of December, 1792, (I believe I am not miftaken, but it is not very material) and the firft information *ex officio*, for that is not the one on which he has been tried, was filed Hilary 1793; and now I fpeak of what paffed in this court. On the fixth of May laft, near nine months before his trial, in Eafter Term, which ended the thirteenth of May, Mr. *Emmet* moved to vacate his recognizance: Mr. Attorney General confented. Mr. ROWAN and his bail appeared in court, and it was vacated, as he was ready to be tried upon that information: next was a motion on his behalf, by the Recorder of the city of Dublin, to appoint a day for his trial in the term following; that

motion

motion was made in Trinity Term, but the Attorney General applied to the court stating, that he had discovered an error in the information, and entered a *noli prosequi;* accordingly no trial was appointed. A new information was filed, and in Michaelmas term, several weeks after the city sheriffs were chosen, a trial at bar was moved for, and a day appointed in this present Term (the twenty-ninth of January). On the eleventh of November last the Attorney General moved to amend the information, by striking out one of the innuendos. The Recorder appeared on behalf of Mr. Rowan, and said he was instructed not to oppose it. On the twenty-ninth of January the trial was called on, and no challenge having been taken either to the array, or to the polls, either principal, or to the favour, the jury were sworn, and tried the cause. There were questions put to some of the jury touching their opinions, whether they had declared them or not, upon the matter in issue: one of them having said, after he was sworn, that he had given some opinion, he was withdrawn by consent; nor was it objected to by the crown lawyers; and these questions, which are said in the books to tend to reproach, were asked, and not objected to.

I must here invert the order of the points, to make it more clear, by following the order of time: the first objection then, is that stated by Mr. Rowan's affidavit to the sheriff's pannel. He swears that *Giffard*, by whom, or by whose sub sheriff, the pannel was arrayed, is conductor of a news-paper, generally considered a government paper; that he has a lucrative office in the revenue, and is in the militia; and he believes he laboured to have such a pannel arrayed, as were prejudiced against him. This I shall first consider in point of law, and then of hardship, as addressed to the discretion of the court: first then, would it have been a cause of challenge upon a demurrer? Clearly not; there is nothing certain nor ascertained in it; is it in law, a ground of challenge, that a man conducts, what is considered, a government news-paper? what is a government news paper in legal estimation? A chimera of the brain. Is it meant to be insinuated that government, or the crown, to use a more proper expression, was at war with Mr. Rowan, or that any thing done, on the part of government, was to be injurious to him? I hope not; nor that any thing he did is to be injurious to government; I trust not. I put it the other way: suppose it had been objected, on the other side, that a juror had published a paper called Mr. Rowan's paper, or the Freeman's Journal, or any paper of that kind; would it be an objection that could have any weight? Undoubtedly not; no denomination of subjects, under that general name, can furnish an objection even to the prosecution.

Then again it is stated that he held an office under government, and was in the militia. If this were to be a disqualification, then mark the consequence: every sheriff in the thirty-two counties

counties of Ireland at large, would be difqualified to return a pannel; which amounts to this abfurdity, that the very grant which qualifies, by law, every fheriff to make returns, does *ipfo facto* difqualify him, becaufe the office of fheriff is under the crown: and if holding an office under the crown difqualify a man, it involves this palpable abfurdity, that the very grant, which makes him, difqualifies him from acting. But it is ftill weaker with refpect to the fheriff of Dublin, for that fheriff is not appointed immediately by the crown, but by election: however I have expofed this objection: upon the other ground I put it, that it would be abfurd that the very office fhould be a direct difqualification, from the fulfilling of the moft important duty of it. But then Mr. Rowan *believes* him to be prejudiced againft him, and that he laboured to return a prejudiced pannel. Would his belief be evidence of favour? Surely not; but the law, not grounded on weak fufpicions, difregards fuch conjectures, and rejects the furmifes of interefted parties. Our law, alfo, appoints a proper time, when even legal objections can only be received. The time for challenging the array, is before *any* of the jury are fworn, and for challenging the polls, when they come to the book; but if the party accufed takes his chance with the jury, he afterwards comes too late to object to them; fo is the language of the law, and the manifeft principle of juftice. But to take it upon the point of hardfhip, which has been infifted upon, there appears to be none; he had three months notice, and near two terms had elapfed, during which time he never expreffed any difcontent againft the fheriff, nor fuggefted to the court, by affidavit or otherwife, that the fheriff was partial, or adverfe to him. He and his attorney muft both have known that this man was fheriff, and yet never applied to have the trial poftponed, or the procefs directed to any other officer; and even in his affidavit, made fince the trial, which is unfupported by any other, he does not ftate that this caufe of complaint came to his knowledge fubfequent to the trial; indeed the reafon of his belief fpeaks the contrary, namely his being the conductor of, what is called, a government paper, an officer in the militia, and in the revenue; which facts, it is prefumable, he could not have been a ftranger to at the time of the trial.

Next comes that objection to the juror *Perrin*, in anfwer to which, what I have already faid, refpecting time, that the challenge fhould have been made before the juror was fworn, and if a challenge had been made, there is not enough in the affidavit, even fuppofing the facts true, to fupport it. It is not fworn that he made any declaration refpecting the matter in iffue, nor in malice, to the defendant. 2 *Hawk. P. C.* 589. *Leech's ed. Irifh octavo;* cited by Mr. Prime Serjeant. The trior's oath illuftrates and is applicable, it is to try, whether the jurors are indifferent upon the *matter in iffue;* but I ftill refort to what I faid before, the objection now

comes

comes too late. A third objection goes to vitiate the verdict as unjuft, founded upon falfe, on uncreditable teftimony. This is a queftion of great extent, and of great confequence to the adminiftration of criminal law ; the object defired is, to be let in, it is faid, to impeach further by new witneffes, the credit of perfons, already attempted to be difcredited on the trial. If that were yielded to, no verdicts for mifdemeanours againft the traverfer could ftand, as long as a man could be found to fwear that the witnefs did not deferve credit. It would be a direct and general invitation to fuch perjury as could not be punifhed by an indictment, and would tend to withhold a part of that evidence by which the witnefs on the firft trial might be impeached, and hold out an invitation to perfons to offer themfelves after the trial, to difcredit the witneffes with fafety, perhaps profit to themfelves. It would wound the conftitution deeply, by transfering the jurifdiction of the jury to the court, and would totally overturn the trial by jury. It is admitted by the defendant's counfel, that no cafe has been found to authorife it, and the cafe cited 7 *Mod.* 57. has been fearched for, and cannot be found : I have found a cafe in page 54, which, fo far as it goes, is againft him ; it would be ftrange and unjuft if it could, but there are other cafes, which go much more ftrongly againft him, where it has been attempted to fet afide the verdict where the witnefs has been incompetent, of which the court, and not the jury, are by law the judges. *Hyan* and *Ballan* cited 7 *Mod.* 54, referred to 5 *Bacon,* was the cafe of a non-fuit, and the court refufed to fet it afide, although the deed, upon which the defendant relied, was fworn to be a forgery ; and *Turner* and *Pearte* 1 *Term Rep.* 717. is much ftronger than this, againft what is applied for. An application was made for a new trial upon affidavit, that five of the witneffes produced by the party, who obtained a verdict, were incompetent, and ought not to be examined at all ; there is an affidavit in anfwer, that the party who called thefe witneffes did not know that there was any objection to them. *Afhurft,* J. faid they came too late after trial. Now there their evidence was to be confidered as a nullity, that they never fhould have been examined at all ; not what credit they deferved, whether more or lefs, which the jury are judges of, not the court. And in that cafe, where the matter was of law within the power of the judges, whether competent or not, though it was fworn that five of them were interefted, and incompetent of courfe, yet the court would not hear the objection becaufe it came too late, and Mr. Juftice *Buller,* a very great lawyer, fays " there has been no inftance of this court's granting a new " trial, on an allegation, that fome of the witneffes examined were " interefted, and I fhould be very forry to make the firft prece- " dent." " There never yet has been a cafe in which the party " has been permitted *after trial* to avail himfelf of any objection " which

" which was not made at the time of the examination." Mr. Juſtice GROSE, in the ſame caſe, ſays, " In the firſt place it does " not clearly appear, that the plaintiffs did not know of the ob- " jection at the time of the trial. It is ſworn very looſely; " and if they knew of it, at that time, that would be a deci- " five reaſon for refuſing to allow it now." And now I ſhall apply this opinion, in this caſe, to the laſt objection made by counſel, as well as to what I have already ſaid; but there it was ſaid by Mr. Juſtice Groſe, that the objection to the witneſs might be an ingredient if the party applying had merits. In 2 *Term Rep.* 113 in the caſe of *Vernon* and others, the aſſignees of *Tyler v. Hankey,* the court would not grant a new trial, to let the party into a defence, of which he was apprized at the firſt trial. I have cited theſe caſes to ſhew, that even in caſe of incompetency, where the witneſs ought not to be permitted to ſtand upon the table, or open his lips,—there after trial, the court would not ſet aſide a verdict upon that ground. But ſee what Mr. ROWAN's affidavit is, even if it could be liſtened to as to his own innocence; he ſays, he heard the evidence of *Lyſter* and *Morton,* charging him with having read, diſtributed and pub- liſhed the paper in the information, in Cope-ſtreet, at Pardon's fencing ſchool, and poſitively ſwears, that their teſtimony was utterly falſe. Now firſt, I ſay, that no trial or verdict was ever ſet aſide, in a caſe like this, upon ſuch an affidavit. It is at beſt the oath of the party to his own innocence; but it is not ſo much; here he does not deny the facts, not one of them; and let me take the words " *utterly falſe*" in every ſenſe they con- vey; if he means falſe in every thing, then he has ſurely made an affidavit ſtating that he has heard the evidence of *Lyſter* and *Morton,* charging him with having read, diſtributed and publiſh- ed the paper, that, he ſays, is utterly falſe. To uſe the ex- preſſion of one of the judges in that caſe I cited, it is a great deal too looſe; the party ſwearing for himſelf does not even con- tradict *Lyſter;* he does not contradict any one of theſe facts ſpe- cifically. I will aſk, could he be found guilty of perjury, upon ſuch looſe ſwearing, ſuppoſing it to be falſe? I ſhould think not. But it is material to another part, that this is the only part of their teſtimony which he has contradicted, and he might, when he undertook to contradict any of the facts, have contradicted the whole, or any other part, as far as the truth would juſtify him, at leaſt upon hearſay or belief; he has not done that.

But it is urged from the bar, upon a point not ſtated in the no- tice, but from the recollection of one of the counſel, unto which no affidavit refers, that I aſſumed to the jury the fact of a meeting, at Cope-ſtreet, of 150 men, at which Mr. ROWAN was preſent, which he has not contradicted; upon that I have built a ſtrong inference of guilt, upon the preſumption ariſing from their ſilence. Here I will ſtate, as accurately as I can, what I did ſay;

what

what I did not fay, which has been imputed to me ; in which I
have the concurrence of my brethren as to their recollection.   I
told the jury, and meant to have told them, as far as my recollection ferves me, that the obfervation made by one of the profecutors counfel, indeed by two of them, firft Mr. Attorney
General, and afterwards Mr. Prime Serjeant, ftruck me, as obvious and ftrong, viz. that the defendant did not contradict by a
fingle witnefs, any one fact fworn to againft him ; I then ftated fome of the leading facts fworn to, thofe facts as I thought
eafieft to be contradicted, and thofe facts which brought with
them, if they were true, the means of defence ; for example,
that there was a meeting in open day at a public fencing fchool,
where from one to two hundred perfons, many of them in volunteer
uniforms, were fworn to have been prefent ; this fact, I told
them, was fworn to by two witneffes, and if the jury believed there
was a meeting of the kind and number fworn to, it was to my
mind, a *volume of evidence:* I fay fo ftill, that the defendant did not
produce any of the perfons to contradict any of thefe facts, or prove
that he did not read, publifh or difperfe the libel in queftion.
He has now made an affidavit, and fee the power of perverting
fancy : Gentlemen argue for an hour upon affidavits, becaufe
the facts fworn to are not contradicted, and they infift upon
thefe uncontradicted facts as truths ; thefe fix affidavits, fay
the counfel, are ftrong and uncontradicted, and therefore the
facts in them muft be affumed ; but on the other hand, Mr.
Rowan has made an affidavit, and he has not to this hour, ventured to contradict all the facts proved againft him on the trial ;
and fhall we not be at liberty in our turn, to affume upon this
motion that he cannot contradict them.   He fwears he heard the
evidence ; he has not ventured to contradict any of thofe facts;
he has not fworn that there was not a meeting of fo many perfons,
nor any thing of that nature.

Now I will ftate what the evidence was: *Lyfter* fwore, that on
the 16th December, 1792, he was at *Pardon's* fencing-fchool,
in Cope-ftreet, in the city of Dublin ; that there was from one
to two hundred perfons prefent in fcarlet uniforms; that NAPPER
TANDY, HAMILTON ROWAN, and others, were fitting at a table ; the witnefs went in from curiofity, and he was told by Mr.
ROWAN, to the beft of his knowledge, that no man in coloured
clothes could be admitted there.   He does not contradict that
converfation with this man—that there was a gallery, to which
he might go ; that is not contradicted—that HAMILTON ROWAN
was very bufy, and walked about with papers in his hand ; thefe
facts, let it be remembered too, that he fwore upon belief and vague
recollection to the beft of his knowledge.   I told the jury this
was not evidence, and fhould be rejected ; but he does not now
contradict any of thofe facts ; then he goes to the publication.
So it was with refpect to *Morton*, what did I tell the jury ?

T   after

after ſtating the act of parliament which declares, if not gives, a power to the jury, to find upon the whole matter, which I told them they had a right to do ; that the credit of the witneſſes was with them, and not with me ; that they were to find, upon the whole matter in iſſue, and that they were the judges of the fact, and the intention. Did I aſſume any fact ? No ; that fact, as well as every other, was to be determined upon belief or diſbelief of the witneſſes. Such may not have been my identical words, but ſuch muſt have been my manifeſt meaning, and the court approved of what I ſaid. And I ſay now with certainty, I never ſaid to the jury, that the defendant's ſilence upon thoſe facts, was to ſupply any defect in the proſecutors evidence ; I diſclaim it. I did not aſſume the fact, nor did I mean or direct that the jury ſhould take it for granted, that there was any meeting whatſoever.

Theſe facts were ſworn to, like the others, by two witneſſes, except the fact of publication, which was the criminal fact, and which was ſworn to by one witneſs only, and ſo I ſtated to the jury, that _Lyſter_ whoſe credit was attacked, if they did not believe, I told them, they ought to acquit. I then left the whole of the facts and credit of the witneſſes and the intention of the paper (if they believed the defendant publiſhed it) to the jury, who were, I told them, to determine upon the whole matter.

But ſuppoſe the fact otherwiſe, and as favourable to the defendant as his counſel wiſhed to have it taken, it cannot avail upon this motion either in law, or juſtice, or fact, or legal diſcretion ; firſt it makes no part of the notice ; next it ſhould have been objected to below. It was the duty of the gentleman who urged it now, and he was not remiſs, to have taken notice of it at the time ; thirdly, it falls under the general rule that any objection which could have been made below, and contradicted or refuted by evidence, cannot afterwards be taken advantage of. It might have been inſtantly anſwered, qualified, contradicted, or adhered to ; but in truth, the general courſe of the defence rejected all idea of diſproof, it was to juſtify that paper ; and ſtanding upon that ground, it ſcorned to deny the publication, I take for granted ; for no attempt was made to contradict a ſingle fact ſworn to by one or other of thoſe witneſſes. But, upon this motion, how is it toaffect our diſcretion ? Does it appear now that any of thoſe facts are contradicted ? What are we then to judge of ? Is it that manifeſt injuſtice has been done, which is the principle that governs motions for new trials. Is there any thing like a new ſubſtantive defence ſet up, which has not been made before ? Is it ſaid by any of the perſons who have made affidavits here, or by the traverſer himſelf, that he can by witneſſes contradict theſe facts ? Not a word of any ſuch
thing ;

thing; and if we are to draw the fame inference from the filence of the affidavits, which was drawn from not anfwering them in the arguments of the cafe; fee how it ftands, what he has not contradicted he has admitted—but I have no occafion for that. This motion is addreffed to the difcretion of the court; that is to the court bound by the curb of legal difcretion, for we cannot indulge our feelings be they what they may, and legal difcretion is as well afcertained as any exprefs point of law adjudications are evidence—we are obliged to follow thefe, as evidence of what the law is. It is faid there is an analogy refpecting the granting of new trials, between cafes of mifdemeanors and civil cafes, and yet, in order to determine this motion, as defendant's counfel defire, we muft abandon that very ground of analogy : the great principle is that, and that alone, which is recognized in *Bright* and *Eynon*, 1 *Bur.* 390, alluded to and adopted in many others, from the cafe in *Styles* to this hour—Has fubftantial juftice been done ? Has the party who requires a new trial been manifeftly injured ? Upon what ground is it we are to prefume an injury done to the traverfer ? He has had fourteen months to prepare himfelf. In trials for their lives, men have often not more than one, and very feldom more than fix months; he had fourteen—they, though confined and in prifon, are fuppofed to have time to defend themfelves in felonies of death—here the party at large, com- plains, invites, provokes the trial. Has he been furprized ? Has he wanted the aid of counfel ? has he been unattended with friends and followers ? Look at the hiftory of the trial. What new defence has he alledged ? has he, even himfelf, contradicted the facts charged againft him ? No ; from what then are we to infer, that injuftice has been done to him? It was faid that whe- ther by right or by curtefy, by indulgence, or connivance, per- fons in his fituation find a way to the matter charged againft them. See how that ftands : there may be very good and fuf- ficient and proper reafons, not to difclofe the name of the party fwearing the information; to protect him from violence or cor- ruption of the party fworn againft. How is this cafe ? The very thing, which moft deferves to be concealed, was made known to him and his agent ; for the perfon, that is to fwear againft him, is difclofed to them, they trace him to the place of his birth, they enquire into his family and connections, they follow him through his private bargains and engagements, they become ac- quainted with his indifcreet, and perhaps immoral conduct ; fhall we prefume, that this man, whofe name was then at the foot of the examination, was unknown to him ? Where are we to look for that fubftantial juftice, by which he can protect himfelf on another trial ? I find it no where; I find it not in the principle of the criminal law ; I find it not in adjudged cafes; I find it not in the found difcretion of the court; he has had every pofible in- dulgence ; he has had every latitude of defence by juftification,

(at

(at the leaft as far as it would go) by infinuation, by addrefs; I believe, and hope he has had, and I truft, in this free country, I am not miftaken when I fuffer counfel to go as large, and take as wide a range, as decent language will admit, to convey every fentiment which may affift his client: can we fay the merits are not tried? Is it faid the merits are in his favour? But fee, as I faid before, how perverting imagination can change the moft common maxim: is it alledged that the juror, who is complained of, exerted himfelf to influence the others? that this was a cafe of a ftruggle amongft the jury? Oh! No; 'ut the cafe was fo clear, that there was not a minute a man in the deliberation. Then where there is not a ftruggle, and it is not faid that he did act partially, or work upon the other eleven, or that by his unjuft means, the verdict was obtained; yet we are defired to ftep out of our way—to go unconftitutionally into the jury box, and fay, that they fhould not have given credit to the witneffes, where the conftitution gives them a power to decide. I am therefore, clearly of opinion, that the verdict cannot, upon any principle of law or juftice, be difturbed.

Mr. Juftice Boyd.—This is an application to fet afide a verdict upon an information. My Lord Clonmel has ftated the affidavits fo much at large, that it is not neceffary for me to take up much time. The counfel in the argument refted the cafe,

1ft. Upon the declaration of a juror againft Mr. Rowan.
2d. Upon the partiality of the fheriff.
3dly. The incredibility of Lyfter the witnefs, and,
Laftly, the mifdirection of the court.

As to the declaration of the juror, there are two affidavits, which ftate it, but it was upon a common fubject; it had no relation whatever to the matter in iffue; it does not appear that this declaration was malicious, and the authority in Hawkins eftablifhes that a declaration to prevent a man from being a juror, muft be pertinent to the matter in iffue, and malicious. The declaration of Perrin, in my opinion, if laid before the court in proper time, was not a ground of challenge in point of law; and I muft conclude it now comes too late; it was an objection meerly to the favour; it is a matter in Pais, to be determined by triors appointed; and here the court are defired to affume the province of a jury and try it here. But I think it now comes too late. In this cafe it does not appear, that juftice has not been done, which is the true ground of fetting afide verdicts. It is no where fuggefted, that the mifconduct of this juror was the caufe, by which the verdict was obtained. The fhortnefs of the time, that the jury were withdrawn, is a ftrong ground to prefume, they were not perfuaded by him.

1

2*dly*, As to the charge of partiality in the sheriff, Mr. Rowan in his affidavit speaks only as to belief; he does not charge it positively. The same observation I have already mentioned, goes to this point; there was not a challenge taken to the array, on the ground of partiality in the returning officer. This being an application to the discretion of the court to set aside the verdict, the question is, has justice not been done? The charge is general upon belief; and yet the affidavit does not say, that the sheriff did procure a partial jury, or that he could procure it; and in this case, as in every other, the not making objections at the trial, is a strong ground to prevent the court from interfering, especially where the traverser in no part of his affidavit, swears he is not guilty; or has a good cause of defence to make upon a new trial, which, in my opinion, are two material grounds, in granting new trials. As to the incredibility of *Lyster's* evidence, I must observe that evidence was offered at the trial, which shews to demonstration, that the defendant was prepared; he produced three witnesses against *Lyster*, for he did produce *Blake, Smith* and *Hatchell*, their evidence and *Lyster* and *Morton*, all went up to the jury; the jury have found their verdict; and this application is made to the discretion of the court, to set that verdict aside and to grant a new trial, to let in further evidence in support of that, which the jury did not credit, that is, of the witnesses, who charge that *Lyster* ought not to be believed on his oath. There is no instance in the books to be met with to warrant such a proceeding.——There are instances, where a court has refused to set aside a verdict, on the ground of incompetency of the witnesses on the former trial, because the defendant had taken a chance of a verdict in his favour. Suppose a new trial granted, what would be the consequence? *Lyster* would be examined before another jury; with the suspicion of the court of King's Bench falling upon him, that he was an incredible witness.

As to the misdirection of the judge;—I attended to every word, as I always do to what falls from his lordship; I recollect the substance of the charge, it had my entire approbation, it was, that the defendant did not contradict, by a single witness, any one fact charged against him. His lordship stated several of the facts, which he thought might be disproved, if not true; the meeting was at noon day, in a public room, and 150 persons present, in uniform; the evidence of *Lyster* was confirmed by *Morton*, but *Morton* had not the paper, but heard the expression, " *citizen soldiers, to arms.*" On the whole the evidence went to the jury, but there was only one witness to the fact of publication. If the jury believed there was any meeting of the kind and number that was so mentioned, the defendant did not produce a witness to contradict one of the facts so alledged. His lordship did not say, that the defendant's silence was to supply the

the defects in the profecutors evidence. All the facts were left to the jury by the court, and each of us made fuch obfervations as occurred to him. By the verdict the jury, it appears, did give credit to the witneffes, and did believe there was a meeting. The defcription given of the meeting was, that there were 150 perfons prefent. Thefe were ftrong circumftances to go to the jury. If you believe there was a meeting, not one of thofe perfons has been brought forward to contradict thefe affertions. I know of no judicial determination of any cafe fimilar to the prefent. In this cafe, the traverfer does not fwear he is not guilty. If this was a civil cafe, here is not ground for a good demurrer. On the whole, I concur with Lord CLONMELL, that this verdict ought not to be impeached.

Mr Juftice DOWNES.—This is an application, to fet afide a verdict of guilty in a criminal cafe, on feveral affidavits. I hope that it will be recollected, that the affidavits have been read without oppofition from the counfel for the crown, and that the court have not given any opinion whether after a verdict of guilty in a criminal cafe, the defendant has a right to have fuch affidavits read, as have been produced in this cafe ; but as they have been read, I fhall examine the grounds of the motion, which is founded on them.

1ft. The verdict is fought to be fet afide (according to the notice) on this ground, that it is *contrary to juftice, founded on falfe teftimony not deferving any credit;* thofe are the words of the notice.

This is a direct appeal from the jury to the court, in a matter folely within the province of the jury ; the court cannot decide on the truth or falfehood of evidence, and yet we are defired to fet afide this verdict on the ground, that the evidence was *falfe,* and that the jury ought not to have believed the witneffes.

No *fact* fworn to by either of the witneffes for the crown, on the trial, was *then* contradicted by evidence, no new witnefs is difcovered, who can, in cafe of a new trial, contradict any *fact* fworn by either of thofe witneffes.

The truth of their teftimony as given on the trial, is *even now* contradicted only by the affidavit of the defendant; the court can make no diftinction between defendants, and no inftance is, or I believe can be fhewn, where the oath of a perfon found, guilty, contradicting the witneffes examined againft him on the trial, has been allowed to fhake the verdict that convicted him : and if it fhould be fuffered to do fo, I believe few convictions would ftand.

But it is faid, that if the verdict fhould be fet afide, *new light* will be let in upon the cafe by the evidence difclofed in thefe affidavits.

But

But what is the new light that is fuggefted; not upon the *merits* of the cafe; it is not alledged that any new ground of defence is difcovered; no affidavit of any of the new witneffes fays one word of the matter in iffue in the caufe, and the defendant himfelf does not in his affidavit ftate, that if the verdict fhall be fet afide, he can at a future trial, produce any evidence, as to the fact with which he is charged.

But it is faid, that new light can be thrown upon the defect of credit in *Lyfter*, the principal witnefs for the crown.

Not by fhewing that any *fact* he fwore was *falfe*, the beft mode of difcrediting a witnefs; it is not fuggefted that the defendant can produce any evidence to that effect.

But, two witneffes can be produced, who will fwear, that *they* think he ought not to be believed, and to let in thefe *opinions*, we are defired to fet afide the verdict.

I fay, to let in thefe opinions, for the particular facts of perjury, which they ftate, could not be fuffered to be proved at the trial.

And I think it is at leaft doubtful, whether if they had appeared on the trial, which has been had, they could (from any thing appearing on their affidavits) have given any evidence at all; for neither of them fpeaks as to *Lyfter*'s general character; whether that be fuch as not to deferve credit in a court of juftice, and it is with refpect to his general character only, that a witnefs can be prepared to defend himfelf, and not againft the opinion of an individual.

But if it were admitted, that a verdict might be fet afide, where a party is furprifed by the prodnction of a fufpicious witnefs, who he had no reafon to fuppofe would be examined againft him; yet this is not that cafe; here it is evident, that there was no fuch furprife; the defendant knew before trial, that *Lyfter* was his profecutor, he was prepared at the trial to impeach his credit; he examined three witneffes for that purpofe, the jury have weighed and decided upon that credit; and can we fay, after the credit of this witnefs has been examined by the jury, that particular facts, fworn by him, in fome of which he was *corroborated* by another witnefs, and *contradicted* by none, ought not to be believed, becaufe perfons come forward and ftate that *they* would not give him credit on his oath: it would in my apprehenfion be a moft mifchievous decifion, if the court were to do fo. And I know not how any verdict could ever ftand, if it were fufficient ground to fet it afide, that new witneffes come and tell us, that the former witneffes ought not to be believed.

My lord has cited cafes on this point, which I need not take up time in again going over.

As to the declarations fworn to have been made by a juror—

Mr.

Mr. Curran cited a cafe, which cannot be found in the book referred to; but fuppofing it has been decided, that a caufe of challenge not known at the trial, is fufficient to fet afide a verdict, I cannot feel, that *mere general declarations*, though fevere ones, relative to the defendants political conduct, made long before the trial, upon a converfation, no way concerning the matter in iffue, would have been fufficient caufe for a challenge. I cannot think that fuch general declarations could form any ground of challenge, for if they would, fuppofe a rebellion in the country, no loyal fubject could be a juror on the trial of any of the principal perfons concerned in it.

As to the objection grounded on the conduct of the fheriff, it is enough to fay, that no particular *act* of partiality is ftated, and that his having endeavoured to procure a prejudiced jury is ftated, only on belief—no act of the fheriff is ftated, upon which that belief is founded ; nor whether it was formed before the trial or not ; and if the defendant had apprehended that the fheriff would mifconduct himfelf, he ought to have taken the proper fteps to have the jury procefs directed to another officer, which could eafily have been done, if fufficient grounds exifted.

Thefe objections—to the witneffes, the juror and the fheriff, are all the grounds, upon which the verdict is impeached by the notice ferved on the part of the defendant; and, in my mind, it would be a fevere and dangerous injury to the trial by jury, if we were to difturb this verdict on *any* or *all* of thofe grounds.

But an objection is taken to my lords charge to the jury, and it is contended, that there has been a mifdirection ; that an illegal charge has been given, and that, on that account, the verdict ought to be fet afide.

When that charge was given to the jury, I thought it a clear, able, fair and legal charge.—I think fo ftill.

I attended to it minutely ; as it was my duty to do; if I had perceived any affumption of any fact, any obfervation in my opinion unwarranted by law ; I fhould have pointed it out to his lordfhip on the fpot ;—and from the manner, in which my humble affiftance has been at all times received by him, I am confident that I fhould have had his thanks for fo doing.

I faw no reafon to object to any part of the charge when it was delivered, and I exprefsly concurred in it.

When, upon the recollection of counfel, without affidavit, of the words of the charge, my lord was ftated to have ufed expreffions to the jury, which conveyed to them—*abfolutely* that there *was* a *meeting* of a great number of perfons—I had no recollection of the fact of a meeting been affumed in the charge.

And,

And, when it was contended, at the bar, that it was put to the jury in words amounting to this pofition or effect, *that the filence of the defendant would eftablifh* a charge, or fupply *evidence* not fully proving the cafe, I muft fay, that the impreffion made on my mind, by the charge, excited no fuch idea. I conceived the charge to have left the fact of the exiftence of a meeting, and the other facts of the cafe, fairly to the jury, upon the evidence given by the profecutors witneffes, without affuming the truth of any of thofe facts, but leaving the credit of the witneffes to the jury. I requefted his lordfhip to give me, in writing, his charge, as to this part of the cafe, according to his recollection of it, and he gave it to me as ftated by him to-day—and the fubftance and effect of it correfponded with my own recollection. As to the obfervation objected to, that *the filence of the defendant was ftrong evidence,* which was the meaning conveyed by the words, a *volume of evidence :* I think the obfervation juftifiable, prefaced, as it is by my lord ftated to have been, and from whofe ftatement I muft take it, in this manner—" if the jury fhould believe there
" was a meeting of the kind and number fworn to by the two
" witneffes, the not producing any perfon who was at that meet-
" ing to contradict any of the particular facts, fworn by them,
" or to prove that he did not publifh the libel in the manner
" fworn." Is this a violation of the maxim, that no man is bound to accufe himfelf? Does this amount to the pofition, that the filence of the defendant will prove a charge? It will not ; it would be monftrous if it were fo held. If no charge is proved, he may be for ever filent ; but where one witnefs has fully proved the fact of publication, if believed ; where he ftated that fact, attended with a number of circumftances, eafy to be contradicted if falfe ; where many of thofe circumftances are corroborated by the evidence of another witnefs, who fwore he was at fuch a meeting as, *Lyfter* defcribed. Is it not a fair obfervation in a judge to fay, (where no manner of evidence to contradict any of thofe facts is given) that if the jury believe ·that there was fuch a meeting as fworn, the filence of the defendant is ftrong evidence—ftrong evidence that the facts which are fworn to have paffed at that meeting, and which might, if falfe, be readily contradicted—were truly fworn.

If no cafe is made out in evidence, by the profecutor, the defendant may be fafely filent, and. the jury ought to be told by the judge, that no cafe is proved ; but if a cafe is fworn to, and fully by the profecutor, if the defendant chufes to be filent, as to the facts, and to reft on the difcredit of the witneffes againft him, he runs the rifk of their being believed ; and if the account they

U
give

give is fuch, and circumftances fworn to by them, ftrike the jury to be fuch, as that they might be eafily anfwered and contradicted if falfe, then if no anfwer is given, *the jury may be well warranted to believe them;* and a charge of a judge, fully and ftrongly putting fuch cafe before the jury, and with fuch an obfervation, would not in my mind be reprehenfible.

Suppofe the only witnefs in a cafe of felony, fhould be an approver, a witnefs whofe credit is reduced to the lowest point of degradation; he may ftate fuch circumftances, as from the facility of contradicting them, may force credit from a jury, and would it be unjuft or illegal for the court to obferve, that where the facts fworn to, were eafy to be contradicted if falfe, it was a ftrong circumftance againft the prifoner, that he had produced no evidence to contradict them; that fuch conduct furnifhed evidence to ftrengthen the credit of the witnefs?

This objection was made for the firft time, when the motion came on to be argued; it is not ftated in the notice that there was any mifdirection; from whence it might be conjectured, that it had not ftruck the counfel, *then,* that there was any ground in the charge, on which the verdict could be attacked; two very able counfel fpoke to the motion for the defendant, without touching upon any objection to the charge.

And the learned gentleman, who took the objection, had immediately after the verdict came in, informed the court, that his client would (if the court thought fit) *then* receive the fentence of the court. It is hard to imagine, that if that counfel, the only one who attacked the charge, then thought that there was a mifdirection in the court, which would have intitled his client to fet afide the verdict; it is hard, I fay, to imagine that he would have informed the court, that his client was willing to appear, and receive judgment, which, if the court had then pronounced, he muft know, would have fhut his mouth for ever from taking any advantage of any mifdirection of the court, if any had exifted.

I think there has been no mifdirection, and therefore, and becaufe I think the other grounds ftated, are infufficient to fet afide the verdict, I think the motion muft be refufed.

Mr. ATTORNEY GENERAL.—My lords, it is my duty to apply to the court to pronounce fentence upon the traverfer.

Mr. JUSTICE BOYD.—ARCHIBALD HAMILTON ROWAN, you have been found guilty by a jury of your country, of publifhing a falfe, wicked, and feditious libel, of and concerning the government and conftitution of this kingdom, with an intent to excite and diffufe among the fubjects, difcontents, jealoufies, and fufpicions of the king and his government; to raife dangerous

feditions

feditions and tumults; to throw the government of this country into
fcandal and difgrace ; to excite the people to make alterations in
the government, and to overawe and to intimidate the legiflature by
an armed force. This charge was exhibited in an information filed
againft you by his Majefty's Attorney General, and the whole
matter was, as it ought to be, left to the jury, who have found,
firft, that the inftrument fet forth is a libel;—fecondly, that
you did publifh it;—thirdly, that you publifhed it with the intentions ftated in the information. The libel is contained in a
printed paper, intitled, " *An Addrefs from the Society of United
" Irifhmen at Dublin, to the Volunteers of Ireland.*" This publication followed and animadverted upon a proclamation publifhed by order of the lord lieutenant and council, to which you
have attributed an intention to create internal commotion, to
fhake the public credit, and to blaft the volunteer honour. This
proclamation has had the fanction of both houfes of parliament.
At this period, and it is upon the records of parliament, the
great body of the Roman Catholics were feeking relief; they
prefented dutiful addreffes, ftating they were anxious to be li-
berated from reftraints they laboured under ;—but you addreffed them to take up arms, and by force to obtain their meafures ;
they were palpably to be made a dupe to your defigns, becaufe
you fay you will proceed to the accomplifhment of your beloved principles—UNIVERSAL EMANCIPATION and RE-
PRESENTATIVE LEGISLATURE.—Seduction, calum-
ny, and terror are the means by which you intend to effect them.
The volunteers are to become inftruments in your hands, and
defpairing to feduce the army, you calumniate them with the
opprobrious epithet of mercenaries. You fay feduction made
them foldiers, but nature made them men. You ftigmatize the
legal eftablifhments for the prefervation of order, as a notorious
police, and the militia, the pride and the ftrength of the kingdom, are to be looked upon as fufpicious. You called upon the
people to arm—all are fummoned to arms to introduce a wild
fyftem of anarchy, fuch as now involves France in the horrors
of civil war, and deluges the country with blood. It is happy
for you, and thofe who were to have been your inftruments, that
they did not obey you. It is happy for you that this infidious
fummons to arms was not obferved, if it had, and the people
with force of arms had attempted to make alterations in the
conftitution of this country, every man concerned would have
been guilty of High Treafon.

The fentence of the Court is—

Mr. HAMILTON ROWAN.—My lords, I am perfectly fenfible of the forbearance of the court in this trial, and particularly during the arrangement of a long affidavit; I hope therefore

U 2

that

that I fhall be allowed a few words, either in mitigation, or in whatever other character I may have a right to addrefs the court, before they pronounce their fentence. (Mr. Juftice Boyd defired Mr. Hamilton Rowan to proceed.) I need not apologife, my lords, for any little errors I may fall into, for I am known to be a man unlearned in the forms of thefe courts, but I fhall as plainly, and as fhortly as I can, ftate every thing as it ftruck my ear and underftanding. My lord, if I underftood rightly, the three heads under which this matter has been argued are, *the evidence*, the *jury*, and *the fheriff*; I did hope that the objections taken to thefe, by my counfel, would have fet afide the verdict.

There are fome parts concerning *the evidence*, in which the court, as well as the profecutor, feem to have been miftaken. They have taken it for granted, that I knew the perfon who was to be brought to give evidence againft me; and it was af-ferted by the bench, that I had ranfacked Connaught for evidence againft the character of *Lyfter*. I do not know what im-preffion this might have made upon fome of the jury; it was indeed corrected at the time, but it was not fufficiently done away; it is plain it was not, for Mr. Solicitor General who was pre-fent the whole time, whofe duty it is, and whofe inclination he declared it to be, to liften with attention and deference to every thing which fell from the bench, has fince repeated the fame affertion. I certainly did fufpect, that the perfon who has now been brought forward, was the man who had lodged the informations againft me; but I hoped that my trial had been poft-poned by the profecutor, from a knowledge of his character, and a wifh to procure more credible teftimony, as to the fact of the diftribution. I had certainly every reafon to fuppofe this had been the cafe, as I knew that feveral of my friends, men who belong to the old volunteer corps, and who probably were at that meeting, if there were any fuch affembly, had been fum-moned on this trial by the profecutor. They attended in the court, but were never called upon, perhaps I am wrong to men-tion this, but had they been called upon, I know the charge ex-hibited againft me by Mr. *Lyfter* would have fallen to the ground, I had been certain of an acquittal.

As to the jury, my lord, I can conceive fome of them to have been very honourable men, and yet prejudiced, much prejudiced; I did not conceive however, that any man would have gone into that box, taking an oath to try me impartially, yet having pub-licly declared an enmity againft me. It was certainly very in-genious in one of the crown lawyers to fuppofe, that the jurors who ufed thofe expreffions, might have thought at that time, that I had been guilty of murder, or fome heinous crime, and had been difabufed before the trial came on, but, without re-curring to my general character, that fuggeftion, in my opinion, falls to the ground, for the converfation was on the fubject of
the

the volunteers; and it is for an addrefs to the volunteers that I
am now profecuted; I certainly did wifh for a revival of the
volunteers, and I did attempt it: I thought they had already
done honour to the nation, that they had been acknowledged
honourable by the legiflature; this I did attempt, if this be a
crime. It has been faid by one of my profecutors, that it was not
with the jurors, but with their verdict that I was difcontented;
I afk, what was my conduct when the verdict was delivered in?
Did that prove a mere difcontent againft the verdict? No. I
thought it a fevere one, unfounded in evidence, but I called for
the fentence of the court; I was ready to abide by that fentence;
and it was not until my return to Newgate, when I found my
prifon doors crowded with utter ftrangers to me, each recapitu-
lating inftances of declared partiality in the jurors, and further
acts of infamy in the evidence, that I had thoughts of fetting
afide their verdict.

As to the fheriff, and the circumftance of my not having made
fome application to the court prior to my affidavit of the day before yefterday, and the queftion of, *when* I became acquainted
with his partiality, the fact is, that it was with the utmoft re-
luctance I now ftood forward, to accufe a man of what muft, in
my opinion, render him infamous. I well knew that in every
public act of my life fince I came to this country, trifling as
they were, I had been calumniated by him; but that was in his
province of editor; he is now become the reprefentative of the
executive power—is he not.—I thought the ftation he now holds,
would give him fome pride, inftill fome fpark of honour into
him, and that, relinquifhing that conduct and thofe proceedings
which were calculated to procure a fale for his journal, in fome
corners of the city, he would confider himfelf bound to return a
jury which fhould be unfufpected. Was it likely that he did not
know of thefe declarations of the jurors? It is not probable.
Before the recognizances were given up, while I was out on bail,
the death of a near relation obliged me to go to England, where
my attendance was neceffary for the arrangement of my private
affairs; I returned however at great inconvenience, and fome pe-
cuniary lofs, to attend this court; yet, during my abfence, I was
branded by this man as a fugitive; and here permit me to obferve, that your lordfhip, in your recapitulation of the events of
this trial, omitted to mention the motion made for me by my
friend, Mr. *Blennerhaffet,* that the examinations againft me
fhould be forthwith returned; Day after day I had attended the
court; the little enquiry I could make, informed me that no fuch
examination had gone up to the grand jury, I believe it was on
the laft day of the term, or it was not motion day, or fomething
of that kind, and there was no order of the court made. It had
been fuggefted to me by fome of my friends, when notice for
this trial was ferved upon me, that I ought to attempt to put it
off; but what would have been the confequence? Your lordfhip

I   has

has faid that *I had called for*, *that I had provoked this trial*, that *I had complained* it was not brought forward; it is true I *did call for*, I did *provoke* this trial; I have *complained* that it was not brought forward. I wifhed to be brought to trial, but I did wifh alfo to be tried by an impartial jury, fummoned by an impartial man; fuch I thought the fheriff of that time * to be, although I was not one of his acquaintance. The very words your lordfhip ufed, fhew why I did not put off my trial. What would then have been faid by that Journal, which is perpetually fligmatizing my conduct, and vilifying my private character? It would have repeated, what was faid in another country, that I was " AN INFAMOUS WRETCH, WHO HAD FLED FROM " THE PUNISHMENT THAT AWAITED ME†." But ftill thofe friends urged me to put off this trial: The fheriff is your enemy— No—I have called for trial, I will truft to his oath of office: though, as editor of a newfpaper, he has acted thus, yet when bound by oath " to return paanels of perfons able and fufficient, and not fufpected or procured, and to do juftice impartially," (thefe are merely the words of the oath of a county fheriff) I hoped he would rife fuperior to his editorial capacity, and act with juftice. Nay even in my firft affidavit, I did not throw out this imputation. As to the fub-fheriff, I know him not, but I am informed that the fheriff himfelf returned the whole pannel upon this occafion; contrary to the ufual cuftom, as I am inform-ed: Why this was fo, I know not; I cannot dive into the breaft of any man; God forbid I fhould be capable of diving into his.——My lord, perhaps what I am going to obferve may be improper, but I once thought that, Intention conftituted Guilt. I thought I heard from the bench, that my intention did not fignify.

Lord CLONMELL.—You have faid nothing improper yet, Sir: go on, you do not feem to recollect the idea perfectly.

Mr. HAMILTON ROWAN.—It was not from your lordfhip.

Mr. Juftice DOWNES.—Certainly it is an opinion no judge could hold.

Mr. HAMILTON ROWAN.—I have been miftaken then, it was fomething like it, it ftruck me fo. As to the paper it has been faid to come from a *Society* of *United Irifhmen*. One of my witneffes was afked was he an *United Irifhman*. I have heard much of United Irifhmen, much calumny here and elfewhere; I avow myfelf to be one, my name has appeared to feveral of their publications, I glory in the name. On entering that So-ciety I took a teft, by which I am bound to feek for the emanci-

* Henry Hutton, Efq.
† Vide the Lord Advocate's fpeech on Mr. Muir's trial, printed by Robertfon, Edinburgh.

pation

pation of every clafs of my fellow-citizens, and to procure (by
fpreading information, for that is the only mode a few men affembled in Back-lane can adopt) a Reform in the Reprefentation
of the People * : a Reform, the neceffity of which has been allowed even in parliament. Thefe are our objects, objects which
I am bound to purfue to their completion. As to the paper, I
honour the head that conceived it, and I love the hand that pen-
ned it. Much ftrefs has been laid upon the words UNIVER-
SAL EMANCIPATION AND REPRESENTATIVE
LEGISLATURE; it may be owing to a want of logical preci-
fion in me, but I do not confider thefe words as carrying the
meaning which has been imputed to them. I did imagine that
the Britifh conftitution was a reprefentative legiflature, that the
people were reprefented by the houfe of commons; that the lords
reprefented the territory, the property ; and that the king reprefented the power of the ftate, the united force, the power of
the whole, placed in his hands for the benefit of the whole. As a
perfon, as a man, I know nothing of the king ; I can know
nothing of him, except as wielding the force of the nation, to be
exercifed for the benefit of the nation † ; and if ever that force
fhould be mifapplied, or abufed, it then remains for the people
to decide in what hands it ought to be placed ‡.

I really feel myfelf in an aukward fituation, thus declaring
my fentiments, feeing intentions different from thofe both of
the author and myfelf are fixed upon that paper, for the diftribution of which I am perfecuted. From my fituation however,

---

* It being the intereft as well as the intention of the people to have a fair
and equal reprefentation, whoever brings it neareft to that, is an undoubted
friend to and eftablifher of the government, and cannot mifs the confent and
approbation of the community.

Locke on Government, fect. 158.

† But yet it is to be obferved, that although oaths of allegiance and fealty
are taken to him, (the king) it is not to him, as fupreme legiflator, but
as fupreme *executor* of the law, made by a *joint* power of him with others ;
allegiance being nothing but an obedience according to law, which, when he
violates, he has no right to obedience, nor can claim it otherwife than as the
public perfon vefted with the *power* of the *law*, and fo is to be confidered as
the image, phantom or *reprefentative* of the commonwealth, acted by the
will of fociety, declared in its laws; and then he has no will, no power but
that of the law. But when he quits this reprefentation, this public will, and
acts by his own private will, he degrades himfelf, and is but a fingle private
perfon, without power, and without will, that has any right to obedience;
the members owing no obedience but to the public will of the fociety.

Locke on Government, Sect. 151.

‡ This doctrine of a power in the people of providing for their fafety anew,
by *a new legiflative*, when their legiflators have acted contrary to their truft
by invading their property, is the beft fence againft rebellion, and the
probableft means to hinder it. *Locke*, Sect. 226. ——When king Charles's
deluded brother attempted to enflave the nation, he found it was beyond his
power : *The people* both *could* and did refift him; and in confequence of
fuch refiftance, obliged him to quit his enterprize and his throne together.
Blackftone, Public Wrongs, B. 4. c. 33. f 5.

having

having an independent fortune, eafy in my circumftances and with a large family, infurrection of any fort would furely be the laft thing I could wifh for. I afk no favour, but I fubmit myfelf to the clemency a d the juftice of the court, and I truft that whatever may be their fentence, I fhall bear it with becoming fortitude.

Lord CLONMELL—I have conferred with my brethren upon what has fallen from you, confeffedly in mitigation and with that view. There are two facts which you feem to infift upon as new. If it made for you, that Mr. Hasset made the motion you ftate, I willingly adopt it. If I had known it in giving the hiftory of this cafe, I fhould not have omitted that or any thing elfe done in this court. You mentioned that the informations fhould have been returned, they were returned into the crown office.

Mr. ROWAN.—My Lord, I meant they were not returned to the grand jury.

Lord CLONMELL.—The proceeding was not by way of Bill of Indictment, therefore what you defire could not have been adopted. The proceedings here were by information *ex officio*, and when the informations were lodged in the crown office, which I am inftructed to fay, was the firft day of Hilary Term, 1793, the firft day the court fat afterwards, the information was filed and the other proceedings had. There is nothing elfe that has not been touched upon. As to the meaning of the libel, I owe juftice to every man, and here and every where I have faid, that no inference can be drawn from any conftruction in your favour that was omitted. I think I will be juftified in faying, that you were well and ably defended by your counfel. Nothing has fallen from you that affected the minds of the court in mitigation, to change the judgment which we have thought proper fhould be pronounced upon you. I fhall not adopt any idea, or fuffer any idea to arife in my mind, from what you laft let fall from you, to increafe that punifhment. The judgment of this court will therefore be pronounced as is the practice in Weftminfter Hall, by the fecond judge of the court. It fhall be pronounced by my brother BOYD.

Mr. JUSTICE BOYD—The fentence of the court is—That you, ARCHIBALD HAMILTON ROWAN, do pay to his Majefty a fine of Five Hundred Pounds, and be imprifoned for two years, to be computed from the 29th of January, 1794, and until that fine be paid ; and to find fecurity for your good behaviour for feven years, yourfelf in the fum of Two Thoufand Pounds, and two fureties in One Thoufand Pounds each.

F I N I S.